The Enlightenment and Original Sin

SERIES EDITOR

Darrin McMahon, *Dartmouth College*

After a period of some eclipse, the study of intellectual history has enjoyed a broad resurgence in recent years. The Life of Ideas contributes to this revitalization through the study of ideas as they are produced, disseminated, received, and practiced in different historical contexts. The series aims to embed ideas—those that endured, and those once persuasive but now forgotten—in rich and readable cultural histories. Books in this series draw on the latest methods and theories of intellectual history while being written with elegance and élan for a broad audience of readers.

The Enlightenment and Original Sin

Matthew Kadane

The University of Chicago Press   Chicago and London

The University of Chicago Press, Chicago 60637
The University of Chicago Press, Ltd., London

Published 2024
Printed in the United States of America

33 32 31 30 29 28 27 26 25 24 1 2 3 4 5

ISBN-13: 978-0-226-83287-6 (cloth)
ISBN-13: 978-0-226-83289-0 (paper)
ISBN-13: 978-0-226-83288-3 (e-book)
DOI: https://doi.org/10.7208/chicago/9780226832883.001.0001

Library of Congress Cataloging-in-Publication Data

Names: Kadane, Matthew, author.
Title: The Enlightenment and original sin / Matthew Kadane.
Other titles: Life of ideas.
Description: Chicago ; London : The University of Chicago Press, 2024. | Series: The life of ideas | Includes bibliographical references and index.
Identifiers: LCCN 2023038222 | ISBN 9780226832876 (cloth) | ISBN 9780226832890 (paperback) | ISBN 9780226832883 (ebook)
Subjects: LCSH: Barker, Pentecost, 1690–1762. | Enlightenment. | Sin, Original—History of doctrines. | Philosophical anthropology—History—18th century. | Theological anthropology—History—18th century.
Classification: LCC B802 .K24 2024 | DDC 190.9/033—dc23/eng/20230922
LC record available at https://lccn.loc.gov/2023038222

♾ This paper meets the requirements of ANSI/NISO Z39.48-1992 (Permanence of Paper).

For Claire, Lou, and Iris

A history is in my mind much the more agreeable and the more valuable (whether the critics will allow it or not) for containing a number of incidents of a less public nature than battles, treaties, and conventions, and the great revolutions of princes and states. I love to see such facts disclosed as bring us more familiarly acquainted with the real characters of the great; and to be informed of what is worth knowing even with regard to those of lower degree.

SAMUEL MERIVALE
to Pentecost Barker, March 2, 1759

CONTENTS

PREFACE

The eighteenth-century Enlightenment is not easy to define. Was it a philosophical movement? A cultural movement? A movement at all? How much did it vary from place to place? What were its priorities? Was it radical? Moderate? Global? European? Spiritual? Secular? Did it give birth to a hopeful modernity or burden the world with new discontents?

This book takes these and other questions into account but approaches the subject from a different angle. It maintains that virtually everything the Enlightenment aimed to accomplish called for rethinking the meaning of human nature. It argues further that this effort was hindered by the doctrine of original sin, a pillar of Christian orthodoxy that on the eve of the Enlightenment stood as the prevailing anthropological faith throughout Europe and the Atlantic. The Enlightenment aversion to original sin was consistent enough to bring rare consensus to such otherwise disparate thinkers as Voltaire and Rousseau. But original sin was even more revealingly a moral and conceptual barrier for relatively ordinary people, like the central character here, Pentecost Barker, an English ship's purser who came into the historical record as an alcoholic Calvinist and left it as a "Rational Dissenter," trying to drag his religious community along with him on his path to enlightenment before landing in front of the highest criminal court in the British Empire. Barker is an atypical subject for intellectual history, never having made a name for himself among the philosophers and theologians. But another argument of this book is that obscure and never-explored stories like his make it possible to know why big ideas like the Enlightenment and original sin made cultural—or common—sense to begin with.

This book is, however, just as much about the indefinite in definitions. "Enlighteners" renounced original sin in its theological specificity, but their surrogate beliefs about human nature developed into anthropological faiths of their own, eventually split by the disagreement that seems to beset faith of any kind. Despite the capacity of original sin to capture the Enlightenment's broad coherence, in other words, the same theological doctrine's core concern with human nature also points to the crux of the disagreements that arose from within Enlightenment thought itself. What is more, the Enlightenment and its legacy have been hardest to pin down where the psychological premise of original sin—the view that selfishness is intractably at the heart of human nature—has been naturalized as a secular anthropological pessimism, so often operating as a counter to a tradition of Enlightenment anthro-optimism, in which faith in improvement and perfectibility extends even to the vexing case of human beings.

This is essentially a history book. It tries to reconstruct a largely forgotten past to explain the behavior of people who have been dead for centuries, and I have tried to preserve the particularity of how those people thought and felt. But the object of their thoughts and feelings was, where I am concerned, the nature of being human. And to the extent that any attempt to conceive of what it means to be human will feel familiar, this is a story about not just the differences but also the continuities between past and present. Another of these continuities is that the same mix of coherence and incoherence that characterizes the Enlightenment also characterizes the strain of modernity that is indebted to it. It is possible to draw from the Enlightenment's varied aims, for example, the positions that coalesce in the nineteenth century—and persist in the twenty-first—as socialism and capitalism. That is another way of saying that Enlightenment modernity too can look streamlined from the outside despite internally permitting a spectrum of anthropological faiths whose capacity to drive ideological division seems unabated.

This might have been two separate books, one a microhistory of Pentecost Barker, his immediate world, and his transformation, and the other an intellectual history of the relationship between the Enlightenment and original sin as it played out across various discursive fields. Ultimately, I found the two stories too intertwined to be told separately. I also think that any rigid distinction between microhistory and intellectual history is unsustainable. I recognize all the same that these historiographic modes encourage different voices, the first more narratological and concrete, and the second more argumentative and abstract. Readers may therefore want to know in advance that the book shifts between these two voices. I hope that the overall effect is nevertheless to illustrate their compatibility and to make clear that either account without the other would have been incomplete.

When it comes to the text, I have reproduced quotations from manuscript sources verbatim, although, when this would hinder readability for no purpose (where, e.g., two periods were accidentally used instead of one), I have made minor editorial decisions without any notice. Pentecost Barker, Samuel Merivale, and other writers of the manuscript sources used here are unknown figures, and, while it was never my intention simply to reproduce what they wrote, I occasionally include passages in the notes that were not crucial to the larger narrative but still may be of interest. Translations are mine unless otherwise noted. For quotations from the Bible, I default to the 1611 King James Bible (RSV), which was the version read by the English speakers in this book.

A final prefatory note—on the image shown on the cover of this book. In this 1765 painting by the German artist Justus Juncker, an apple, the symbol of original sin, lies illuminated on a pedestal, framed as an object of study, with small bruises and a cut in its skin indicating that it may be overripe. It is flanked by two symbols in their own right. The bee calls to mind an Enlightenment trope for socialization through unceasing labor, while the butterfly, born a lowly caterpillar, is a metaphor for metamorphosis. It is the bee that looks ready to ingest the apple as the butterfly keeps its distance. But both will likely be fed by the fruit, as secular thought is so often nourished by theology. The image, in other words, captures much of what this book is about: a symbol of religious orthodoxy, verging on decay as it is bathed in light, while two rival symbols of a new regime of anthropological faith are juxtaposed, rendered in realistic detail, and effectively coming into focus.

CHAPTER ONE

Anthropological Faith

What really matters is not what I think about the Church today, or about Capitalism, or military processions, or about Communism; what matters is whether I believe in Original Sin.

T. S. ELIOT
to Stephen Spender, June 1932

With a godly name in an ungodly world, Pentecost Barker was bound from the beginning to have a complicated life. Born in 1690 on the southern coast of England into a household that made wine casks and barrels, Barker knew that family prosperity was always haunted by the prospect that it depended on someone, somewhere, getting drunk. But the moral tension grew unbearable by the time he was a teenager as he held onto the religion of his parents, pursued his own career as a ship's purser, and failed himself to abstain from the intoxicating substance he found all around him. A godly Presbyterian, Barker was also, by his own admission, "a drunkard."

Those facts of life alone were in conflict. "Wine is from God, but the drunkard is from the devil," the Puritan minister Increase Mather warned in a sermon on the evil of addiction.[1] But it was the details of their interaction that made the facts of Barker's life unmanageable. By the time he reached his twenties, his career had come to depend on his credibility, which he sought by going inside the homes of elites—naval captains, local politicians, money lenders—and proving that he could be trusted to oversee a ship's supplies during its long voyage at sea. The problem was that the same socializing so often required social drinking, which was a problem made worse in his hometown of Plymouth, where the elites were typically mainstream Anglican Christians whose favor Barker worried he would lose if he turned down their invitations to drink. As he built his reputation, he accordingly drank politely in polite company, returned home to binge, and berated himself for the moral failure of his excesses. And then he got back on his feet, resuming his quest for prosperity and the divine favor it suggested by repeating this hopeless pattern of aspiration, drinking, sin, and regret.

I first came across Barker's life by chance and by way of the one surviving volume of his diary, which he wrote in middle age on the interleaved blank pages of another book, Edward Leigh's *Critica Sacra,* an interpretive English dictionary of Greek words in the Bible.[2] The blank pages that Barker filled with his handwriting were bound into Leigh's book to assist the reader who wanted to take devotional notes on the text—the sort of reader that in theory Barker might have been but in reality was not.[3] He almost never references the book inside of which he wrote his own, which itself imparts a story of desperation.[4] By his own reckoning in his early forties, he was "scores of pounds in debt" and had been "for more than 20 years," and he may have had no resources to purchase an empty octavo volume of the type often used by more prosperous diarists. Still, he had to write somewhere to control his urge to drink, so he turned to the nearest blank pages he could find.[5] This was a diary troubled in content and troubled in form, and it seemed worth writing about for that reason alone.

But Barker's drinking, ambition, and guilt also started to connect to something larger—a cultural shift in the eighteenth century that lies at the threshold of modernity. Several years after finding his diary, I discovered hundreds of letters that Barker wrote at the end of his life to his friend Samuel Merivale—a radical minister and another important figure in this book—in which it became clear that, after suffering through years of personal struggle, he had pulled himself back from the edge (at this point from the brink of suicide), abandoned religious tradition, and embraced the ethos of the Enlightenment, which he found made it easier for him to stop hating himself for what he could not control.[6] At the center of that transformation was, unmistakably, his renunciation of original sin, a Christian doctrine that said that human beings were depraved, ancestral sin was inescapable, and self-control was an illusion. That doctrine had perfectly captured who Barker as a younger man imperfectly was. But by later middle age and by his own estimation it had grown incompatible with who he was becoming: an optimist about human nature, a believer in his own agency, and someone whose years of failure were finally yielding to control over his addiction. By the end of his life, with his personal change more fully realized, Barker was, in fact, only rarely referring to himself by his conspicuously Christian name

Pentecost. In his letters to Merivale, he was typically "Philalethes." The defiant philosophe François-Marie Arouet found in "Voltaire" an escape from a last name that sounded like *à rouer*, French for "to be beaten." In the same spirit, a heretical purser from Plymouth had found in Philalethes, Greek for "lover of truth," a way to stop advertising the orthodoxy of his youth.

Dramatic as it was on its own terms, Barker's transformation was even more striking alongside another obscure figure I had written about at length, a Leeds clothier named Joseph Ryder, whom Barker almost remarkably mirrored. Both were born in provincial England in the 1690s and died there in the 1760s; both were pious Dissenters who struggled to make it into the emerging middle class; both authored spiritual diaries, married but failed to have children, and managed to outlive most of their peers despite their lifelong conviction that death was always around the corner. But there was a crucial difference. Joseph Ryder had put the brakes on the Enlightenment influences that trickled into his life as soon as they challenged original sin, the same doctrine whose rejection marked the beginning of Pentecost Barker's spiritual and intellectual transformation.

Dissent—a broad category of non-Anglican (or "nonconformist") English Protestantism and in many ways the legacy of Puritanism—had come by the middle decades of the eighteenth century to be split between those who upheld the tenets of the Reformation and those who were starting to believe that their former guiding light, Jean Calvin, had "defaced the beauty of the Christian Religion," to quote from a letter one apostate minister wrote to his congregation before his resignation.[7] These divided people nevertheless sat together in the same chapels, which meant, among other things, that unorthodox ministers found themselves preaching to orthodox listeners. Joseph Ryder, the Leeds clothier, noted the discord that could follow such sermons, but he also noted that the congregational grumbling eventually subsided, except on an occasion in the 1750s when a heterodox minister dedicated a sermon to tearing apart original sin. That was the tipping point. Dozens of Ryder's fellow parishioners stormed out and founded a new chapel across town, while those who stayed behind reinvented themselves as one of the first Unitarian congregations in Britain, founded under the last minster Ryder heard before he died, the polymath Joseph Priestley. Ryder could admit to himself that he had trouble grasping abstract theological concepts, like the Trinity and predestination. But, like the people who abandoned his chapel, he had no trouble at all understanding the theological importance of original sin in capturing, in his words, "the depravity of our nature."[8]

Barker and Ryder were therefore not at all mirror images of one another—or, if they were, it was only up to the point where Barker walked away from his earlier beliefs, which remained reflected by Ryder and orthodoxy on the other side of the looking glass. Even more at odds with Barker, however, were the godly people who fled the transitioning Leeds chapel where, despite his reservations, Ryder stayed put. These diehard Calvinists renounced the ethos of the Enlightenment as it had taken shape in what had come to be called *Rational Dissent*. And, like evangelical congregations across the Atlantic, their new congregation across town in Leeds rested Christian rebirth on the act of embracing original sin and the presumption of their depravity. This was a defining conversion experience of evangelicalism, and I had not paid much attention to it until after finding Barker I started to see it everywhere.

For an archetypal example, consider the story of Jean Guillaume de la Fléchère, one of the most exemplary lives held up by evangelicals at the time. His decision to take the path *away* from what contemporaries often called the *enlightened age* was the moment of his great spiritual awakening. As explained by one of the founders of Methodism, John Wesley (under whose spiritual guidance the Swiss-born Fléchère was reborn and anglicized as "John Fletcher"), a meaningful spiritual life required recognizing the meaninglessness of Enlightenment values. Fletcher, as Wesley explained in a hagiographic funeral sermon, had in early life been "of a high and ambitious turn," which was "sufficiently refined for religious as well as scientific pursuits": "He aspired after rectitude, and was anxious to possess every moral perfection. He counted much upon the dignity of human nature, and was ambitious to act in a manner becoming his exalted ideas of that dignity." No less was Fletcher "rigidly just in his dealings, and inflexibly true to his word": "[H]is sentiments were liberal, and his charity profuse; he was prudent in his conduct, and courteous in his deportment; he was a diligent inquirer after truth, and a strenuous advocate for virtue." But for the reasons listed above it was no wonder, Wesley concluded with an ironic twist, that Fletcher should "cast a look of self-complacency upon his character." His achievements had become his downfall. "While he was taken up in congratulating himself upon his own fancied eminence in piety, he was an absolute stranger to that unfeigned sorrow for sin which is the first step toward the kingdom of God . . . a perfect stranger to the true nature of Christianity."[9]

Wesley's moral was unmistakable. Caught up in the idea of improvement by way of science, liberal sentiment, amassing good deeds, and a misguided belief in his self-worth, Fletcher had consistently failed in early life to recognize what Wesley described as the "entire corruption and depravity of his whole nature," the universal truth of self-perception that Methodists and evangelicals believed made salvation accessible only by way of Christ's redemptive sacrifice.[10] Being born again—the individual experience that in the aggregate propelled Wesley's Great Awakening—required waking up to one's own depravity. This was a point, in fact, made over and again in evangelical writings. An early biographer of the Methodist organizer Selina Hastings described the moment of her conversion by lifting whole sections from this same sermon of Wesley's with only the pronouns altered: "*She* aspired after rectitude, and was anxious to possess every moral perfection—*she* counted much upon the dignity of human nature, and was ambitious to act in a manner becoming her exalted ideas of that dignity . . . *her* sentiments were liberal, and *her* charity profuse; *she* was prudent in her conduct, and courteous in *her* deportment. . . ."[11] This was not a furtive act of plagiarism—Wesley's sermon was known well enough that its language could be borrowed without attribution. But that only makes the case another way. Embracing original sin after rejecting the Enlightenment was so fixed in form and function as an evangelical trope that the personal narrative of rebirth hardly needed to be personalized.

These were different trajectories, but they pointed to the same conclusion: original sin was the conceptual threshold between confessional and Enlightenment Europe. Whether people rejected or affirmed this theological doctrine effectively indicated whether they were likely to be drawn to or drawn away from the Enlightenment.

Why that was the case is a story that has remained untold. Maybe surprisingly so. The antithetical relationship between the Enlightenment and original sin was not only felt by contemporaries like Barker, Ryder, Fletcher, and Hastings, not to mention Samuel Merivale (or Merivale's young daughter Jenny, another figure we will meet). The antithetical relationship was also logical, or, more particularly, theological.

Augustine of Hippo had laid out the doctrine of original sin in the fourth century in an attempt to explain the existence of evil in the world.[12] After grappling with various possibilities, he concluded that the blame lay not with God but with human beings, who were delivered into a perfect world and quickly found their way into the forbidden. In Augustine's telling, Adam and Eve's disobedient act of eating from "the tree of the knowledge of good and evil" (Gen. 2:17) set human evil in motion. And, by the lust-driven sex that precedes the birth of everyone else, the human depravity first on display in Eden is passed through the species like a sexually transmitted moral disease.[13] Just as importantly, Augustine thought that his doctrine also guaranteed the necessity of Christ for salvation. If Adam ensures that all people are born with sin, Jesus offers the only way out. The implications of this salvific monopoly troubled some theologians, like Augustine's contemporary Pelagius, who wondered about all the souls in the world who had never come across the Christian message. But Augustine could accept that such people were born in the wrong place or time and effectively threw them into the fire. This too was a function of original sin. It justified its own heartlessness. Who among a depraved species deserves salvation anyway? Not least, Augustine used original sin to explain human nature, no example of which was as laden with biblical symbolism as an episode from his adolescence, when he and his friends stole ripe pears from a neighbor's tree just to feed the fruit to the pigs in a gratuitous celebration of the forbidden. "It was foul," Augustine wrote, "and I loved it. I loved the self-destruction, I loved my fall, not the object for which I had fallen but my fall itself."[14] In miniature, this was the Fall writ large, with Augustine's youthful capacity for senseless evil speaking to the depravity of the whole species: to our supposed selfishness, our lack of self-control, and our inability to comprehend, among other things, the moral knowledge in pursuit of which Adam and Eve too had stolen fruit from a tree.

Given all this, how could enlighteners ever improve the world after coming to know it with clarity? "Unregenerate man," wrote John Fletcher, "is nothing more than a chaos of obscurity, and a mass of contradictions."[15] Without reliable self-control, how could there be dependable self-organization, whether in government or in the liberalized economy, the latter of which was especially unsettling if self-interest was just another form of depravity? What was the point of human rights if most humans were hardly worth saving? Even where enlighteners remained committed to Christianity, they had little interest in giving Christ exclusive power as a savior or in smearing humanity with Adam's guilt. Where the Enlightenment's rationalist religious outlook was most coherent was where it embodied the very universalism that Augustine hoped original sin would prevent.

These tensions were acutely felt in the eighteenth century, and we will turn to them in more detail. But as this story unfolded further for me, it became clear that the same basic tensions were felt and recognized by authors who wrote about the Enlightenment after the fact, including its early critics and historians. The critics were for their part trying to recover original sin in its Augustinian fullness to push back against secular modernity. Writing in the aftermath of the French Revolution, the counter-Enlightenment philosopher Joseph de Maistre found in original sin the doctrine "that explains everything and without which nothing is explained."[16] In particular, it explained that rational constitutions like those through which France cycled in the revolutionary 1790s were hopeless. "Man," Maistre insisted, "is too wicked to be free."[17] The more reliable political path was to submit to the authority of throne and altar, whose origins should stay buried and obscured in the sacred and mysterious past.[18] Charles Baudelaire, only one of Maistre's many nineteenth-century admirers, was perfectly consistent with these associations when he grew "bored in France because everybody here resembles Voltaire" while in *Les fleurs du mal* (1857) casting the underlying truth of the human condition as *l'immortel péché*—the sin that never dies.[19]

Between France's humiliating defeat by Germany in 1870 and the fulfillment of revanchism in 1914, Maistre's cultural and political vision resonated with a range of disillusioned French authors, from the syndicalist and latter-day Augustinian Georges Sorel to the founder of the anti-Semitic Action Française, Charles Maurras.[20] A full-spectrum antidote to Rousseau, the revolutionary tradition, and the perceived threats posed by individualism and self-organization, original sin also emerged in the wake of the Dreyfus affair as a counter to alleged Judaizing influences in Christianity.[21] The fullest defense offered by any fin de siècle writer came, however, from the literary critic Ferdinand Brunetière, who looked for inspiration not to Maistre but to the Augustinian bishop Jacques-Bénigne Bossuet, Louis XIV's mouthpiece and one of the Age of Enlightenment's great bogeymen. With an eloquence even his enemies admired, Bossuet claimed that original sin was the crucial plot twist in the Christian narrative, demanding, among other things, political submission to kings whose claim to rule by divine right had been threatened from one side, he thought, by rationalists like Thomas Hobbes and Baruch Spinoza and from the other by the political and religious chaos of the mid-seventeenth century. Brunetière accordingly found in Bossuet the paragon of "the classical spirit" as well as the inspiration for his own conversion to orthodox Catholicism in 1895, after decades of living as an avowed rationalist and freethinker.[22]

These French authors were widely read, and they struck a nerve in the anglophone world, especially among a group of Modernists whose conservatism was coming to rest on their renunciation of the ethos of both the Enlightenment and its progeny, as they saw it, Romanticism.[23] While struggling as an itinerant professor during the First World War, a young T. S. Eliot taught classes on French and English literature in which he put forward original sin as a theory of everything.[24] Avidly reading the same French authors on the recommendation of Irving Babbitt—Eliot's former professor at Harvard whom one contemporary tellingly dubbed "a minor Brunetière"—Eliot set his sights on Rousseau.[25] In Eliot's words, Rousseau was an insincere egoist who fabricated "the fundamental goodness of human nature," glorified spontaneity over form in art, and embodied "several conflicting tendencies" in the culture he shaped—"excess in any direction . . . escape from the world of fact, and devotion to brute fact." Here too the antidote could be found in what, echoing Brunetière, Eliot called "the classicist point of view," a category of French literary periodization that, as Eliot explained on his class syllabus, captured "the ideals of the seventeenth century" and lay in "essentially a belief in Original Sin—the necessity for austere discipline."[26] A fellow critic and poet, T. E. Hulme—according to Eliot "the most remarkable theologian of my generation"—had drawn on the same French authors to say the same thing, although he found yet another regrettable source of modernity in Rousseau's failure to recognize that literature should cast "man" as "by his very nature essentially limited and incapable of anything extraordinary."[27]

As did Eliot, Hulme thought that original sin had dominated the century of Pascal (here they were descriptively on target).[28] And both Hulme and Eliot were confident that it was only a matter of time before what Brunetière called *classicism* would come back to challenge the dominance of Rousseau and his naive followers.[29] Hulme was killed in the trenches in 1917, but years later Eliot's faith was undiminished. "What really matters," he wrote the poet Stephen Spender in the summer of 1932, "is not what I think about the Church today, or about Capitalism, or military processions, or about Communism; what matters is whether I believe in Original Sin."[30] That is an astonishing thing to say under any conditions but especially in 1932, amid the perceived decline of religion, economic collapse, and ideological division on the cusp of unthinkable violence.[31]

But ominous developments in the 1920s and early 1930s seemed only to affirm the tension between Enlightenment modernity and original sin. And it was on this tense foundation that serious Enlightenment historiography took shape. The American historian Carl Becker had long been aware of the Augustinian recrudescence, particularly around Brunetière. In a book review of Brunetière's *Bossuet* (1913), Becker identified the French critic (not before praising his literary gifts) as the leader of a "Bossuet cult," while years later, in his *City of the Heavenly Philosophers* (1932), he pushed back against the cult's aims when he defined the Enlightenment's first article of "faith" as the rejection of the view that "man is natively depraved."[32] Ernst Cassirer, one of Weimar Germany's most celebrated philosophers, reached the same conclusion in a book published the same year, months before he had to flee Nazi Germany for safer harbors. "The concept of original sin is the common opponent against which all the different trends of the philosophy of the Enlightenment join forces," Cassirer asserted in *The Philosophy of the Enlightenment* (1932).[33] Like Becker's comment to the same effect, his line is buried in the middle of a dense book. It was also drawn out only in relation to Pascal, whose Augustinian pessimism he used to capture the worldview of the seventeenth century, and Rousseau, whose optimism he characterized to capture the more hopeful philosophy of the eighteenth century. But the point he was making about original sin was obvious enough: this bedrock Christian doctrine was the Enlightenment's antithesis.

Closer to home for Cassirer than Brunetière's Bossuet cult was the theologically tinged pessimism of a younger generation of German intellectuals. In Davos, Switzerland, in 1929, Cassirer participated in a high-profile debate with Martin Heidegger, ostensibly to hash out the legacy of Immanuel Kant, although both philosophers found themselves more fundamentally arguing over what one historian aptly calls "normative images of humanity."[34] It was obvious that the up-and-coming Heidegger shunned any Christian idea of redemption—if Augustine's human beings confront their existence in the face of divine righteousness, Heidegger's confront theirs in the face of nothingness. But even Heidegger acknowledged the cues he took from Augustine and Luther.[35] And as Cassirer later noted, Heidegger's philosophy drew its salience from the religious issues it resembled: residual Augustinianism ran through the importance Heidegger ascribed to anxiety about death; it captured his concept of being, which he defined not by human potential but by limits or finitude; it was evident in the responsibility, often characterized as guilt, that he suggested people carry for the harsh conditions of existence.[36] One could add to the mix that Heidegger's ancillary concept of "thrownness" calls to mind the biblical metaphor of eviction: much as Adam and Eve were ejected from Eden, an act that for Augustine and Luther forever defined the human condition, we too, Heidegger thought, are defined by the way in which we are "thrown" into the world by forces beyond our control. Cassirer's optimistic view of human nature sounded, in contrast, that like of Pelagius. Far from stressing our limits, Cassirer argued at Davos that powers once claimed for the divine were within human grasp. And where Heidegger's keyword was *finitude,* Cassirer's was *spontaneity,* the process that brought shape to the world through symbolic forms projected by a human mind possessed with limitless powers of self-determination.[37]

If original sin played a subtle role in Heidegger's thought, it was an active principle, to take one last but critical example, for the German political theorist Carl Schmitt. Drawing on Bossuet, Maistre, and yet another disillusioned liberal, the Spanish theorist of dictatorship Juan Donoso Cortés, Schmitt had already recognized the importance of theology to politics in his *Political Theology* (1922), in the 1927 article "The Concept of the Political," and in a 1932 book of the same title that expanded on the article.[38] But there was a difference in emphasis in the edition of *The Concept of the Political* known as the *third edition*, which appeared in book form in 1933, only months after the publication of Cassirer's *Philosophy of the Enlightenment*.[39] Schmitt had multiple reasons for the quick turnaround. He could be more openly anti-Semitic in the wake of Hitler's seizure of power in January 1933—like Heidegger, he joined the Nazi Party at the earliest opportunity.[40] He also wanted to respond to the criticisms of his work offered by the political philosopher Leo Strauss in correspondence.[41] Strauss had been Cassirer's doctoral student, but in his aversion to liberalism he was more ideologically akin to Schmitt, and in several letters written in 1932 a young Strauss applauded Schmitt's early work for resting a political theory on what Schmitt had called an "anthropological confession of faith."[42] Even so, Strauss maintained that the book's failure to be emphatic about the distinct political virtues of a *bleak* confession of faith made Schmitt open to misreading, as if he supported the relativistic position he was arguing against.[43] Schmitt's forgotten third edition was therefore at pains to stress that, when it came to capturing both what political thought should and should not be and what the Enlightenment was and was not, it was original sin, in its theological specificity, that ultimately mattered.

Yet Strauss had never mentioned original sin in his letters to Schmitt. Cassirer had been the one to invoke the doctrine in early 1932 expressly to set it in contrast to the waning spirit of the Enlightenment. And it was very possibly Cassirer's book that made Schmitt even more emphatic in claiming that bad behavior is never morally innocent, as in Hobbes, who recognized nature as bleak but cast it as sinless. Sin had to carry Adam's guilt. In case some readers could not put the pieces together, Schmitt added this unambiguous line to his 1933 edition: "[T]he denial of original sin destroys all social order."[44] "This statement tolerates no contradiction," writes Heinrich Meier about the revision: "Credo or non-credo, order or disorder."[45] No more, we could add, does the statement tolerate Enlightenment political thought: if the denial of original sin destroys all social order, and if the Enlightenment uniformly denied original sin, then, with one broad stroke, nothing produced by Locke, Rousseau, Montesquieu, or any other eighteenth-century luminary ever rises to a legitimate theory of politics.

We have admittedly veered from Pentecost Barker, but only to notice that the same distinction that the ship's purser made in the mid-eighteenth century continued to resonate and on a much broader scale. From its origins to the Weimar Republic—from Locke and Bossuet to Cassirer and Schmitt—the Enlightenment was consistently cast by both its detractors and its defenders as the antithesis of original sin. Rarely do such diametrically opposed authors agree. And again it makes sense to ask why this aspect of the story alone—the antithetical relationship—has never been subjected to sustained study. But almost as soon as the serious histories of the Enlightenment began to appear in the early 1930s, the idea that opposition to original sin was the operative concept largely disappeared from historiographic view.[46] There is a reason for that. Much of this larger story very much should be told in the terms I have used up to this point. It is to our detriment that we have forgotten—if we ever fully knew—how crucial original sin was to the Enlightenment's defenders and its detractors. But in these terms alone the story of the Enlightenment and original sin cannot be told fully.

~

During the eighteenth century, and for a century and a half afterward, critique of the Enlightenment was dominated by political and social conservatives who basically followed Bossuet and Maistre in targeting it for its supposedly characteristic humanitarianism. But among the many things that the Nazi seizure of power and its aftermath called for reconsidering was this broader narrative, in which the Enlightenment simply represented humanitarianism, which original sin, a pillar of Christian orthodoxy, simply opposed. A view was already emerging from the left by the mid-1930s—and overwhelmingly from victims of the Nazis—that humanitarianism was subordinate to the Enlightenment's instrumentalist hyperrationality.[47] The further possibility was raised by Max Horkheimer and Theodor Adorno in the 1940s that fascism, a destructive turn in anti-Enlightenment ideology, was not simply antithetical to Enlightened modernity but one of its expected consequences.[48] How, therefore, could any narrative in which original sin was vanquished by the forces of progress and disenchantment not sound triumphalist and naive? To witness the binary opposition unraveling required looking no further than the fact that, despite wanting nothing at all to do with the theology of original sin, virtually the entire Frankfurt school appreciated Joseph de Maistre for highlighting the excesses of individualism.[49]

A further complication, although one never spelled out, is that original sin itself figures unexpectedly in the Enlightenment's legacy. Pentecost Barker's case will make clear that, on the one hand, encounters with the world beyond Europe could unsettle religious belief, not least belief in original sin. The alternatives to Christianity exposed by global comparisons could, for example, highlight the unfairness of assuming that only people with direct awareness of Christ could be saved from hell.[50] Experience could demonstrate even more radically that other religions rested on modes of self-perception that could better handle existential problems. The broader world held this potential to undermine orthodoxy wherever experience led to the simple exercise of comparing and contrasting. But, even with that admitted, it is also true that original sin undermines the core progressivist assumption of Enlightenment conjectural history, an eighteenth-century conceit of filling in the blanks in the record of the past by supposing that people move historically through stages of increasing sophistication.[51] In the empires Europe assiduously built during its Age of Enlightenment, such stadialist and Eurocentric assumptions underwrote the judgment that countless people were ill-equipped to advance to modernity.[52] Here there was nothing liberating about rejecting original sin, a doctrine that, as formulated by Augustine, at least had the virtue of being indiscriminately universalist. To view original sin solely as an impediment to humanitarianism is therefore to miss the way in which this theological doctrine could, however inadvertently, play the role of impeding other such impediments.[53]

To witness the irony deepen, consider original sin's relationship to slavery and racism. The conditions of being enslaved were, on the one hand, justified by Augustinians as postlapsarian facts of life. Even if perpetual bondage had once contradicted "the law of entire nature as it was before the Fall," as the Puritan author William Perkins argued, it was consonant with "the law of corrupted nature *since* the Fall."[54] The venerable historian David Brion Davis went so far as to call original sin the religious doctrine most "closely connected with slavery" and "the most powerful ideological force" that stood in the way of ideas of liberation in "Western culture."[55] But Davis also recognized that fading belief in original sin did not necessarily lead to an optimistic view of human nature.[56] Nor did it lead to any decline in the Atlantic slave trade, which did not peak until the final decades of the eighteenth century.[57] It is hard not to wonder, then, whether the *assault* on original sin, whatever the motives, directed some defenders of slavery away from the rhetoric of universal sin and toward the differentiated categories of race.[58]

One case in point is *polygenesis*. As the name indicates, polygenesis assumed that humankind had multiple points of origin. That assumption could resolve the monogenist Bible's failure to account for indigenous Americans in the human migration story told in the book of Genesis, but it was also a virulent heresy in early modern times in threatening both the inerrancy of scripture and the dependence of original sin on universal human descent from Adam and Eve.[59] Polygenesis could therefore make inroads where belief in original sin had already been attenuated. And as the Atlantic slave trade showed no signs of decline, it was also a ready-made justification for racist claims rooted precisely in different origin stories.[60] David Hume—arguably a polygenist and certainly no Christian—asserted in 1753: "[T]here never was a civilized nation of any other complexion than white."[61] Voltaire—without any doubt a polygenist and hardly less allergic than Hume to traditional religion—thought black Africans were a "species" as different from whites as "Spaniels from greyhounds" and "incapable of the highest intelligence."[62]

Even in the writings of some monogenists, however, there is a link between, on the one hand, religiously heterodox confidence about overcoming the effects of the Fall and, on the other, an emerging sense of racial superiority.[63] Carl Linnaeus—the paragon of Enlightenment taxonomy and also a firm believer in human descent from a single couple—was nicknamed the "second Adam" by his contemporaries for having reclaimed the power to name that the first Adam lost through sin.[64] It was the same Linnaeus whose taxonomies gave Europe one of its earliest racial classifications, with "Europeaus" described as "clever, and inventive . . . governed by laws," while "Africanus" was "passive, inattentive, and ruled by impulse."[65] All this is to say nothing of the way in which Rousseau's valorization of the state of nature fueled the trope of the "noble savage." Rousseau's insistence that "natural man" was depraved not by nature but by society may have done its part to subvert traditional conceptions of the Fall, but the associated belief that moral innocents still existed throughout the world required imagining these living Adams and Eves, in all their primitive naturalness, as devoid of any viable society or culture.[66]

The deepest irony running through this story, however, is that the Enlightenment reaction to original sin can look less like a rejection than a repackaging. "Some exalt our species to the skies and represent man as a kind of human demi-god, who derives his origin from heaven, and retains evident marks of his lineage and descent," as David Hume wrote about anthro-optimistic moral philosophers before acknowledging that "others insist upon the blind side of human nature, and can discover nothing, except vanity, in which man surpasses the other animals, whom he affects so much to despise."[67] How different was this back-and-forth over human nature, which occurred *within* the Enlightenment, from theological debate that had been occurring since the early centuries of the church?[68] Hume's anthro-pessimists sound like Augustine no less than his optimists sound like Pelagius, who had responded to Augustine in the early centuries of Christianity with the interlocked counterarguments that human nature is innocent at birth, that the tendency to behave badly is socially conditioned, and that the human capacity to act with agency is the precondition of salvific moral conduct.[69]

Nor was it simply that the Enlightenment held its own anthro-pessimists and anthro-optimists along a line that runs parallel to theology. Sometimes the lines of argument *were* parallel, but sometimes they met. The Jansenist Pierre Nicole—one of the earliest authors to imagine how to transform the vice of selfishness into rational self-interest, an eventual core assumption of Enlightened political economy—was committed to original sin. He also wrote a series of essays in the 1670s in which he used the evocative phrase *amour propre éclairé* (enlightened self-love) to explain that excessive regard for one's own interests could underpin economic self-organization. Nicole reasoned that the deep anxiety of death engendered by self-love (the more we love ourselves, the less we want to lose that thing we love) encourages us to form social and economic bonds of interdependence that can help stave off life-threatening situations and lessen our anxiety. Just as economically tinged was his argument that enlightened self-love makes us long for greater material comfort, which can serve to keep us both engaged with the material world and interested in emulating the productive behavior of others.[70] But the crucial qualification was that Nicole did not want to live in the world he helped envision. He demurred that a society so animated would be brutally susceptible to the extremes of egoism. Implicitly recognizing original sin as a line in the sand, the leading historian of Jansenism has described Nicole as "pre-Enlightenment" but never properly part of it, having never "ventured to pronounce the pursuit of self-love morally good": "[N]o Jansenist ever did." When later enlighteners "audaciously stood Nicole on his head by christening the passions generally and self-interest particularly as productive of 'true virtue' and 'acts of the most enlightened charity,' contemporary Jansenists could not find words suitably strong—'horrible,' 'abominable,' 'scandalous,' to name just a few—with which to characterize this 'travesty of vices into virtues.' "[71] The distinction here is important: there very much was something audacious about enlightened political economists standing Nicole on his head, which is to say removing theology and morality from the equation for economic purposes. But no less important is that de-moralizing amour propre reaffirmed the Augustinian description of selfishness as the primordial human motive force.[72] However transformative in its consequences, the shift in moral perspective that was so pronounced in political economy was also rooted in a continuity of anthro-pessimistic psychology.

The relationship between the Enlightenment and original sin was therefore never so simple. But that only enriches the story. To be sure, enlighteners were unusually coherent in their aversion to this theological doctrine. They tried to get to the bottom of the meaning of being human by self-consciously using their terms, criteria, and texts—systematic natural history, fact-finding, observation, induction, and so on—while refraining from defining human nature as "evil." They thought, just as characteristically, that, whatever their problems, humans could handle themselves. Maybe that meant that the species could be improved; maybe it could only be managed. But the most cynical Enlightenment solutions to the problems of human nature still stand in contrast to Bossuet's infantilizing assertion that a semidivine king is required to hold people in check, not to mention the broader Christian belief that human shortcomings require divine intervention.[73]

Yet the Enlightenment's echo of Augustine vs. Pelagius drives home the equally important point that, in the eighteenth century, theorizing human nature was hardly less elusive than it had previously been. Little surprise, then, that surrogate theories of human nature in the eighteenth century were so varied. What is more, this internal divergence points to the fact that the Enlightenment's philosophical *incoherence,* no less than its consistent opposition to the *theology* of original sin, rests on the foundation of anthropological faith.[74]

By invoking that word *faith,* I do not mean to detract from the subject enlighteners were overwhelmingly trying to sort out, which was "man."[75] The point is that, despite the language of common sense used by all sides, propositions made about the subject of man depended on and functioned like belief, with all its differing major premises and latent irreconcilability.[76] Of course, a remarkable faith was also required by pious Augustinians who believed that Adam's sin had been transmitted to the rest of humanity. But was it any less remarkable to believe that society could be ordered and organized by a species whose individual members were allowed to dedicate themselves wholly to themselves? Or to believe, more optimistically, that humankind could be led without the usual forms of coercion to transform itself and become reliably selfless in its actions?

There were also, admittedly, plenty of Enlightenment authors who professed a more moderated faith that the extremes could be reconciled or at least accommodated. In his *Essay on Man* (1733), Alexander Pope thought that human nature occupies "a middle state . . . with too much knowledge for the sceptic side . . . and too much weakness for the stoic's pride."[77] Voltaire and Rousseau were generally opposed to one another on the anthropological spectrum, but both found something to admire in Pope's poem and the moving target of the "middle state," as did Pentecost Barker, who memorized lines from it a few years after it was published and months before his death still maintained that he "never yet met with a truer Account of Man."[78] Just as much, for that matter, did Adam Smith try to accommodate what the Scottish Enlightenment as a whole cast as the polarities of anthro-optimistic *Stoicism* and anthro-pessimistic *Epicureanism*.[79] In his first book, *The Theory of Moral Sentiments* (1759), Smith reflected the influence of his professor at the University of Glasgow, Francis Hutcheson, who argued that all people possess a natural benevolence that leads to broad human sociability. In the second book, *The Wealth of Nations* (1776), Smith sounded more like Bernard Mandeville, who argued that we perform virtue only as a by-product of our selfishness.[80] Because Smith's first book also argued that people can restrain themselves by internalizing social perceptions, it can be read as the moral and psychological assurance meant to minimize the risk of the social and economic wager made in the second book. Taken together, that is, *The Theory of Moral Sentiments* and *The Wealth of Nations* make a coherent argument that something very much like Pierre Nicole's *amour propre éclairé* can lead to both unprecedented economic prosperity and a new secular morality. But not for nothing did economic historians long regard the tension between these two books as evidence of an "Adam Smith Problem," a characterization that may have been overdrawn but still had the virtue of acknowledging that anthropological extremes informed the most conciliatory thinkers.[81]

Even, then, where the polarities of anthropological faith are ideal types, they are no less revealing to think with. They rendered the Enlightenment philosophically incoherent in direct proportion to how purposefully they were exaggerated. And the purpose for which they were exaggerated was so often to generate broader social and cultural visions that only made the divergence in faith more pronounced. The polarities of anthropological faith, in other words, structure the Enlightenment's tensions and incoherence. And the resulting structure again echoes theology. Much as Augustine's major premise sustains an orthodox package of doctrines, and much as Pelagius's alternative implies a more universalist ethos, what regularly flowed from Enlightenment anthro-pessimism was a programmatic view focused overwhelmingly on the self, while the aim of Enlightened anthro-optimists was to sublimate self-love into something more egalitarian.

All this is to say that the explanatory power of original sin in Enlightenment scholarship understandably may have faded after the mid-twentieth century, when this theological doctrine was simply framed as an obstacle to Enlightenment humanitarianism. But framing it in such a way was always missing the fuller story, which, I hope, this book manages to tell. Put simply, enlighteners were commonly opposed to original sin, but they were opposed to it *differently*. Taking seriously both those facts—the opposition and its varied forms—makes this theological doctrine and its implications all the more revealing. The opposition casts light on the motives of contemporaries and the reasons that they found such a profound difference between the culture of Enlightenment and the culture of religious orthodoxy. But the different forms taken by that opposition point to the divergences of the Enlightenment's own anthropological faiths, which may have required a conceptual space set apart from religious orthodoxy to come into their own but still took shape with much the same thing—faith—that had stood for so long between the theologians.

So where does this leave Pentecost Barker, not to mention some of the other figures we will come to meet? If their stories are defined by personal transformation, what is faith, anthropological or otherwise, if not belief in its hardened, unswerving form?

It is in large part the intractability of faith that has made these individual cases worth trying to unravel. It was not simply by reading heady books that Barker underwent a transformation. He would eventually read the headiest books the century could offer, much as he would call himself a *Rational Dissenter* or use words like *éclaircissement* as he made reasoned arguments that orthodoxy was riddled with contradictions.[82] But when he made his midlife leap of faith in a more optimistic direction, his motives came from emotionally charged experiences and encounters. Many authors otherwise characteristic of the "Age of Reason" arrived, in fact, at one of their most lasting insights in thinking about personal change occurring along these very unreasonable lines. "Reason is and ought to be a slave to the passions," wrote David Hume in order to say that people change their minds not because of a compelling argument but because of experiences emotionally stirring enough to jar them loose from their ingrained habits.[83]

Barker thought about the motive force of emotion too.[84] He did not go as far as Hume in marginalizing reason, but he recurringly cast his former self and the ethos of orthodoxy as restrained by fear, while his later self and the hopeful new age he saw looming on the horizon were animated by love. Barker's formulation was more revealing than he realized. The ambiguity of *love* captures the Enlightenment's internal tensions by way of another route: anthro-pessimists and optimists also made common recourse to this same emotion—in, for example, the formulation amour propre—even as they disagreed about whether the love should terminate at the individualist self or be sublimated for the sake of the other. We will come back to love and its ambiguities. But for now the point is that Barker too was drawn to the idea that emotions are indispensable in making sense of dramatic changes, like his own eventual aversion to original sin, or his embrace of the ethos of the Enlightenment, or the transition from the ancien régime to whatever exactly was coming next.

By virtue of the vagueness of terms like *love,* the question of what encourages a leap of faith or a change of heart is also begged. But the paper trail Barker left behind permits the reconstruction of the context, experiences, and events that make such emotions and their objects intelligible. It may well be true, then, that there is a frustrating intractability implied in the notion of anthropological faith or, for that matter, in the notion that minds can much more easily be changed by encounters charged with convergent feelings, which are not exactly easy to curate. But Barker also offers a chance to look more closely into why such changes do occasionally occur. Here we could say that the anthropologically pessimistic and optimistic operate in yet another way: on one side stands mountainous evidence of people bound to their beliefs, on the other an obscure purser, open to the world and the possibilities it has to offer, and willing, when nudged, to see things another way.

All this leads to a final preliminary remark, this one about method. Up to a point I am sympathetic to an approach characteristic of the history of ideas. In a review of the French translation of Ernst Cassirer's *Philosophy of the Enlightenment,* Michel Foucault captured what this approach entails at its most illuminating when he praised Cassirer for his singular focus on "the theoretical," the realm of philosophical discourse that in its very isolation from context can help define what Foucault called *forms* of cultural knowledge and restore for the sake of analysis what he described as "the simultaneity and generality of all that was contemporary in the eighteenth century."[85] Given that Foucault and Cassirer took such different approaches to studying knowledge, it is significant that on this point they stood on common ground. For my part, I would add that, because the acceptance of original sin was so broad and deep, because the confrontation it met from strands of Enlightenment discourse was so multidimensional, and because the cases for and against it were so often rooted in the logic of theological concepts, occasionally considering ideas in the abstract—as we will—can offer some clarity about the scope and interaction of the various cultural and intellectual forms of anthropological faith.

But my aim is to try to understand what emerged from the interaction of ideas with arguments, experience, belief, and emotion. What follows therefore better qualifies as intellectual history in its concern with the embedded rather than the free-floating.[86] A caveat is called for here too, however. Most of the subjects we will come to meet are not well-known intellectuals but relatively ordinary people, where the *relatively* is really intended. Anyone preserved in detail in an eighteenth-century archive is, of course, already exceptional, whether because they took the time and had the ability to write something down or because they had something written down about them, which usually meant they had defied or deviated from norms. Archival survival is always tied to some condition of power (literacy, leisure, the law, etc.), and power was obviously distributed unevenly.[87] For that reason it may be worth bringing to light anyone who managed to beat the archival odds. But I also really intend the word *ordinary*. Beyond statistical anomaly, people like Barker—neither elites nor well-known authors—have a capacity to reveal something that wide angles and the widely known can both easily fail to capture.

This may be especially true when it comes to views of human nature, which are self-referential not only culturally but also at a deeply personal level, at which they are born, remade, rejected, and reaffirmed in the service of self-perception. Certainly, the ideas associated with the Enlightenment and original sin play some role in explaining motives. The logic of those ideas—*ideology* in a basic sense—has an explanatory reach precisely in relation to what Foucault found useful in Cassirer: the discernment of cultural knowledge and its production.[88] But if emotion is always somewhere in the mix, and especially if calculating reason takes a back seat to it, then, where self-images undergo the rare process of being turned upside down, ideas will not fully explain the transformation. What is more, if access to the evidence of emotion therefore becomes all the more indispensable, then intellectuals—the sorts of people who in their printed works excelled at burying their unreasoned decisions—are less revealing than are the kinds of people who had no illusions about their cultural importance.

More than it is an intellectual history of intellectuals, this book is therefore an intellectual history of nobodies. It looks at the people whose ideas, experiences, beliefs, and emotions have been marginalized in the effort to understand the genealogy of concepts like the Enlightenment and original sin. If this approach helps counter the condescension of posterity, so much the better. But my intent was also practical. It is by virtue of being unimportant enough to risk expressing how they felt that the nobodies—who were in my view not nobodies at all—turn out to be where the real story is found.

CHAPTER TWO

"Do Not Call Yourselves Christians"

Is it not amazing that Horace and Virgil &c &c should entertain higher thoughts of the dignity of the noble Creature Man (his intellectual part at least) than we Christians. The Doctrine of Original Sin must have occasioned this as preached by too many. They have made the Benevolent Supreme a greater Tyrant than Nero and mankind more wretched than the Brute Creation.

PENTECOST BARKER
to Samuel Merivale, March 12, 1761

If time travelers came to the twenty-first century from the eighteenth, they could be forgiven for thinking that original sin had been idolized in the intervening years. Adorning the machines that much of the population displays in their houses and offices, carries around in their pockets and purses, and clutches in their hands is a bitten apple, sometimes glowing, sometimes glimmering, but ubiquitous enough in either case to seem like a totem of a global religion. If the same travelers gave the matter a little more attention, however, they would surely be just as struck by how much the machines bearing the image of the bitten apple defy the religious meaning it invokes. In the typical Christian telling, Adam and Eve's disobedience was, among other things, a universal cause of mental disorder.[1] But by way of the electronic devices—instruments of self-organization and biometric self-management as much as computing—the disorder can be ameliorated. Add to the mix Apple's cheery aesthetic, and the message is not at all that we are unfixable. The first proposed logo for the Apple computer went so far as to make the point in early modern terms. It was a mock seventeenth-century engraving of Isaac Newton sitting under a tree on the family farm, waiting for the fruit to drop.[2] The image suggested that Newton went back to the very sort of place from which the first parents of humanity were expelled before, like the personal computer, he transformed the world.

In the effort to revise the image of an atheistic and pagan Enlightenment hell-bent on assailing the Catholic church, recent histories have rightly emphasized the Enlightenment's compatibility with religion, latent in its residual Christianity.[3] But redressing the balance should not come at the expense of recognizing the obvious.[4] People in the eighteenth century could believe in a monotheistic god or a deified nature—they could be as vestigially religious as the symbol of a bitten apple on an iPhone—while still posing an existential threat to *orthodoxy*. Countless contemporaries were aware of this. As they saw it, watered-down spirituality was as worthless as no spirituality at all. "If you have never felt the weight of original sin," wrote the Methodist George Whitfield, "do not call yourselves Christians."[5]

Whitfield's point was basically familiar. When Pelagius challenged the doctrine of original sin in the early fifth century, Augustine smeared him by association with the pagan "heresy of Pythagoras and Zeno," which in so many words said that Pelagius should not call himself Christian either.[6] Augustine was already linking belief in original sin to faith in Christ as the exclusive path to redemption. And, as did other later defenders of the doctrine, he drew on suggestions made even earlier by Paul. "Without faith [in Christ] it is impossible to please God," Paul wrote in his letter to the Hebrews (11:6), while explaining in his letter to the Romans (5:12) that the reason God was nearly impossible to please was that "all have sinned."[7]

But the beginning of the early modern era nevertheless saw arguments in support of original sin intensify, in large part because of the Augustinian monk Martin Luther and his breakout idea, *sola fide*, a concise Latin phrase that captured the view that believers are saved not by moral conduct but by *faith* in God *alone*. As one of the leading historians of the Reformation has argued, the doctrine underneath *sola fide* was, fundamentally, original sin. It was original sin that offered both the first evidence and the lasting explanation for the utter depravity of the species.[8] It was the assumption of our depravity that for Luther revealed a vast chasm between human beings and their perfectly righteous creator. And it was that chasm, opened by Adam's sin, into which good deeds, confession, communion, indulgences, and other supposed bridges between humankind and God fell hopelessly short of reaching the other side.

The Catholic church rejected Luther's argument that faith *alone* was the way across the chasm. But even as the church was antagonized by the Protestant reformers, it did not pull away from original sin. In its fifth session in 1546, the ecumenical Council of Trent made clear that the first sin was committed by Adam, affects everyone, is transmitted by sex, demands infant baptism, and can be pardoned only through the grace of Christ.[9] Catholics would admittedly give more potency to baptism to deal with the problem of inherited sin. So, for that matter, would even some of the most unlikely Protestants.[10] But any threat posed to original sin continued to arouse fear in mainstream theologians across the spectrum for a reason fundamental enough to make this a rare pillar of early modern Christian orthodoxy: in the absence of original sin, Christ's sacrifice would lose its necessity.[11]

By the eighteenth century, it was becoming clear, all the same, that, despite any post-Reformation consensus around original sin, the doctrine was under attack. Electronic databases indicate, for example, that uses of the term *original sin* in printed works in English declined over the course of the century as uses of other religious terms like *Trinity*, *predestination*, and *baptism* stayed constant (and while countervailing cultural keywords like *improvement*, *happiness*, and *progress* shot up in use).[12] But more revealing is the way in which the doctrine's defenders mounted their defenses, appropriating the keywords of the Enlightenment critique of religious orthodoxy. In one of the longest works he wrote in a career that included some forty thousand sermons, John Wesley made his case in *The Doctrine of Original Sin* (1757), which carried the empirically tinged subtitle *According to Scripture, Reason, and Experience.*[13] Jonathan Edwards called the first part of his epic apologia "Wherein Are Considered Some *Evidences* of Original Sin from *Facts* and Events, as Founded by *Observation* and *Experience*. . . ." John Fletcher did not reference scripture at all, titling his long defense of the doctrine *An Appeal to Matter of Fact and Common Sense; or, A Rational Demonstration of Man's Corrupt Nature* (1772). When G. K. Chesterton quipped that original sin is "the only part of Christian theology which can really be proved," the line was virtually handed to him by a team of eighteenth-century writers.[14]

None of these arguments were hard to grasp when they came down to the ubiquity of bad behavior as original sin's proof. But as further testimony to the seriousness of the threat, the supporting arguments were not always so simplistic. A subtle defense—and a further appropriation of Enlightenment ideas—came from Jonathan Edwards, who in *Original Sin* (1758) drew on Lockean psychology to argue that original sin is no harder to wrap the mind around than the assistance that, Edwards believed, God has to provide to preserve human identity. Yes, Edwards admitted, it seems incredible that Adam's sin could be transmitted throughout the entire species. But, without recourse to God, no Lockean could sustain the notion that personal identity holds together through our lapsing memories and episodic consciousness. One must believe, Edwards concluded, that with mind-bogglingly constant attention God overrides the endless cognitive disruptions and guarantees the continuity of being. With that belief established, Edwards thought it was only a small step to accepting that God could impute Adam's sin to everyone.[15]

While defenders of original sin co-opted Enlightenment language and ideas, defenders of the Enlightenment represented their beliefs in the subverted symbols of original sin. Take the apple and the tree. Denis Diderot and Jean-Baptiste le Rond d'Alembert's *Encyclopédie; ou, Dictionnaire raisonné des sciences, des arts et des métiers* (1751–72), the Enlightenment's most self-conscious major achievement, reads as if it was structurally designed to subvert Augustine's major premise. As early as his 1750 prospectus, Diderot had written that he wanted to organize the entire encyclopedia around the concept of interrelated "branches" of knowledge, and in his "Preliminary Discourse" d'Alembert noted that he hoped that what he called the *encyclopedic tree* would help accomplish Diderot's goal.[16] The eventual organization of entries was more modestly alphabetic, while the linkages were facilitated by cross-references. Even the image of the tree had to wait for its graphic appearance for nearly three decades beyond the publication of the *Encyclopédie*'s first volume. But when it did appear as a foldout inside the first volume of the 1780 index, it was a thing to behold, covering, when unfolded, a two- by three-and-a-half-foot sheet of paper, over twice the size of the already impressive folio volume.

Mapping secular information as trees was not fundamentally new. Since the Middle Ages, visual metaphors of "roots" and "branches" had lent themselves to the representation of lineage, moral virtues, and the stages of life.[17] The shape of trees was also used pedagogically in the seventeenth century, in some of the ways in which, for example, the Académie des Sciences sought to find the *enchaînement* or "interconnectedness" of knowledge.[18] These kinds of trees were innocent enough. But the type of learning that Diderot and d'Alembert wanted their encyclopedic tree to represent veered into heterodoxy. There was an unmistakable element of subversion in how much its three main branches, labeled *Memoire, Raison,* and *Imagination* dwarfed the small branch marked *Théologie.*[19] Diderot and d'Alembert also drew their inspiration not from anodyne family trees but from Francis Bacon's *Advancement of Learning* (1605), a philosophical work written in English rather than Latin with the implied aim of reaching a wide audience. The same aim and audience were implicated in the language of cultural renewal in which the *Advancement of Learning* articulated the inductive method, which the Enlightenment adopted as its own orthodoxy. It sounds banal in isolation—to draw generalizations from data rather than trying to force experience to square with authority. But Bacon boldly claimed that his method would restore human understanding to "its perfect and original condition" or, failing that, at least get to "a better condition than that in which it now is."[20] It is also true that framing things this way recognized shortcomings in unaided human understanding, which Bacon readily admitted "distorts and discolors the nature of things by mingling its own nature with it."[21] But if epistemological limits could be broken by better technology, methods, and collaboration—all human inventions—then the power to remedy lapsarian ills no longer belonged exclusively to Christ.[22]

Diderot and d'Alembert aligned their aims with Bacon's to drive home the same point: the new epistemological method, writ large, promised to better the human condition in ways that original sin denied. And it was against the background of that promise, different in scale and scope from other arboreal metaphors, that the subversiveness of the *Encyclopédie*'s tree lay, too, in the fact that it was a tree. Adam and Eve had stolen from one kind of tree of knowledge in the Bible. Now a different tree of knowledge was promising to set things right, not only for epistemological confusion, but also for the other woeful consequences of the Fall: labor and death.

As elsewhere, the signifiers were multilayered. Representations of labor in dozens of the *Encyclopédie*'s engraved plates can ominously foreshadow a world of humans toiling as "docile automatons."[23] But wherever they imagined technology permitting less arduous labor, those same representations still looked to a world slowly unburdened by inherited sin. In the same spirit, the *Encyclopédie*'s images of human anatomy stand in contrast to sixteenth- and seventeenth-century anatomical figures, whose bodies were exposed in order to illuminate their animating souls, often through allegorical representation of the Fall.[24] The *Encyclopédie*'s anatomies were instead aimed not at the immaterial soul but at what Diderot described as "a more perfect knowledge of the human body."[25] In their treatment of humans as machines, the further implication was that medical science of one kind or another held the potential to extend life dramatically. Only a small step was required for Benjamin Franklin to muse in a letter to Joseph Priestley that in the brighter future "all Diseases may by sure means be prevented or cured, not excepting even that of Old Age, and our Lives lengthened at pleasure even beyond the antediluvian Standard."[26]

Alongside Bacon, the encyclopedists identified another of their guiding lights as John Locke, whose view that the nascent human mind was a blank slate "levelled consciousness" in assuming that everyone has an unwritten starting point in life.[27] And, if the mind and the self are clean before receiving outside impressions, what mechanism in the body imputes Adam's sin from one generation to the next?[28] No less did Locke's politics imply an element of religious heterodoxy. When he rested his political theory on an abstract state of nature rather than the book of Genesis, he chose nature as a better authority on such matters than scripture.[29] That suggestion took on greater force, as we will see, when it was set against absolutist arguments that were specifically coming to invalidate self-rule on the basis of original sin.[30] In his later years, Locke brought these implications to the surface, musing in his most widely read religious work that original sin is a doctrine "little consistent with the justice or goodness of the great and infinite God."[31]

Completing the encyclopedists' English trinity alongside Bacon and Locke was Isaac Newton, the "great genius," according to d'Alembert, who "gave philosophy a form which apparently it is to keep."[32] In the million plus words he devoted to theology, Newton did not directly touch on original sin, although the doctrine was inconsistent with his view of moral freedom, not to mention being part and parcel of other later additions to Christianity that he clearly rejected, like the trinitarian Godhead.[33] But when it came to the mythic view of Newton, the takeaway was obvious. The apple that he watched drop from the tree in 1666 was a new kind of fall—a literal one. As Newton later recounted to a biographer, why did it "not go sideways, or upwards"? The whole mystery was that it fell downward.[34] What is more, its very literalness—an apple falling downward from what turned out to be a tree of knowledge in its own right—gave it allegorical meaning.[35] Contemporaries appreciated the irony. The Cambridge philosopher Robert Greene thought Newton was yet further evidence that all our knowledge comes from an apple.[36] Voltaire wrote that, much as Milton authored a brilliant epic drawn from the "ridiculous triffle" of Adam and Eve, "Newton walking in his Gardens had the first Thought of his System of Gravitation, upon seeing an Apple falling from a Tree."[37] By the end of the century, Newton's story had become so mythic, wrote the philosopher Georg Hegel in his *Habilitationsschrift*, that "people derive assurance [from Newton's apple], forgetting of course that an apple was present at the beginning of the universal misfortune of humankind."[38]

The early Enlightenment's subversion of original sin and the Fall was by no means limited to the *Encyclopédie* or its English heroes. René Descartes was accused of rejecting original sin. He may have denied the charge, much as he denied his reputed atheism, but there is a good chance that this was in an attempt to save his skin.[39] The more obviously godless Thomas Hobbes built his political case on a view of human nature as pessimistic as Augustine's but conspicuously bypassed Christianity for a materialist major premise.[40] In his Jewish upbringing, Baruch Spinoza was spared the encounter with original sin by way of religious inheritance, but at the end of his life he still took a parting shot at it for having muddied the waters of his precondition for political theory, the study of human nature.[41] Even Gottfried Leibniz has been described as *hyper-Pelagian* despite his ostensible defense of religious orthodoxy.[42]

As the eighteenth century progressed, antagonism to the doctrine grew only more axiomatic. "Many a sober Christian," wrote Edward Gibbon, "would rather admit that a wafer is God, than that God is a cruel and capricious tyrant."[43] Joseph Priestley called original sin a "strange doctrine . . . injurious both to our Maker and ourselves."[44] "[In] spite of the fall," wrote Immanuel Kant, "the command that we ought to become better human beings resounds unabated in our souls; consequently we must also be capable of it."[45] For Denis Diderot, "man is as God or nature made him, and God and nature do nothing evil."[46] Benjamin Franklin thought original sin was "a Bugbear set up by Priests (whether Popish or Presbyterian I know not) to fright and scare an unthinking Populace out of their Senses."[47] For Voltaire, it was a notion worthy of Augustine, an author "who passed his life in perpetual self-contradiction." "What ought to be said upon the subject?" he asked in his *Philosophical Dictionary* before offering the simple answer: "Rien" (nothing).[48]

Like his nemesis Rousseau, Voltaire did in fact have more to say about original sin. But none of it was favorable, even in his most pessimistic work, *Candide*, a novel whose provocation was the earthquake that laid waste to Lisbon in 1755 on a Sunday morning that also happened to be All Saints' Day, a coincidence that drove home for Voltaire the absurdity of believing in a God who would allow his most devoted followers to be crushed under the weight of the city's collapsing churches. Equally worthy of ridicule was any philosophy that tried to rationalize away suffering with the optimistic belief that we live in the *best of all possible worlds*, a phrase *Candide* turns into a satiric mantra by invoking it in the face of so much evidence to the contrary.[49] As a friend of Pentecost Barker's put it, the whole point of *Candide* was "to ridicule *whatever is, is right* by proving ludicrously that whatever is, is best."[50]

But if Voltaire mostly took up the theme of cosmic evil in *Candide*, he also framed the book as a reappropriation of Genesis and the traditional view of human evil. Candide, the protagonist, is expelled from a place that he naively thinks is paradise and then forced with his friends to journey around the globe, traveling to among other places El Dorado, a feasible dreamworld for the Anglophile Voltaire with its constitutionalist government, religious toleration, and scientific achievement—the same friend of Barker's called "Pais D'Eldorado (like the Golden Age) the only rational chapter."[51] But after learning nothing Candide returns in the book's final pages to a garden. It is no Eden, however. It is just a garden. None of this is in any sense optimistic. Even if we might learn—or relearn—how to cultivate our gardens, we cannot in any deep sense cultivate ourselves. But his secular anthro-pessimism notwithstanding, Voltaire was equally clear in saying that *doctrinal* original sin had nothing to offer. If the overarching conceit of *Candide* did not make that obvious, he tellingly let the dreaded Inquisition and the clueless Pangloss extol the doctrine's virtues.

Rousseau's views were no more born in optimism. He first rose to fame when the Académie de Dijon held an essay contest in 1750 on whether the arts and sciences help purify morals. A Calvinist by upbringing, he was awarded first prize for his firmly negative answer, his *Discourse on the Moral Effects of the Arts and Sciences*, an indictment of Enlightenment self-flattery with little to separate it from the skepticism Augustinians held toward the redemptive power of moral conduct. But when a few years later the same academy held another essay contest—on the origin of inequality and whether it is authorized by the law of nature—he spelled out his case by locating inequality in society. Steeped in the latest scholarship, he found human beings as naturally capable of pity as of self-preservation. And in a telling judgment the Académie de Dijon, funded by the political elite, passed over his entry, the *Discourse on the Origin and Basis of Inequality among Men* (1755), a social theory masquerading as conjectural anthropology, and instead split the first prize between two essays that did not just defend inequality but expressly did so on the basis of original sin.[52]

While making his novel argument, Rousseau coined the word *perfectibilité* to relish the irony that it was by striving for material improvement that people had walked down the path toward inequality.[53] He was in this sense socializing the narrative of the Fall—recognizing the ubiquity of bad behavior but identifying society rather than nature as the cause.[54] But the difference in equality's origins was crucial: the social can be remedied. Rousseau accordingly characterized the right kind of perfectibility—moral improvement—as a goal that could come into closer view through social and political reform (a case he argued in *The*

Social Contract [1762]) or, more fundamentally, through education reform, which he explained more fully in *Émile* (1762), a book in which the proper route to self-formation begins after the narrator announces: "[T]here is no original perversity in the human heart."[55] In fact, it was that line—*perversité originelle* being as unmistakable a reference to original sin as Baudelaire's *l'immortel péché*—that authorities in Geneva cited before publicly burning the book.[56]

When he turned to autobiography, Rousseau did make clear how difficult the right kind of perfectibility could be to achieve. But his allusively titled *Confessions* (1782) was in many ways his most potent subversion of the doctrine. Augustine's *Confessions,* the locus classicus of original sin, had interpreted every uncontrollable sexual urge, selfish cry of an infant, and gratuitous act of theft as a sign of natural depravity. Rousseau's *Confessions,* the locus classicus of secular self-writing, instead interpreted masochistic sexuality, petty misdemeanors, and jealousy as socially conditioned. Augustine found reason only for self-recrimination when he looked inward. Rousseau found a new basis for psychotherapy. ("It took Freud to 'think' Rousseau's feelings," wrote Jean Starobinski. The psychoanalytical terminology came later, but the impulse to mend the self through analysis of past experience and the recovery of early memories of repression came straight from Rousseau.)[57] And if for Augustine no trait attested to human depravity more than uncontrollable sexual urges, for Rousseau understanding the process by which society can make a perversity of sexuality was, among other things, a crucial step toward ending the cultural reproduction of guilt.

When Ernst Cassirer called original sin the Enlightenment's *common opponent,* he may not have realized how right he was. As Paul-Henri Thiry d'Holbach put it in an age whose leading lights assigned themselves the task of ridiculing the ridiculous, doctrinal original sin was no more or less than that: a "ridiculous hypothesis."[58] However different the arguments were in the details, however different the motives, it is hard to find any enlightener who did not agree.

But this is the other point to bear in mind: the oppositional relationship between the Enlightenment and original sin did not just take random expression in the eighteenth century. It was articulated at nascent moments of cultural self-awareness, as if opposition to original sin was itself partly constitutive of the Enlightenment.

One of the first recorded uses in French of the phrase *siècle éclairé* (enlightened age) was sardonic. Mocking the presumption that some people at the time were feeling "well enlightened," the French historian Charles Sorel wrote in 1671: "[O]ne hardly hears of anything but lights. One puts this word everywhere in place of where one used to use 'mind' or 'intelligence'; and it often happens that those who use this word apply it so badly, that one might say they see nothing at all with all of their lights."[59]

If Sorel's characterization reflects the diffusion of the secular metaphor of light, it is further suggestive of the invocation of *les lumières*—what would (or Sorel suggests may have already) become currency for *enlighteners*—by Jacques-Bénigne Bossuet, Sorel's contemporary and arguably the early Enlightenment's most formidable enemy. In one of his many sermons on original sin, Bossuet insisted: "[F]rom our origin, our senses are rebellious: from the womb, where reason is immersed in and dominated by the flesh, our soul is the slave, and burdened with this weight. All the passions we have, and often all together, and even the most contrary ones, are in turn [also rebellious]." For these reasons, Bossuet concluded, "God takes the lights [les lumières] out of us, as He did to Adam": "[We] are struck with the wounds of ignorance and lust. All good, even the least, is difficult for us; evil, no matter how great, is attractive to us."[60]

Bossuet was expressing his consistent argument that from our moment of origin—both as individuals and as a species—original sin makes inadequate our capacity for self-control in the face of irrepressible passions and inclinations. But he was also saying that we have as little control over our *reason* and our *senses*, two keywords of an emerging Enlightened outlook that was coming to rest on rational and empirical criteria. Our reason, he writes, is dominated by the flesh, while the senses are unavoidably "rebellious." Here Bossuet seemed to operate on a second-order level of reflection, suggesting that people who were subverting tradition in favor of reason and the senses could already be captured as *les lumières*. He was not, in other words, simply making an Augustinian case against moral optimism. When he reproachfully describes *les lumières* as "hopeless" because of original sin, he seems aware both that this was a perfidious new cultural ethos and that its followers were enlighteners for the same reason they were worrisome: they threatened the doctrine he defended and the religion that depended on it.

Similar associations, in similar tropes, can be found elsewhere in the seventeenth century, in some cases even earlier. As others have noted, in the 1620s Francis Bacon cast his entire restorative project—restorative precisely because it promised to restore what had been lost in the Fall—in the secular language of light.[61] But if we are looking for the first English author to use the more pointed phrase *enlightened age* in writing, the distinction belongs not to a major figure like Bacon but to a worldly parson committed equally to Edenic allusions and actual gardening and a writer, like any good pastor, tuned into the mundane as a generator of metaphors of the extramundane.[62] This was John Laurence, an unassuming author of an unassuming gardening primer, *The Gentleman's Recreation; or, The Second Part of the Art of Gardening Improved* (1716).

Laurence begins his book by imagining that the Fall had never occurred. In such a world, the flicker of human existence spent in Eden never would have ended. And since Eden was underneath it all a garden, humankind would still be gardening and benefiting from all it entails. "Had Man continued in the Garden of Eden as he came out of the Hands of his Maker," Laurence wrote, "I doubt not at all but Contemplation and Devotion would have been his chief Exercise and Delight; as most suitable not only to the State, but to the Place of Innocence," which is to say to the garden itself. Indeed, Laurence continued: "[I]f Angels were confined to these lower Regions, they would seek the Retirement and Pleasure of a Garden, as most agreeable to their heavenly Dispositions."[63] Gardening here was existential palliative, *Candide* minus the cynicism. Why did God place us in a garden at the start of what was supposed to be endless earthly delight? Because it was a garden.

Gardens were the essence of paradise for Laurence no doubt because he was a committed gardener. What is still surprising is his suggestion that gardens possess salvific potency in relation to the Fall. "There are many Ideas of Pleasure that have lain buried in the Ruins of corrupt Nature for want of being easily roused, and made to exert themselves by proper objects," he wrote. "Proper objects" in the most direct sense pointed again to gardening, an activity that the invocation of "corrupt Nature" already suggests Laurence believed held redemptive power. That suggestion turns explicit in the next sentence: "[W]e might soon see a more virtuous and *enlightened Age*, if it were but rescued from the intolerable trammels of Logick and Rhetorick, the aversion and Bane of Youth, and some of the easy Parts of Natural Philosophy, Practical Mathematics, and Gardening Operations substituted in their place."[64]

If Laurence knew that he was novel in using the phrase *enlightened age*, he drew no attention to the moment, which may itself be telling of how easy it was to set these two words in apposition. The phrase was also already pointed. Laurence did not just place gardening and being enlightened on one side of the equation and moral corruption on the other. He groups the enlightened age and gardening together with natural philosophy and mathematics, and he contrasts all of them to the exemplars of medieval learning: logic and rhetoric. It is not simply that his enjoyment of his own pastime and writing about its pleasures made him offer gardening as a symbol of an enlightened age. He was expressly saying that the enlightened age includes what he calls "the easy Parts"—the basic understanding—of natural philosophy and mathematics.

This too seems to have been his point. It could trivially be said that Eden would have continued forever had the Fall never occurred. But, given that it did occur, it is a bold thing to assert that where gardening in a postlapsarian world matters is where, along with the right kinds of intellectual pursuits, it can offset the effects of original sin and save people from moral decline.[65] Laurence was not just disparaging the medievalism of logic and rhetoric. He was subverting original sin. By the redemptive power he ascribed to gardening—and natural philosophy and mathematics—he was giving the road to salvation a more secular lane. Either it is an incredible irony, or it is incredible that it is not an irony at all. Even the phrase *enlightened age* seems to have grown out of a garden.

Something similar might be said of Francis Bacon, the more noted English author of the secular metaphor of light. One of Bacon's concealed influences was the practice of keeping waste books, which lent themselves to his inductive method.[66] In Bacon's London, waste books were mainly used by artisans and commercial types to organize and administer their businesses. But farmers likely kept waste books too.[67] The logic of the metaphor was already agricultural and for that matter easily made biblical: waste books captured rough data that were uncultivated like the waste land on a farm and like the waste land that might be cultivated to re-create Eden. When Milton writes in the opening lines of *Paradise Regained* "I who e're while the happy Garden sung, / By one mans disobedience lost now sing / Recover'd Paradise to all mankind, / . . . And Eden rais'd in the wast Wilderness," he was only echoing Isaiah 51.3: "[God] will comfort all [Zion's] waste places; and he will make her wilderness like Eden, and her desert like the garden of the Lord." Without too much exaggeration, we could say that Bacon's "new organon" too was born in a garden, with the additional irony that his concealment of his sources looks like theft from the gardeners.

Not all early English uses of the phrase *enlightened age* relate so directly to Eden, depravity, and the Fall, but they still imply a tension—and an awareness of the broader meaning of the tension—between original sin and being enlightened. In 1721, for example, George Berkeley lamented that the essence of what he called the *enlightened age* was that it has "taught us to laugh at everything that is serious as well as sacred."[68] Maybe Berkeley had in mind that laughter itself was sometimes seen as a consequence of the Fall, although the more immediate context for his remark was the South Sea Bubble having burst, an occurrence he directly blamed on rising self-interest and corruption.[69] But the bishop also had irreverent freethinkers in his sights, here as elsewhere. (Samuel Merivale would later write Pentecost Barker about Berkeley's *Alciphron* [1732]: "[T]here is too much acrimony against the free thinkers who are set in a very despicable light, & too great a tenderness for the Church & clergy.")[70] If being enlightened consisted only in knowing how to ridicule, Berkeley reasoned, then such an enlightened state would always do little to stop private interest from eroding public spirit.[71]

But no early use of *enlightened age* is as implicated in the story of Pentecost Barker (to which we are finally about to turn) as one that occurs in an exchange between James Foster (1697–1753) and John Brine (1703–65).[72] Now obscure, Foster was in his day a celebrity preacher and a heterodox one.[73] He had turned away from bedrock Calvinist principles like the Trinity in his twenties.[74] And by his thirties he was targeting original sin in his published sermons, many of which addressed human nature and, as he believed, its benevolence. Foster's apostasy infuriated the Calvinist Baptist minister John Brine, who among other things was the uncle of Barker's correspondent Samuel Merivale. (John Brine and his nephew Merivale had, as we will see, nothing in common ideologically—a "brine" in Barker and Merivale's lingo meant a religious bigot.)[75] Brine read James Foster's works and found them tantamount to atheism. He accordingly dedicated hundreds of pages to showing that Foster and his heretical cohort were destroying Christianity with their new cultural spirit. "[They] seem to account it the Glory of this inquisitive and *enlightened Age*," Brine wrote, "that Religion is thought to contain nothing mysterious, or above the Comprehension of Men."[76]

The particular thing Foster had said to make Brine tag him as a representative of the new enlightened age was that, despite the Fall, human beings still reflect the divine image in which they were made. Brine could concede that the Bible said that in the beginning humankind had been made in a divine image. Foster, for his part, could concede that Adam and Eve had made a mistake. But such concessions did not get to the heart of the dispute. For Foster, alleged consequences of the Fall like sickness and disorder might bedevil human behavior, but not because of an innate moral defect. Bad behavior occurred through an act of will. As Foster saw it, people like Brine had therefore misrepresented the Fall when they had "taken their estimate of human nature" from the "brutal part" of humankind while ignoring its "intelligent and moral" part. Such cynical selectivity explained why the same pessimists "have understood particular passages of scripture which give the character of the most profligate and abandon'd sinners, as describing the natural temper of mankind." Not only should bad people not represent the whole of the species, but bad human tendencies are also of our own making: "Human nature, even in its present state, is a reasonable nature. . . . Our rational and moral powers, by which we resemble the Deity, are the chief excellency and advantage of our nature: By these we are eminently advanced above the brute creatures, rendered capable of the pleasures of society and friendship, and of improvement in knowledge and virtue."[77]

For Brine, all this was an unmistakable refutation of original sin. There was an obvious reason, he thought, that Foster was trying to demonstrate that we all still reflect the divine image: he wanted to defend real improvement in knowledge and virtue while affirming a basic instinct for moral benevolence and sociability, the human traits that made self-improvement not only possible but also likely and desirable if the mind could be properly directed. For Brine, on the other hand, "profligate and abandon'd sinners" were not at all exceptions offered by God to prove an optimistic enlightener rule. Such sinners *were* the rule. If original sin meant anything at all, it was precisely that sinners represent the natural temper of humanity—a temper that distorted the image in which we were made. "If Man is a fallen Creature," he wrote, "he is not what God made him, nor bears his Image." Equally to the point, "*all* Men are Transgressors," he insisted, before appropriating Foster's Enlightenment criteria to drive home his point: "Reason itself affords us evident Proof of this melancholy Truth."[78]

Pentecost Barker, Samuel Merivale, and others in their milieu intimately knew the Foster-Brine debate. Equally well-known was the argument with which Brine concluded, which came forth in what Merivale sarcastically described as a "doughty dialogue" between a Calvinist, a Socinian, an Arminian, a Baxterian, and a Deist. The point of the imagined exchange was didactic and obvious: any doctrinal wavering in the assumption of human depravity doomed Christianity.[79] "Baxterianism," the religious outlook of Richard Baxter, who represented the slightest deviation from Calvinism among Brine's theological examples, wavered on original sin and made room in the salvific equation for the power of moral conduct. Baxterianism in turn led to Arminianism, which in its mid-eighteenth-century iteration signaled a more obvious swerve from Augustine's key doctrine. Arminianism degenerated to Socinianism, a religious philosophy that denied Christ's divinity and opened the door to deism and hence, for Brine, atheism. This was degeneration by theological inexorableness, and, as we will see, the basic argument was made with remarkable consistency: by Calvinists who feared the rising moralism of their own religious brethren; by Catholics like Bossuet, whose only modification was to place Lutheranism and Calvinism at the beginning of the degenerative sequence; and in the years since by historians across the ideological spectrum.[80] There could be disagreement among such people about what exactly would lead to the elevation of human nature. Brine put his finger on the popish veneration of moral conduct; Bossuet put his on Protestant individualism. But the argument was fundamentally the same: with the loss of original sin, Christianity faced an existential threat.

The other thing that stands out is that these arguments were made on a second-order level of reflection. Cassirer and others were not reading into the evidence when they found the Enlightenment's common opponent in original sin. They could have gone further. In the metaunderstanding of Brine, Bossuet, Laurence, evangelicals, Dissenters, canonical enlighteners, and who knows how many others, the rejection of original sin was both a threat to religious orthodoxy and a defining characteristic of a cultural moment that contemporaries expressly called the *enlightened age*.

With his aching foot propped up on a pillow, a seventy-year-old Pentecost Barker felt enough temporary relief from his gout to finish a letter to his confidant and faithful late-life correspondent Samuel Merivale. This was April 25, 1760.

Barker had started his letter earlier in the day to express dismay on being "censur'd by our Calvinists for writing the words Rational Preacher." The oblique reference was to an increasingly toxic dispute within Batter Street Chapel over the Unitarian minister John Hanmer, whom Barker was trying to install in place of the late Peter Baron. Barker had gone to Merivale to see whether he wanted the job for himself. But Merivale knew that, especially since Plymouth's other Dissenter chapel, Broad Street, had embraced Rational Dissent, Batter Street had taken in Broad Street's ideological refugees and become a haven for the orthodox.[81] Merivale had zero interest in ministering to such a congregation.

Barker understood Merivale's rationale, but he still had his own commitments to Batter Street. Peter Baron, his dear friend for decades, had been uncontroversial but open-minded. Baron "can bear to have his opinions debated," and with respect to those "too dogmatic for me . . . I can agree to differ," Barker had explained to Merivale, who needed no explanation because he had known Baron for decades and felt the same. Merivale, for his part, could appreciate from the authoritative side of the pulpit how adept Baron had been at preaching on one level to the orthodox and on another to those who, like Barker, were now dissenting from Dissent. No less important was that Barker had committed decades of his life to Batter Street. Baron's death was no time to walk away from their cherished chapel. It was an occasion to ensure that the congregation would not backslide into orthodoxy, at which point Barker worried that "there will be no rational Dissenters [left] in this once famous town."[82]

When he resumed his letter to Merivale, the anger over the row in Plymouth redirecting his mind from his painful foot, Barker moved on from the local matter of replacing Baron to the general problem of orthodoxy. What made the majority of traditionalist parishioners so obstinate could be reduced to their unwavering belief in absurd doctrine. Barker complained that they still believed in predestination, a harsh notion that gave individuals no agency in their salvation. He complained that they still thought Jesus needed to be a god for there to be a God ("since I lost the Trinity, which was once a darling tenet, I have had no doubt of the Unity," as he put it). But the devastating comment he reserved for original sin: "What a piece of Wisdom to say to God, We left thee in a Garden, because Adam sinn'd there—Shall the son of a Man, whose Father got drunk in an Alehouse, say to God, I left thee in an Alehouse?"[83]

The antideterminism of Barker's analogy had a long history.[84] For a thousand years, Pelagianism had been defined by its opposition to original sin on the grounds that denying free will deprived human beings of their ability to make moral progress. A biblical passage favored by Pelagians (Deut. 24:16) used terms even closer to Barker's: just as "the fathers shall not be put to death for the children, neither shall the children be put to death for the fathers: every man shall be put to death for his own sin." Or, closer to home in Reformed circles, there was the argument made by Simon Episcopius, a Dutch Arminian. Arminianism was nominally the religious philosophy of Jacob Arminius, another Dutch reformer, although one who saw a greater danger in predestination than in original sin. But Arminius could not control his movement from the grave, and, after his death in 1609, Arminianism slowly drifted in the direction favored by his more Pelagian disciples. Episcopius, the most important of these by the mid-seventeenth century, had written in 1643 in his *Institutiones theologicae* (1678) that, if read properly, the story of the Fall had made unequivocal that only Adam was responsible for his own sins.[85]

Barker was therefore making anything but an unfamiliar argument, at least in the fundamentals. But he was doing something distinctive by articulating that argument around his particular sin. In the logic of his alehouse analogy, Adam was the kind of person Barker had been, a drunkard, original sin was analogous to being blamed for your drunk father having lost control, and Eden was the alehouse. The last part sounds like a subconscious revelation: Barker had by later life finally gotten his drinking under control, so did he really mean to compare the alehouse to paradise? But he looked back with a mix of remorse and fondness on the sociability of the White Alehouse in Plymouth, above all his watering holes, where he had spent his early years with his closest friends, almost all of whom died young. For its male sociability and mindless drinking, the alehouse had been a sort of paradise for unmoored men. And hardly less than Eden it was designed to lead one into temptation.

What else Barker was indicating by analogy is that original sin was inconsistent with his own experience. This is a recurring theme in Christian theology: the notion that original sin should be understood along the lines of its existential intuitiveness. An abstract concept like the Trinity required one to accept what Barker saw as a flat-out contradiction. But arguments for and against original sin so often came down to easily observed evidence of selfish behavior. Augustine himself hardly had to look further for proof than the case of whining infants, clamoring for their mothers' breasts during the opening seconds of life, attesting to the selfishness that animates us from the origin of the species and the origins of every individual member of it. In the same vein, but with subversive intent, what Barker was doing with his alehouse analogy was cutting the knot of philosophical debate with a different set of observations. He had been a drunkard, and now he was not. Here, in other words, experience attested to the way in which sin could be overcome. And part of the explanation for Barker was that he had abandoned the dismal, fatalistic self-perception that he found embedded in original sin, a doubly criminal doctrine for failing philosophically to capture the reality of his own agency while bolstering a mode of self-perception that rendered that agency indiscernible.

It is hard to overstate the centrality of original sin to Barker's transformation, not to mention his articulation of the difference between confessional and Enlightenment culture. In his diary, Barker asserted that "without self-denial we can't be Christians."[86] This echoed the language of Christ. "If any man would come after me," according to the gospel of Matthew (16:24), "let him deny himself and take up his cross and follow me." But even more was self-denial an expression of the mortification of the flesh as it took shape in the Pauline tradition, which orthodox Dissent embraced. As Paul put it in his letter to the Romans: "[I]f you live according to the flesh you will die, but if by the Spirit you put to death the deeds of the body you will live" (8:13). The English word *flesh* came from Paul's use of the Greek σάρξ (*sarx*), which in the pages of Barker's copy of the *Critica Sacra* was defined not as "human being" but as "homo corruptus."[87] The "self" of Barker's "self-denial" was corruption embodied. And self-denial was therefore a crucial part of an effort to resist the endless temptation of fallen man: to find redemption in spiritual life through acts of restraint that mortified—killed—life corporeal. The phrase *without self-denial we can't be Christians* has original sin written all over it.

But that was how Barker defined Christianity in 1730. Three decades later, the object of the prepositional phrase *without self-denial* had been turned upside down. In his letters to Merivale, he instead believed that "no man can be a Christian *without being a Deist*."[88] *Deist* had unambiguously been a dirty word for Barker in the diary, where he lines up with other orthodox Christians (e.g., John Brine) in reviling deists for having watered down belief to the point of it being nonbelief. He confessed to his diary more than once that things were so bad and his piety so faltering that he was "tempted to deism," which in context was shorthand for saying that he was on the verge of losing his religion, all the more immediate of a danger because of the heretical views taking shape at the time within English Dissent.[89] In later life, that is, Barker was using the exact same word to identify himself that he had once used to capture the enemy.

And by doing so he was again taking direct aim at the Augustinian tradition. In a different letter to Merivale, this one written in May 1762, a few months before his death, he found another occasion for astonishment as he reminded Merivale that the majority of Batter Street congregants held on to faith in original sin: "Is it not a crime to believe that the whole creation of rational Beings must have perish'd everlastingly, had not [Christ] stepped in & Savd a few . . . that every Man, Woman & Child descended from Adam must have perish'd for his eating the forbidden Fruit & without any one actual sin, had not the Son been more merciful than the Father . . . ? And what's the English of this, but that I was then in the Loins of Adam, & sinned, as he did, tho I knew nothing of it till 5000 years after? Is it any wonder that a Man of sense turns Deist?"[90] Barker was now not only saying that original sin was absurd. He was reappropriating the trope of criminality. Contrary to everything he once believed, humankind's original sin had not induced it to behave criminally. The real crime was the doctrine itself. What is more, recognizing that this pillar of orthodoxy was twisted should therefore compel a personal transformation. A man of sense, acting on his sense and then seeing original sin for what it really is, should *turn* deist. George Whitfield compressed the alternate view into the memorable line we saw earlier: "If you have never felt the weight of original sin, do not call yourselves Christians." In early life, Barker agreed. In later life, he was saying just the opposite. People should not call themselves Christians, in what Barker later saw as the appropriate universalist sense, until they had *ceased* to feel the weight of original sin.

But what has to be stressed here too is the metaunderstanding. For countless eighteenth-century people who fell across the ideological spectrum, rejecting original sin—and being open about it—was precisely where it was appropriate to invoke the metaphor of light in its new secular sense. This was no less true for Barker. In one of his final letters to Merivale, written as the dispute at Batter Street was about to turn into a case for Lord Mansfield and the Court of King's Bench, Barker admitted: "[F]or a long while, I kept the objections against their harsh Doctrine to myself, without coming to an Eclaireisment [*sic*] or to the point with any one nor to any minister but you. But since you lent me [David] Hartley &c, my mind has brighten'd and I am persuaded that we have found the Pearl of great price."[91] Barker's language requires some decoding. *Harsh doctrine* broadly meant orthodoxy, but, as we have seen and will continue to see, nothing made orthodoxy as harsh to Barker as inherited sin. In the same vein, *Hartley &c* does signal the importance that Barker ascribed to David Hartley, one of the century's shrewdest theorists of emotions. But here it is the *&c* that is telling. It implies a cultural coherence. Barker just as easily could have written "Locke &c" or "Rousseau &c," much as in the epigraph that opens this chapter he writes "Horace and Virgil &c &c" to capture the protomodern pagans. What he meant, in other words, was something broadly cultural, the boundaries of which were ever more expansively delineated by the range of authors he was now reading with Merivale: Locke, Voltaire, Rousseau, Bayle, Shaftesbury, Mandeville, La Mettrie, Hume, Toland, and dozens more. Not least, he uses the word *Eclaireisment,* a spelling that can easily be corrected as the French word *éclaircissement,* literally, "enlightenment." Barker never finished the eighteenth-century equivalent of high school. He picked up French not through formal training but on the fly during his time in the navy. His spelling and grammar are understandably imperfect. But the meaning of what he was saying here is obvious. His mind had been brightened and enlightened in part because of the orthodoxy that, through the process of *éclaircissement,* he had left behind.

We will come to what he thought about the fuller meaning of *enlightenment* later on. But first we need to figure out what brought about this dramatic transformation. Original sin was not just a theory of human evil. It was a theory of human nature and the basis of self-perception. This makes the question all the more significant. Not many things are as entrenched as a self-image. So what did it take to shake Pentecost Barker loose of the tenacious, dismal view he had of himself?

CHAPTER THREE

Pentecost Barker

Never was so great a sinner all things considered, as this miserable Pentecost Barker.

Diary of Pentecost Barker, June 27, 1731

Few words from the Bible have been more culturally long-lasting than the forenames—Adam, Barack, David, John, Mary, Paul, Sarah, and so on—whose meanings have mostly been forgotten. The Whig provocateur John Wilkes once made the point to Samuel Johnson that Elkanah Settle, a contemporary playwright, might have achieved more fame had his fanatic-sounding name not put off potential readers. "There is something in names which one cannot help feeling," he said, with an implied sense of assurance, that his own name no longer made one feel that "Yahweh is gracious," the literal meaning of יוֹחָנָן (*Yôḥānān*), or, for short, "John."

This is one of the ironies of Puritan culture: even as people of a cooler religious temperature persisted in naming their children after biblical heroes, the infamous biblical literalists of the time were innovators. For instance, "Praisegod Barebone," the namesake of a short-lived English parliament in the 1650s, baptized his son "If-Christ-had-not-died-for-thee-thou-hadst-been-damned" before the son renamed himself "Nicholas" and became an economist.[1] Birth registers in Puritan strongholds hold countless other examples: Stedfast, Renewed, Safe-on-Highe, Rejoyce, Muche-Merceye, Increased, Sin-denie, Faint-not, Constant, Christophilus, Thankful, Accepted, Lord-is-near, Discipline, More-Fruit, and, straight to the point, Reformation.[2] Biblical literalists deviating from the script looks like a contradiction, but it was this deviation that helped maintain the spirit of their literalism. If no one would hear in *Abigail* the Hebrew for *my father is joy*, then a more obviously hortatory name like *Rejoyce* could convey the point more directly. It captured an idea that parents wanted their children to embody, and it obviated the problem of illiteracy in ancient languages. What one cannot help but feel about these godly named people—what one was supposed to feel—is their social and spiritual set apart–ness from vain and idly named pagans and the profane.[3]

Set apart–ness was no doubt part of the feeling Gregory and Susana Barker wanted to encourage when they gave their firstborn the name *Pentecost*.[4] On the Christian calendar, Pentecost commemorates the moment the Holy Spirit entered the apostles, quieting their doubts, and rousing them to spread the gospel. It was seen by Protestants as a sort of birthday of their religion, and it was a poignant name to give a child on his own birthday, reflecting, at once, the family's link to orthodox Dissent, the origin of their religion, and the possibility of direct experience with the divine. *Pentecost* also turned out for a time to have reflected the feelings of the person it named. By virtue of being born into a pious household, he may at first have had little say in his religion. But years later, when given the chance to reconnect to the Puritan ethos that lingered in Dissent, he did so in a public conversion, laden with the symbolism of regeneration on yet another birthday, the day he turned thirty, which was also the loaded age at which Jesus began his ministry.[5]

Being Pentecost was nevertheless not easy. The piety of his parents and their religious culture fit uneasily with growing prosperity in Plymouth, where Barker was born in 1690, and where after a life lived largely on the move he would die and be buried in late 1762.[6] Since the sixteenth century, Plymouth had been the most important naval town in the southwest of England, the part of the country that pointed to the open Atlantic and the expanding empire. The Elizabethan privateers Walter Raleigh, his cousin Richard Grenville, and his half brother Humphrey Gilbert all came from surrounding Devon. John Hawkins and his cousin Francis Drake, both of whom began their lucrative maritime careers in the slave trade, came from the town of Plymouth itself. So did the Puritans who set out for North America before establishing what, loyal to their point of departure, they called Plymouth Colony.

All this happened while Plymouth was still small. It had fewer than five thousand inhabitants when Francis Drake was the mayor in 1581 and hardly more by 1660, when it ranked only as the twentieth biggest town in England.[7] But by Barker's lifetime it began to reflect its growing importance demographically. The first national census for the United Kingdom would not appear until 1801, although by then Plymouth had pulled ahead of other major towns (York, Newcastle, Oxford, Cambridge, etc.) to become England's seventh biggest city. If even then it still paled next to London or Manchester, it had long since acquired a crucial purpose. Construction began in 1690 on Plymouth dockyard, now Devonport and the largest naval base in Western Europe, although already throughout the eighteenth century one of the Royal Navy's two crucially important "western dockyards" along with Portsmouth.[8] Coincidentally, 1690 was the same year Barker was born. Not at all coincidentally as it relates to the dockyard, the year marked the beginning of a series of global wars with France that would last until Napoléon's final defeat at Waterloo. War, empire, and the needs of the fiscal-military state grew dramatically in scale over the course of the eighteenth century. Barker's Plymouth, which helped ensure the navy's dominance and reach, grew along with them.[9]

The moral difficulty for Barker in all this had less to do with the immediate effects of war and empire than with the related part of the economy that mattered to his family: Plymouth's booming trade with Europe in alcohol.[10] Exactly when Gregory Barker established himself as a wine cooper is unclear, but it had happened by the time Pentecost was a young man, from which point there would be a dozen apprentices living in the Barker household and helping make barrels used to store wine for trade and prolonged voyages. The busy household scene was in one sense telltale evidence of economic prosperity in the category of the middling sort. But it was those same apprentices, "wicked servants" Barker called them, who helped lead him—and possibly his sister, Susan—into temptation.[11]

In this world of mixed signals—godly parents on one side, debauched apprentices on the other, and through their economic interdependence the production of a morally complicated substance that boosted family prosperity—what was never in question was the value of hard work.[12] Like their religious predecessors, Dissenters of Barker's generation prized relentless labor not only for its economic benefits but also for its power to suggest spiritual salvation. As one of Barker's minister's preached: "[W]e should be diligent, not only to be called and elected, but to know that we are so."[13] But what to do when the tangible result of such worldly diligence was alcohol?

In theory, there was an obvious answer. As Barker put it in his early forties, by then in the general business of his father, "without much watchfulness this selling of wine will keep me out of heaven."[14] Hopeful prosperity and hopeless excess could be navigated, that is, by the techniques implicated in the practice of *watching*, a cultural keyword for the godly that signified relentless examination of one's behavior, interior life, and an outside world laden with providential meaning.[15] Watching could nevertheless be difficult to put into practice, especially when it was complicated by the countless opportunities "wicked servants" offered to sin—opportunities made all the more inviting when Barker's mother, Susana, died in February 1708. This was "the greatest affliction that ever befell me," Pentecost wrote twenty years later. His mother had been his spiritual collaborator in the endless effort to resist temptation, and, with "her watchful Eye being gone," he capitulated: "I gave my Self unto all *Iniquity*. . . . O what *Wickedness* did I fall into soon after her Death!"[16] *Iniquity* and *wickedness* were code in the diary for drinking, and it was now drinking and all it entailed that replaced Barker's mother as the guiding force in his life: "From one end of the week to the other, we [i.e., he and his friends] spent our Time in Alehouses, Taverns & Sometimes bawdy houses, tho as to the latter I can't say that we used to compleat the Acts of Debauchery in them but went chiefly for idle Chat, & to sport ourselves with loose Winches without committing the gross act of lewdness with them."[17]

How accurate were these characterizations? If the mix of contrition and bragging common to confessions of recovering addicts is already formulaic, diary writing in the Puritan tradition was more so as diarists exaggerated to demonstrate suitably pious self-persecution. A major template for the genre came from *Grace Abounding to the Chief of Sinners* (1666), an autobiography written by John Bunyan, a pious minister who was hardly the "chief of sinners." Barker remembered himself as being "more criminal, more sinful, abominable & vile" than any of the friends he drank with, which rings a little hollow when he explains what happened to those friends. The closest among them, the "Idol of my heart," drank himself to death in his thirties, and "3 or more" had died "beyond Sea, 1 came home & died in a miserable Condition, others died of Distempers produc'd by Excesses & did not live out half their Days."[18] That Pentecost was the one who lived to tell the tale at the very least suggests he could maintain a measure of distance, one of the likely effects of the watchfulness inculcated by his mother. But, all that said, the fact that he spent so much of his time with these men, about whom he had no reason to lie, means something just as likely. He may not have been the worst sinner who ever lived, but he no doubt deserved some of his self-recrimination.

Other details of Barker's early years can be inferred or gleaned from stray comments in his later letters. He once told Merivale, for example, that he might have been a minister "had not the old J. Bedford frightened [him] into stammering when [he] was about 8 years old."[19] The same teacher pressured Barker to learn Latin not calmly and comprehensively but "as fast as they could teach [him]": "So awed I was by his severity that I could not read a chapter to gain the world, yet I went in again about 13 and stayed 2 years." Where all this may have been headed is hard to say.[20] Throughout his late-life letters, Barker complained that he could not read Latin as well as he would have liked to, although Samuel Merivale would occasionally send him long Latin excepts, and he never asked for a translation.[21] French too he seemed to understand well, even if not perfectly, in part thanks to naval voyages that took him to French-speaking parts of the Mediterranean.[22] Greek was more difficult, which may explain his near indifference to the *Critica Sacra*, a Greek-English biblical lexicon. As he put it toward the end of his life: "I lament in vain my ignorance in Greek, that my dear mother should take me from school, when I had come so far as to be able to construe the 1st and 2nd chapter of the Acts." Although at that point he cared about Greek less because of the New Testament than because he would not live long enough to see the first full English translation of Plato's works.[23]

We also learn from stray comments that, while he was in his early twenties and possibly earlier, Barker was in love with a woman named Peggy Lace whose sudden death in 1711, a "shocking Providence," gave him more incentive to drink.[24] He says nothing about her in any more detail. But that he ended up finding a wife not long after Peggy's death suggests some degree of instrumentality in his eventual marriage, which took place on August 15, 1712. Suggestive too is Barker's neglecting to mention his wife's name in his diary. Other sources indicate that her name was Alice Beer, an almost incredible surname given Barker's great vice.[25] Her father, John Beer (or sometimes Beere), was important enough to become mayor of Plymouth in 1717. That connection no doubt helped Barker briefly become constable for his ward, and it almost certainly helped his career as a purser.[26] We can also imagine that courting a reputable woman required some sobriety. But that is all we can do with relevant details missing from the sources.

The 1710s saw prospects improve for Pentecost's sister too. Named after her mother rather than a biblical virtue, Susan may have faced her own problem with alcohol. That was already a possibility with so much drinking in the house. It is also possible that she was affected by the event that touched off her brother's years of heavy drinking. "That she was expos'd to many Temptations from the death of my dear Mother to this day of her own death is most certain," he wrote the day Susan died, before expressing his hope that "the Errors of her Conduct were not willfully allowed and indulged by her."[27] Whatever mistakes she had made, he prayed they were not entirely her fault, but he continued to lament that "her case was attended with many Difficulties." Some assurance came from believing that she had "gone to appear before a God infinitely Good" and that "all the favorable allowances for her Failings & Infirmities will be made that are consistent with the Eternal Justice."[28]

Clearly, something had made him anxious for her soul. But whatever it was she managed to marry a young minister, Peter Cock, in the 1710s. Along with a particular "discourse of Sophron's [Peter Baron] against keeping bad company," Susan's new husband, a lifelong friend of Barker's, may have played a role in encouraging her brother to become a parishioner at Batter Street, where his entry is recorded on November 6, 1720, shortly after his thirtieth birthday.[29]

Two years and nearly four months later, on February 27, 1723, Barker began a spiritual diary for the purpose of controlling his drinking. Judging by the only surviving volume, which was written from October 28, 1729, to June 27, 1731, this was an artifact of the genre of Puritan diary writing.[30] It reflects belief in Puritan doctrine. It references Puritan authors and their eighteenth-century Dissenter counterparts.[31] It reflects the way Barker read like a Puritan—as both a watchful observer of Providence and a consumer of works of practical divinity. And in formal terms it is written like a Puritan diary, which is to say that it was not a vehicle for Barker's egoism but an instrument of self-discipline.[32] Here Barker looks more like the earliest Puritan diarists than he does some of his nearer contemporaries, who often could not help but undermine the aims of the genre by becoming self-conscious authors, filling their diaries with tables of contents, frontispieces, flourishes, and other features that deviated from the pure practice of piety. Given his notes on his devotional reading, his sermon glosses, his records of the day's deliverances, and the way in which he wove these concerns as a matter of necessity into the *Critica Sacra*, there is reason to believe that Barker cared less about keeping a diary to be an author than about protecting himself from his great vice.[33]

There were signs from the very beginning that the diary was not the success Barker had hoped it would be. A passing comment made in the extant volume references his near drowning from drunkenness in April 1723, which would put the incident shortly after he began writing.[34] By the time he commenced the surviving volume, the diary's failure to keep him sober was even more obvious. He made it through October 28, day 1 of writing. By day 2, he was drinking moderately. By day 3, he was drunk. By day 4, he was hungover and full of regret: "O must this new book contain records of my wretched conduct, & treacherous Behaviour so very soon!"[35]

Was Barker an alcoholic? Did he accordingly write not just a Puritan diary but an alcoholic's diary? In the eighteenth century, the word *alcoholic* was used not to describe people but rather as a modifier in the language of chemistry (*alcoholic thermometers, alcoholic vapors,* etc.). The operative word during Barker's lifetime—and the one he applies regularly to himself—was *drunkard,* which captured what *alcoholic* now means in relation to outward behavior, which is to say someone who drinks to excess with damaging consequences. The case has been made that being called a *drunkard* at the time nevertheless did not carry the association of being an *addict* in a modern sense. The discovery of addiction instead occurred only when alcoholism came to be seen as a problem beyond the control of the alcoholic, a change in perception clearly noticeable in the late eighteenth century and the early nineteenth. Characteristic of the eighteenth-century view was, the argument goes, the opinion of the American evangelical Jonathan Edwards, who saw drunkenness as a condition drunkards could surmount.[36]

This narrative has some merit, but the story is more complicated and more interestingly so in its suggestion of some of the deeper implications of the Puritan ethos.[37] The language of being *addicted,* for one thing, appears front and center in Puritan admonitions. Increase Mather subtitled his influential *Wo to Drunkards* from 1673 *Two Sermons Testifying against the Sin of Drunkenness: Wherein the Wofulness of That Evil, and the Misery of All That Are Addicted to It.* Being *addicted* to something in seventeenth- and eighteenth-century English could admittedly just mean adhering to that thing; and, much as people could change their minds about what beliefs they adhered to, by the logic of this early word usage they could also change their habits in relation to some substance to which they were addicted.[38] But already overlapping this common sense of the word in the eighteenth century was being addicted by virtue of *immoderate* devotion, which veered into suggestions of losing the sort of judgment necessary to maintain self-control. The Essex Dissenter minister John Mason, for example, wrote in his *Treatise on Self-Knowledge* (1745), a book Barker later owned and admired, that "self-acquaintance shews a Man the particular Sins he is most exposed and *addicted* to," before relating these very sins to "the temptations which [we] have least power to resist."[39]

What also merits rethinking is the cultural timing of alcoholism. For a long time, the progenitor in the history of the diagnosis of alcoholism was the physician Benjamin Rush (1746–1813), who made four central points. According to an influential sociology of drinking: "First [Rush] identified the causal agent—distilled liquor. Second, he clearly described the drunkard's condition as a loss of control over drinking behavior—as compulsive activity. Third, he declared the condition to be a disease. And fourth, he prescribed total abstinence as the only way to cure the drunkard."[40] But were these really novel criteria? Richard Baxter, a writer whom Barker read throughout his life and arguably the most widely read of all late Puritan and early Dissenter authors of practical divinity, tackled the problem of drunkenness in a long section of his *Christian Directory* (1673) where a drunkard appears as someone who "*would* drink too much if he *had it* [alcohol], and is not restrained by his *will*, but by Necessity."[41] Baxter also expressly identified the causal agents, which for him were wine and ale rather than distilled liquor, although that is a distinction without much of a chemical difference.[42] Just as interesting is that he prescribed the equivalent of abstinence to treat the problem: if a drunkard given access to alcohol will drink too much, then the best thing to do is to inhibit access or to restrain by "necessity." Finally, he pointed to the limits of willpower where the drinker operates in a state of ignorance. He can admittedly assign agency an important role when he writes that one cause of being a drunkard is weak reasoning and weak faith in the face of "a beastly raging appetite." But "another cause" of drunkenness is drunkards' "*not-knowing* that their excess and tippling is really a hurt or danger to their health."[43] Knowing about such consequences should otherwise make one exercise restraint. But how can people be fully responsible for not knowing what they do not know?

Baxter was also foreshadowing later medical orthodoxy in associating drinking with disease. He does not identify the disease as drinking in and of itself. He emphasizes the various pathologies that drinking causes. But this nuance lines up with much modern medical understanding according to which "alcoholism becomes a disease when loss of voluntary control over alcohol consumption becomes a necessary and sufficient cause for much of an individual's social, psychological, and physical morbidity."[44] Morbidity for Baxter was these things too—along with being a danger to his own health, a "drunkard" was "an enemy to thy family," "a heinous consumer of thy pretious Time," and so on. What, for Baxter, was even more damning, more worrisome, and more tied to the Puritan ethos was a sort of moral morbidity, the assumption of which gave him occasion to invoke the language of depravity so often seen in relation to original sin. In his words, a drunkard was "the *shame of humane nature*":

> Thou representest man in the likeness of a Beast, and worse: As if he were made but instead of a Barrel or a sink: Look on a drunkard filthing and spewing and reeling and bawling, and see if he be not uglyer than a bruit? Thou art a shame to thy *own Reason,* when thou shewest the world, that it cannot so much as shut thy mouth, nor prevail with thee in so small a thing. Wrong not *Reason* so much as to call thy self

> *Rational*; and wrong not mankind so much as to call thy self a *man*: *Non homo sed amphora*, said one of *Bonosus* the drunken Emperour when he was hang'd: *It is a barrel and not a man*.[45]

Puritans were not always the killjoys tendentiously represented in later literature and historiography. In the messiness of reality, people who were called and sometimes called themselves *Puritans* drank, had sex, and found other ways to engage in the pursuits of the material world.[46] But the prescriptive advice that emerged from so much of their literature of practical divinity—even from relatively moderate voices like Baxter's—was still strenuous. And if believers like Barker took the advice seriously, they must have embodied it to some degree. All this is to say that, if godly opinion makers were formulating the definition of *alcoholic* and *alcoholism* before the letter, then their receptive readers may have been precocious alcoholics. They obviously were not the first people to drink too much. What they pioneered under the influence of moral advice that both admonished and anticipated the alcoholic was their suitability for the diagnosis.

This raises possibilities related to Barker's changing outlook. In still the most thorough history of alcoholism, the American psychiatrist George E. Vaillant argued that, despite the complex etiology of alcoholism, "alcoholics . . . invariably suffer from impaired morale": "If they are to recover, powerful new sources of self-esteem and hope must be discovered." Vaillant believed that "religion provides fresh impetus for both hope and enhanced self-care." But if religion serves this role, he was careful to say that it is because "in ways that we appreciate but do not understand, [it] provides forgiveness of sins and relief from guilt."[47] All this can be taken to mean that, if not all religions provide such forgiveness and relief, then not all have this therapeutic effect.

It is beyond the scope of this book to talk comprehensively about religion with respect to its role in aiding recovery from addiction. But we can easily tell what Barker later thought about the self-esteem encouraged by his earlier faith. As a Rational Dissenter, he looked back on his orthodox years and found relentless sin and guilt. Contrary to self-esteem, Calvinism encouraged what was supposed to be a spiritually healthy—although for someone with addictive tendencies an emotionally unhealthy—dose of self-loathing. The whole point of the alehouse analogy—Barker's alcohol allegory against original sin—was that it showed the unfairness of being accused of Adam's sin. How well suited was Calvinism to provide the relief from guilt that a drunkard needed when the same religion encouraged its adherents to take the blame for something someone else did?

Barker may not have read the passages I have quoted from Baxter's *Christian Dictionary*, although, given his affection for Baxter and Baxter's pointed comments on drinking, it is almost unthinkable that he did not (in which case we can wonder how *non homo sed amphora*—"not a man but a barrel"—would have struck a wine cooper). But he reasoned the same way. He too thought the problem was spiritual. "A Man in Covenant with God should have . . . reason to be afraid that he is a Drunkard," he admitted to his diary.[48] No less worrying was what drinking was doing to his health. Some of the damage was magnified by his anxiety. By his own admission he was "what the world calls the Hypo and what many are apt to laugh at." Hypochondria nevertheless induced real trauma. It was the "hypos," he wrote, who "have more need of their Prayers" than anyone else "under bodily afflictions."[49] Barker suffered too from what he called *apoplectic* fits, a vague term that in the eighteenth century described the presentation of symptoms rather than a single disease.[50] The symptoms may have been stroke-like. He may have suffered from epilepsy or panic attacks. Concrete details are missing. But what is clear is that his fits were memorable and haunting.[51] So, for that matter, was his insomnia, a predictable outcome, as he well knew, of his binges, a condition for which he sometimes took opium.[52] He copied a line from the seventeenth-century essayist Francis Osborne to serve as an epigraph on the opening page of his diary and a reminder to be industrious and wakefully attuned to spiritual dangers: "Leave your bed upon the first desertion of sleep; it being ill for the eyes to read lying, and worse for the mind to be idle; since the head during that laziness is commonly a cage for unclean thoughts."[53] The words must have reverberated during the sleepless nights when he was too drunk to get out of bed but still trapped in his "cage for unclean thoughts," listening to his heart pound (a detail he does often give), and cycling through the ways he was slowly destroying his body and soul.

Running throughout the diary, it is worth saying too, are also Barker's concerns that his health was endangered by his gluttony, especially after eating meat. An aspirational vegetarian, Barker was all but guaranteed to fall short of his aims if he had been drinking and meat was available. And, as predictably, he purged after indulging. It is not wrong to consider him bulimic in the functional sense in which, with regularity, he lost control, binged, and then purged. But that is not to say that his practice was therefore unusual. Purging—usually by emetic—was a form of what would later be called *heroic medicine*, a set of approaches aimed at restoring humoral balance by ridding the body of fluid or substance—sweat, blood, the contents of the stomach.[54] Probably more unusual were the motives for the diet he tried to maintain. He deviated from

Presbyterian orthodoxy as it came forth in the writing of Thomas Edwards, who treated vegetarianism as an offshoot of heresy.[55] But neither did he perfectly line up with contemporary vegetarians like Benjamin Franklin, who thought a meatless diet was both healthy and ethical (until he smelled a savory fish cooking over a campfire, saw it had devoured other smaller fish, and rationalized his way back to being a carnivore in time for dinner). Franklin's vegetarian diet had been inspired by Thomas Tryon, a seventeenth-century author who advocated for vegetarianism where acquiring food required doing violence to "inferior Creatures" who "cry and send forth their Complaints to their maker."[56] In his diary Barker seemed to care about only what meat was doing to his body.[57]

But to the extent that nothing more reliably opened the floodgates than drinking, what meat was doing to Barker was ultimately about what alcohol was doing to him, which is another way of saying what I have already suggested. The language in the diary indicates that he, if anyone, had internalized the prefiguratively modern Puritan condemnation of drinking. He could identify the substance. He knew it was by various routes a danger to his spiritual and physical health. He could not stop himself. And he had nothing close to a proven self-image for ameliorating his addiction. Some of his low self-esteem was admittedly reenforced by drinking itself—drinking was his big sin, and his sinfulness only affirmed his self-hatred. But the self-perception that made an escape route from his addictive behavior so elusive was primordially encouraged by the belief that guilt was inescapable and that self-loathing was therefore a suitable desire. What Barker would later describe as "the fetters" of Luther and Calvin therefore presented a stifling paradox.[58] Orthodoxy laid out the diagnostic terms of alcoholism and its morbidities while prescribing a model of self-perception that, in its harshness, made a cure all the harder to find.

Yet it was worse than that. Barker's bind was as economic as it was emotional, psychological, spiritual, or physical. In one sense, there was an emerging view in Britain that drinking was tied to the difficulty of "managing populations" and maximizing personal productivity.[59] Barker could certainly lament his efficiency, especially when hungover, much as he could regret the days wasted at the alehouse. But his more particular dilemma came from the dependence of his prosperity on the thing he was trying to avoid. By way of one job or another, the money he made could always be traced to alcohol.[60] In his last diary entry, he looked back over the decade that had passed since joining Batter Street: "I have now been in Covenant with God—10 years & 3 months, have daily kept an account of my actions for more than 8 years, and yet alas, I have made a very small Improvement in the Christian Life, nay have reason to fear, that I am upon the Declension rather than the Growth in Grace. Sad case indeed how many records of Drunkenness, Discontent, and worldly mindedness doth this volume bear against me. . . . Never was so great a sinner all things considered, as this miserable Pentecost Barker."[61] What Barker understood is that the "drunkenness, discontent, and worldly mindedness" that he found everywhere in his diary and in his life were inextricable.

By Barker's reckoning, the first day of February 1730 marked the eighth anniversary of "a daily account of my conduct" written to use "divine assistance" to "suppress . . . that accursed Inclination that was within me to follow strong drink."[62] This was Barker in a state of optimism: "[T]ho' I have many times gone too far, yet I trust I do not allow myself to drink extravagantly," as he recalled he had done so catastrophically in the past. As the month wore on and he nearly wore himself out social networking, it was clear why he was so often inclined. It was a far too regular occurrence to be led from "one Glass to another till I could drink no more, & brought up that which I had drank. Good God Defend me! What am I still a Drunkard after having made so many Remonstrances against it & suffer'd so very much by it?"[63] The next day he went to go hear a sermon but was too hungover to pay attention. He returned home, pulled out his diary, and came back to his self-recriminatory habit of recalling how long he had been a congregant at Batter Street: "It is enough to fill me with Eternal Horror and Despair, that after more than 9 years & 4 Months being in Covenant with God I am still so very fickle and inconstant." The previous night of excess "should be a Day of Humiliation and sorrow to me as long as I live": "I let down my Watch. . . . I was off my Guard and as Soldiers in such a case meet with a severe Punishment, so may God chastise me severely in this world and punish me Eternally in the next." In the lament, Barker reveals why it was all but guaranteed that he would let down his watch again and again. He was "ensnar'd" in the company of "a Man in power here, one of the principal Inhabitants": "I was fond of being known to him."[64]

This was why Barker complained of worldly mindedness in the same breath in which he bemoaned his drinking and discontent: he was constantly ingratiating himself with local elites to build his reputation. As he put it on another occasion: "[T]here are many sins within me, such as Ambition, Pride, & a Desire to appear Somebody in the World, & to be able to say, I am acquainted with this and that and the other Person, who I think are men in some power and make a figure in the world. Wretched man that I am! May God forgive me for Christ his Sake, and may I in the afterlife be more watchful, live more by Faith in an unseen world."[65] Or on yet another occasion and straight to the point: "[T]o ingratiate my Self with Persons of figure and in power, I comply with things that I should abstain from were I in better Circumstances."[66] Whatever prospects of independence lay in the future, Barker in his here and now needed the favors of men who could provide the social and economic capital necessary for his main line of work.[67] He held down several jobs earlier in his life—cooper, wine merchant, lighthouse keeper.[68] But the job he held the longest, the one that brought him the greatest number of personal connections, likely the greatest amount of wealth, and the one that made drinking so complicated in his early middle age was as a ship's purser, the Royal Navy's provisioner and overseer of a ship's consumable goods.

Victualing ships "was not the most heroic branch of the navy," Linda Colley has written, "but it was the most vital" in allowing for ever more distant and ambitious voyages by keeping men in relatively good health.[69] Victualing ships was also, however, the most corrupt branch of the navy. According to Samuel Pepys, the renowned diarist and the naval administrator most responsible for the first round of the victualing system's major reforms during the Restoration: "[A] purser without professed cheating is a professed loser, twice as much as he gets." The core reason, writes the naval historian N. A. M. Rodger, was that the system "not only encouraged the pursers to fraud but virtually enforced it."[70] Pursers were held financially responsible for many of the goods and services they doled out, which ranged from food and drink to candles, bedding, and credit. These were also entrepreneurial men, constantly looking to turn a profit in a system without any regulation, and almost guaranteed to skim from the top to do so.

Pepys understood that the problem was structural, and toward the end of the reign of Charles II he tried to fix the system by making it more responsive to central oversight, which called for more detailed and honest accounting from pursers while realigning the victualing board to take over much of the role of financing provisions from local creditors. The implementation of reforms was nevertheless uneven, while the pursers remained chronically underpaid. Well into the eighteenth century, wages amounted to a few shillings a month at most, even as the transactions pursers oversaw, like issuing credit to sailors, grew more complex. Pursers unsurprisingly continued to find ways to augment their wages. They consistently angled, for example, for built-in "commissions," which were revenue sources that varied according to the amount of supplies they used, the size of the ship they were assigned to, the kind of activity the ship was engaged in, and so on.[71] If such angling was not already suspicious, other built-in customs allowed for skimming extra income off the top, like the "purser's pound," a deliberately short weight, seven-eighths of a pound that was designed to compensate for loss due to evaporation or spoilage and also ready-made to encourage the "creative practices" found throughout pursers' accounting books.[72] As Ned Ward put it in *The Wooden World Dissected* (1707), the period's most influential if tendentious anatomy of the navy, the purser is "the man can boast, that he never purchas'd his preferment with money, for it was his want of it, that got him shuffl'd into his Post, that he might clear off his Debts at the Sailors Cost." The purser was the captain's "Privy-Counsellor" who will "take the meat from other mens bellies"; "he's the most excellent alchemist in Nature, for he can transmute rotten pease, and musty Oatmeal, into pure Gold and Silver"; "in him Miracles are not ceas'd, for he ofttimes turns Water into Wine, and Wine into Water." Throughout the eighteenth century, editions of *The Wooden World Dissected* continued like Ward's one-liners, and the perception they drove home was obvious: pursers were not to be trusted.[73]

The diary offers no evidence that Barker deserved any of these insults, least of all the worst of them. But there is evidence that he was entrepreneurial. And in that spirit his visits to the homes of elites may have been driven by the search not just for social capital but for financial credit, which he may have used to do more than provision ships with perishable goods. After Pepys's reforms, perishable goods were authorized by the ship's captain and mostly paid for by the Victualling Board. But pursers still had to acquire credit to purchase other "necessaries" for a naval voyage: candles, bedding, lamp oil, tobacco for the sailors, coal and firewood for the galleys.[74] Pursers might also still do the sort of related work on the side that required capital investment. Barker, for example, tried to consolidate his work as a cooper and wine seller with his work as a purser in the 1740s and again through his London wine shop in the early 1750s (more on this in the next chapter).[75] That he was referencing selling wine in his final diary entries is a good indication that he was already trying to consolidate his ventures by 1731.

But whether it was to find work on ships or to acquire credit, during the diary years Barker still had to walk into the homes of Plymouth's elites and convince them that he was reputable, credible, and reliable.[76] If that effort was not already complicated by the prejudice against his vocation, it was made worse by the fact that the creditors were overwhelmingly Anglicans while, at the time of the diary, Barker was anything but a Rational Dissenter. He was an avowed Calvinist. Hence the dilemma we opened this book with. Orthodox Dissent of the sort Barker embodied in early middle age was commonly associated—even by Barker himself in later life—with fanaticism and enthusiasm. Abstemiousness would have only confirmed the stereotype. Yet acceptance of the wine that polite company offered meant opening the door to one of his binges.[77]

The perils of social-capital drinking on a slippery slope made life stressful enough. But the drinking itself also appreciably contributed to Barker's debt. After a Sunday sermon in the late summer of 1730, Barker despaired that he could not help but "to sin without control and to drink inordinately," before offering the explanation: "[Drinking] could not be done without Money and to get Money I did things which must not be committed to writing. I borr'd money and as I think began with a shilling and proceeded to pounds and have continued borrowing from one and another to this very day so that I am scores of pounds in debt, and have bin in debt for more than 20 years."[78] It is a revealing comment. The problem was not just that he had to drink politely with his lenders, which, given his addiction, meant drinking excessively on his own later in the evening. The problem was also that all the drinking meant spending some of the money that, through the complicated nexus of seeking credit, he had already compromised his self-control to borrow. If he could not control the sin of drinking, how could he ever manage the debt that supported it? The solution to his debt and drinking therefore was not simply more money or more credit. In that case he would likely just spend more on drink, fall more into debt, feel more anxiety, and then despairingly feel more need to drink.

Things got only worse toward the end of the diary when he started selling wine, which put him in the position of being a retailer of the object of his addiction. Now, still more palpably, he had to face the dilemma of alcohol as the source of both sin and salvation. His debts persisted. And, surrounded by the product that offered a route to solvency alongside the benefits and dangers of intoxication, he lost control, often by drinking as the wine passed between the cask and the bottle.[79] In these bouts of drunkenness, two major currents run through the diary: his suicidal feelings of self-loathing and the growing incompatibility between his behavior and religious orthodoxy.

As some of the lines from the diary that I have already quoted suggest, Barker was no different from countless Puritans and Dissenters who saw their success in the world as an auspicious sign of their spiritual prospects. By itself, this was always a set up for a potential spiritual problem: a measure of economic success could lessen anxiety about salvation, but economic *excess* was no more promising than poverty. That made striving in the world as dangerous as any medicine that in heavy doses becomes a poison, especially as the commercial eighteenth century shifted the cultural standards of what counted as "moderate" and "excessive" profit and worldliness. As tricky as all this already was, what compounded the dilemma was again that Barker was also retailing in a morally ambiguous substance.

But Barker did not endlessly suffer because of these tensions. He was pushed by them toward a new religious outlook and, along with it, a new self-perception. In the final months of the diary, at the end of February 1731, amid his work as a wine merchant, he experienced one of his obscure fits, after which he began to argue with his wife—whether drinking was involved he does not say. Then he "broke forth into most outrageous language" and "talk'd of hanging or destroying" himself.[80] Weeks later, and "after 20 years & ½ being a profest xtian," he faced danger as great as anything he had yet confronted before recording this remarkable admission: "I am tempted to Deism." A large part of the reason? "I am so much in debt that instead of exercising my thoughts about religious matters, they are day and night employed about the unhappiness of my worldly circumstances."[81] By the next month, growing debt was again leading him to the bottle. He recognized that he was "not free from suspicion of being a drunk."[82] Nor was the suspicion without justification. Two days later, he abused wine and "strong drink."[83] In another two days, he drank too much wine while bottling it. Here, however, he jettisoned the spiritual motive for feeling bad about his actions and gave his behavior a medical gloss. "I have behaved pretty well today," he wrote on May 3, 1731, "but the Devil would persuade me that I have drank too much, whereas I don't know that I have drank more than 5 small glasses of wine so that if I should perplex myself about this I think I should give myself needless trouble. As to the thoughts that I have been vext with I believe they may be a part of my Distemper and a Disease rather than a Sin."[84]

Here we have to pause. A ship's purser is teetering between early modern and modern notions of drinking in the pages of a humble Puritan diary that was written—effectively hidden—inside another book. His religion is telling him that five glasses of wine is too much and therefore a sin. The more secular voice emerging in his head is telling him he may have a disease. One view of drinking he associates with orthodoxy; the other he expressly bundles into deism. A major cultural change is being contemplated in miniature and in obscurity.

But then the thought that maybe it was not all his fault—and any relief that may have come from that thought—vanished. Days later he listened to the devil and returned to his orthodoxy. On May 6, he recorded the line we came across earlier: "[W]ithout much watchfulness this selling of wine will keep me out of heaven." On May 8, he noted: "I must go [to communion] tho it be with a doubting faith, lest the power of Melancholy increase so far upon me, that it ends in actual Despair & I come at last to lay violent hands upon my Self & put an end to a wretched life here, to begin a much more miserable & tremendous one in the world of wicked spirits." After rejecting the idea that he could blame his drinking on disease, he again expressed suicidal thoughts ("I could even destroy myself") because of selling and consuming wine, confusion, "madness," and his seeming drift from his faith.[85] The gap between his religiosity and his worldliness was growing. His minister exhorted him "to the Duty of Self Examination," but he could "range nothing in tolerable Method": "I afterwards spent some time with a godly Minister, and tho I drank a glass or two of wine more than common yet I trust that I did not willfully offend. . . . O let me pray for submission & resignation to the will of God. It is the desire of my soul tho my flesh rebels against it."[86]

Barker was at a turning point. One solution to the problem was to end it all, a reliable route to hell and not ideal. Another was maybe too ideal. It was to stop drinking, an unrealistic option while he was surrounded by wine and poised to make money from it. But there was a third option. He could abandon the religious outlook that made him despair about his drinking. This is not to say he could then drink with abandon. He still had to confront the physical damage and the other social morbidities. But as hinted at by the medical gloss of "5 small glasses" as a symptom of disease rather than depravity, he may have been contemplating a softer view of human nature—a retooling of self-perception—that could help him drink less and then feel better about himself emotionally, spiritually, and physically.

What turned these pressures into motive forces was not deism in a purely intellectual sense. Admittedly, ideas and carefully made arguments could be the catalyst of change for some of Barker's contemporaries. In later life, Benjamin Franklin recalled that reading the "Boyle Lectures"—high-profile sermons given in London to put Newtonian science in the service of religion—"wrought an effect . . . quite contrary to what was intended by them": "[T]he arguments of the Deists which were quoted to be refuted, appeared to me much stronger than the refutations."[87] But Franklin's experience cannot account for Barker. If the intellectual encounter with deism had been compelling enough to effect a change, why did not Barker become a deist as soon as that religious philosophy was made available to him, which was long before the diary?[88]

We can also rule out that Barker was a closet heretic waiting to be given permission to reveal his true beliefs. Among Calvinist or Reformed denominations, English Presbyterianism had comparatively few mechanisms for maintaining orthodoxy, like the consistory, a council of elders that elsewhere in the Reformed world policed new ideas. The absence of these modes of discipline may have already conditioned English Presbyterians to be susceptible to new ideas. It also mattered that in the late seventeenth century the denomination had fallen under the influence of figures like Richard Baxter and Daniel Williams, who were undogmatic when it came to doctrine.[89] But a more dramatic change occurred in the wake of the Salter's Hall synod, a meeting of English Dissenter ministers in 1719 at which a slim majority of Presbyterians, in opposition to the other main factions, the Baptists and Independents, refused to force their coreligionists to subscribe to the Thirty-Nine Articles, the Protestant confession of faith that dated back to the early years of the Reformation.[90] The vote against subscription caused a polarity shift in the meaning of *Presbyterian* and *Independent* (the Baptists were more evenly split down the middle). Once known for their relative tolerance in the days of Oliver Cromwell, the Independents came to be associated with conservatism. The Presbyterians, the more austere Calvinists of the previous century, became an eighteenth-century haven for the heterodox.[91] If there was ever an opportune moment for Barker to embrace heterodoxy, Salter's Hall was it. Barker often simply writes "1719" in his later letters to Merivale to signal that this was, in fact, a pivotal moment in Dissent more broadly. But it was conspicuously the year *after* Salter's Hall that Barker openly made his covenant with God as a congregant at a steadfastly traditional Presbyterian chapel, Batter Street. If anything, 1719 only seemed to make Barker more orthodox.[92] The record of sermons in his diary makes even clearer that Batter Street ministers were anxious about what was happening to Presbyterianism. By all indications, Barker understood exactly which doctrines were being interrogated and was anxious along with them.[93]

What pointed Barker in a different direction was instead a set of more mundane and emotional pressures. And what was ideally suited to turn those pressures into transformational forces was the experience of seeing others doing things another way.

European contact with the non-European world posed all manner of theological problems for orthodox Christians. Pre-Columbian people in America challenged the narrative of Genesis by their mere existence. According to the Bible, Noah and his family had been the only people to survive the flood, after which Noah's three sons and their wives went off to settle the known world—Ham to Africa, Shem to Asia, Japheth to Europe. There was no fourth son and therefore no obvious way to use the Bible to account for a fact already apparent to Europeans by the early sixteenth century: people had been living for a long time on huge continents in the Americas separated by oceans too vast to be crossed by Old World ships. The theological problems extended beyond biblical literalness. If there was no descent from Adam by way of Noah, then there was no original sin.[94] For this reason, it was crucial to believe, as Jacques-Bénigne Bossuet was only one of many to put it, that God "wanted all human races to be reduced to the one race of Adam, so that all men, according to body and soul, depend on Adam's will and freedom."[95]

How much these theological abstractions mattered to ordinary people can be hard to tell. Complications and contradictions arising from the juxtaposition of the narrative of Genesis to distant experience might first have to be pointed out. No less heretical than doing that, at least in the sixteenth century and the early seventeenth, was the solution to the problem known as *polygenesis*: the view that humans arose from multiple points of origin rather than the single point depicted in the monogenist Bible.[96] Even where there was awareness of biblical inaccuracies, without having something at stake to drive home the latent implications it was easy enough to go on with business as usual. For Barker, however, there *was* something at stake. What gave non-Christians enough importance to be included in his diary was how adept they were at avoiding the temptations into which he was constantly led.

The success of others where he had failed could sometimes be found in books. The same Francis Osborne whom Barker gave pride of place on the opening page of his diary had written something about indigenous Americans that resonated with him enough for him to record this in the diary: "[T]he Indians, by the great moderation they use, are well able to digest raw flesh."[97] This was in fact the only observation Barker noted in the main body of his diary from his reading of Osborne—that indigenous Americans could do something he could not when they ate meat with enough restraint to avoid indigestion. Which is not to say that Barker was then ready to walk away from his beliefs. But why write any of this down at all? What is more, if the point was about moderation, why did non-Christians on the other side of the world possess that virtue?

Reading Osborne did not make Barker raise theological questions, like whether moderately tempered, healthy "heathens" could ever make it to heaven. But the possibility that in the diary-keeping years Barker was beginning to believe that such people could be saved (he fully believed this during his later years) is raised by a different moment of exposure to the broader world, when he linked geographic and cultural knowledge more directly to emotion. "How affecting is it," he wondered in one of his diary entries months after reading Osborne, "to consider the state of the World. How little do we know of Gods dealings with the Children of Men? What can one say of the Condition of poor Heathens in another state?"[98]

The catalyst of these feelings was Barker's one rumination in the diary on the slave trade. Why only one is itself a question worth asking. John Hawkins was, as we noted, not just from Plymouth. He had set out from Plymouth's port in 1562 on his precedent-setting slaving expedition to Africa, giving himself the ignoble distinction of being England's first modern slave trader and Plymouth that of being the first English port directly involved in that trade. But during Barker's lifetime the slave trade had come to be dominated by Bristol, Liverpool, and London, leaving Plymouth to focus on other facets of empire and the economy, namely, shipbuilding. It may be relevant too that Barker served only on warships in the Mediterranean, not on ships that crossed the Atlantic.

What Barker was willing to say about the slave trade on this standout occasion is nevertheless significant. After the line quoted above—"what can one say of the Condition of poor Heathens in another state"—he continues:

> I was told last Night, that the Negroes at Guinea sell one another to our English Merchants; ~~by load~~ they are brought onboard our ships for Sale. Good God, that humane Creatures should deal thus by one another! And what can one say to it, that profest Xtians should thus deal with their fellow Creatures? Did they carry them from their own Country to teach them the Gospel, 'twould be very commendable, but they trade upon a part of themselves, for there is no doubt, but ~~a Negr an Ethiopian~~ a Negro hath a rational Soul, ~~as well as~~ as capable of Immortality as that of a European, and I never read the 18th of Revelations & 13th but I think of our Guiney Trade. How it can be justified I can't see, but this I firmly believe, that God will deal very favorably by these poor Creatures in another State. May I so manage, as that as the last Day, I may not be among the Number of wicked Christians, for if I am, amazingly dreadful must my case be![99]

Why Barker uses exclamation marks to express astonishment is unclear. On the one hand, when he writes "I never read the 18th of Revelations & 13th but I think of our Guiney Trade" he uses the present simple verb tense, which suggests that *whenever* he reads Revelations 18:13—the text of which is "cargoes of cinnamon and spice, of incense, myrrh and frankincense, of wine and olive oil, of fine flour and wheat; cattle and sheep; horses and carriages; and human beings sold as slaves"—he always thinks of the slave trade. In that case, he knows the slave trade well, and maybe even thinks about it often, but in any event calls it to mind when occasioned by this biblical passage about Babylon before its fall (which looks not unlike prosperous, commercial, and slave-trading Britain in the 1730s). On the other hand, he writes as if he was hearing about the details for the first time. Was it therefore the details that explain the surprise? Maybe. But what he puts in writing is not all that detailed. Yet another qualification is that, for all his talk of what is and isn't "humane," Barker, still at this point an orthodox Protestant, would have approved of captivity for religious conversion. ("Did they carry them from their own Country to teach them the Gospel, 'twould be very commendable.")

The previous night's conversation seems in any case to have made him consider the slave trade more fully, after which he could not help but undermine some of the same orthodoxy he otherwise displays in his diary. One sign of cracks in the foundation is the erasures. He started to write the word *negro* before writing *Ethiopian*. It may be that he was using both words interchangeably—*Ethiopian* came from the Greek for *black skinned* and was used in this generic sense in the King James Bible (see Jer. 13:23). But why did he draw a line through both words before returning to his first word choice? Why the expression of hesitation? Did he reconsider his initial wording because, as first stated, it was too theologically challenging in signifying such a large number of non-Christians from the African continent? Did he then turn to *Ethiopian* as an alternative because in a more precise sense Ethiopia was a Christian kingdom? Or more radically, at least in a theological sense, did he return to writing the word *negro* because he decided that, in fact, he did want to ensure that the statement he was about to make about "rational souls" should apply to *non*-Christian Africans, which the word *Ethiopian* may have been too ambiguous to signal clearly? That last possibility squares with his final word choice, which ends up being central to the premise of his underlying theological proof. Premise 1: A rational soul makes one capable of immortality. Premise 2: Africans have souls as rational as any European's. Conclusion: As capably as Europeans, "heathens" can go to heaven.

What, then, did he mean by *capable*? One possibility is relatively tepid. It is that rational capability is simply the condition that makes one suitable for exposure to the gospel, which would then remain key to salvation. And because all people are rational, non-Christian Africans can be instructed in the Bible as easily as, for example, the unreformed in Europe. A second possibility is more theologically heretical. It is that already in the diary Barker was entertaining what in later life he would come to hold as an article of faith: the view that rationality by itself made one predisposed to behave morally. Here the implication was, in other words, that moral behavior justifies salvation regardless of any exposure to the gospel. What ultimately matters is not faith in Christ. What matters is moral conduct. This is exactly what Barker professes thirty years later in his letters to Merivale. It is the opposite of what he professes on virtually every other page of the diary.

What makes likelier the possibility that Barker was already contemplating the saving power of works is that it gels with the most striking of the broader cultural encounters in the diary. In the spring of 1730, several months before his entry on the slave trade, he stepped outside books and hearsay and into the realm of direct experience when he met three men from Bengal. This happened not on the open seas but in what he refers to as "Morely," by which he almost certainly meant the small village now called Moreleigh in Devon, where the men were en route to Plymouth for their return trip back to Asia.[100] Why they were there is never made clear in the diary, but their presence is not surprising given what historians now know about the "counterflow to colonialism," which brought South Asians to the British Isles throughout the seventeenth and eighteenth centuries.[101] Maybe equally unsurprising, considering that in the early eighteenth century such encounters were not yet so routinely racialized, Barker notices these men for their status (they were "gentleman-like") rather than for the color of their skin.[102] What is surprising, however, given his ostensible beliefs, is that Barker commended their conduct to such a degree that he wondered if, despite the "heresy" of being Muslim, they were good candidates for salvation.

Even more intriguing about this encounter is that, in sermons at Batter Street, Barker had been explicitly told to be suspicious of Islam. A few months earlier, he opened his diary to record a minister's claim that Christianity is "free from inconsistencies and contradictions wherewith it is charg'd by some," the "some" being at first a proxy for deists. But in the same sermon the minister, a young and himself more orthodox Peter Baron, broadened the comparison to include the other Abrahamic faiths.[103] Baron first conceded that Christianity can appear irrational. Then he pivoted: "[T]o the Mahometan Religion it is vastly preferable. No such ridiculous Follies are to be charg'd on this as on that. . . . Whoever hath look'd into the Alcoran hath there met with a great deal of Stuff strange and surprizing. It gives the Reins to Men's furious Lusts and heady passions, and then it promises a Paradise much fitter for Swine than for Men." But the best thing about Christianity, Baron concluded, is that it "lays down a very satisfactory acct of the Depravation of Mankind": "This is of great Concern . . . that we may see how vile We are, that we may be able to acquiesce in God's Afflictive Dealings and under a sense of our sad State be qualified for Grace and Mercy."[104] The steps of Baron's argument were not exactly logical, but they were clear enough to Barker, who wrote them down without dissent: Christianity is consistent; or maybe it is not perfectly consistent, but it is not as bad as Islam; and in any case what makes Islam even worse and Christianity even better is that *only the latter has a doctrine of original sin.*[105]

The implications of how all this fits together—or, from another angle, starts to fall apart—are again remarkable enough for us to pause. Christianity is being held up as superior to Islam for the express reason that Islam has no doctrine of original sin, a doctrine that can *laudably* explain "how vile We are" as a species. In this characterization, original sin is the central pillar of Christian orthodoxy, and the recognition of the vileness it entails, which in Baron's words is to say the "sad State," is held up as a precondition for salvation. But, by the same logic, if one backed off the belief that such vileness is necessary for salvation instead laying stress on moral conduct, then what purpose would the presumed vileness serve? It would only encourage self-loathing to no end. Competing theories of salvation are here inextricably tied to self-perception.

The other thing that is so striking here is that Barker was directly told that not just any religion but Islam very specifically was inferior to Christianity.[106] We know he was told all this because he writes it down. But whatever tacit approval his recording of the sermon suggests on the day he heard it, he superimposed none of its argument onto the Muslims he met months later. He instead seized on the Bengalis' abstention from alcohol, especially in the case of the man to whom he talked in detail. As he later recounted in his diary: "I was impressed and surpriz'd to find so much good sense, humour & complaisance in such a one. . . . I observ'd that he & two Indians more with him went early to Bed [while] some Englishmen (pretendendly [*sic*] Christians) stay up very late drinking and carousing." There may be a rhetorical motif in the admission that a heathen's behavior could lead to Christian self-improvement. "These poor Heathens or Mahometans should be such a Reproach to us Christians! What a Report will this Man carry home with him concerning the Inhabitants of Great Britain," Barker writes in the same entry. But beyond all expectations he finishes with this observation: "I believe these Heathens or Mahometans if they live agreeably *to the Light they have* will have the most favourable Construction put upon their Actions, by the most merciful God, and be in a much happier Condition at the Day of Judgment."[107]

Barker's encounter with the Bengalis did not change him overnight, but knowing what we know about his later life this must have been a crucial moment. Against the backdrop of his problem with alcohol, it gave him an occasion to think comparatively about religion, to perceive a "light" precisely where there is no original sin, to question orthodoxy implicitly, and to read cultural comparison against his personal problem. There was something potent about the fact that these three Muslim men maintained what he could not: self-control in the face of alcohol. Even though a minister had expressly called Islam inferior to Christianity for the specific reason that it has no doctrine of original sin, Barker's experience with Muslims evinced anything but such inferiority, nor did it offer the occasion to reason that the absence of original sin—the inability to see one's own vileness and depravity—made the Bengalis anything other than models of piety. The metaphor of light that Barker invokes in relation to the Bengalis had, even further, nothing to do with Christ. What was enlightened enough to get them into heaven—and by implication to get anyone else into heaven—was their behavior, or, as Christian theology might put it, their *works*. Barker was inching toward that nightmare scenario that haunted the orthodox in which renouncing original sin opens the door to tolerance of other religions for the very reason that it elevates moral conduct and, by association, diminishes self-loathing. When Peter Baron railed against Islam, he was making a theological case: he was saying that only those who suitably felt their vileness were qualified for the grace Christ offered. Barker was here confronted with a direct experience that made him implicitly reject that case. How easy it must have been for him to wonder too whether a softer view of human nature—the absence of original sin—offered a sounder basis for self-control, especially given that he would come to believe exactly this in later life, much as he would read the Quran in English translation and be interested in what he found there.[108]

Given these theologically challenging episodes and the subtle cracks in the foundation, did Barker continue his spiritual diary in another volume after he wrote the last sentence on the last blank page in the *Critica Sacra* on June 27, 1731? There is good reason to believe he did not. His dilemma was worsening. Work may have generally had a spiritual mandate, but *his* work immersed him in drinking, despair, and self-loathing. He could either avoid the situations that made drinking an immediate temptation and slide into poverty. Or he could keep working in proximity to alcohol, trying to pull himself out of debt while finding a way to rethink the spiritual implications of his excesses. Drinking was, at once, a personal failing, a spiritual problem, and an economic necessity complicated by the salvific promise Dissenters generally discerned in their material achievements. The likelihood that in 1731 Barker was already seeing original sin and the self-perception it entailed as the culprit—and seeing its rejection as the solution—is suggested further by the way in which consuming alcohol would come to be replaced by what enlightened culture had to offer. Three decades later he would confess to Merivale that to write to him was "more pleasurable . . . than . . . drinking."[109] In a different letter, he would claim that an "Extract from [Jean] Le Clerc" that Merivale had just sent him "suit[ed] [his] taste indeed better than a large hamper of Tokay, Champs, Burgundy, [M]ethuens Port, Lacry in [Lacryma] Christi . . . [of] any wine whatever."[110]

This was Barker at the end of his life, proud of holding views that others saw as heretical, and dismayed by those around him who still believed in what his diary, thirty years earlier, recorded as articles of faith. But in that otherwise puritanical diary the forces that would bring him to his later views were already present. The experience of a culturally complex world and the emotional and economic meaning implicated in his drinking were pushing him closer to renouncing original sin and the view of human nature that made self-loathing so easy. That renunciation may not have paid his debts or instantly restored his health. But finding fewer reasons to hate himself was a promising start.

CHAPTER FOUR

The Intervening Years

Loin de rien décider sur cet Être Suprême,
Gardons, en l'adorant, un silence profond,
Sa nature est immense et l'esprit s'y confond,
Pour savoir ce qu'il est, il faut être lui-même.

(Far from determining anything about this Supreme Being,
Let us keep a profound silence as we worship it,
Its nature is immense and merged with the mind,
To know what it is, you have to be it yourself.)

Unknown author, ca. early eighteenth century

Enlightenment historians were once fixated on the stars, the luminary authors whose ideas, having survived the era in printed bestsellers, offer a tangible basis for Enlightenment thought. The influence of social and cultural history eventually directed attention to different kinds of sources.[1] Now decades old, this shift in focus has revealed a great deal, maybe above all else that the Enlightenment was not simply a confined philosophical movement. But the more recent observations can still feel as indirect as inferences about exoplanets. If the stars are no longer so bright that they dissolve all bodies in nearby orbit, a telescope reveals little beyond disturbances in light and other artifacts that ultimately depend on a nearby star's effects.

Distant images can also mislead. The impressions drawn from the book trade, for example, are generally taken to mean that consumers and sellers were ideologically in line with the books they bought and sold. Undoubtedly that was often true. Yet the godly Leeds clothier Joseph Ryder bought heretical books solely to keep them from innocent eyes.[2] On the other side of the transaction, the bookseller who sold

Pentecost Barker an English translation of La Mettrie's *Man a Machine* (1747)—"downright atheism," Barker rightly called it—was "a preaching Methodist" who was oblivious, as Barker laughingly told Merivale, to the book he was selling.[3]

Structures discernible only from a distance are at their least revealing, however, when it comes to the motives that led people to change. That makes the sources Barker left behind unusually valuable, especially given the contingency of their survival. Dissenters wrote spiritual diaries to maintain their faith, not to explore unorthodox ideas. If they lost their connection to orthodoxy, their spiritual diaries had failed. And unless they were willing to use them to rethink the genre and its underpinning faith, those diaries came to an end. If on the other hand they decided to record their heterodox views using other written forms, as did Barker with his letters, whatever later writing they produced needs to have survived for the sake of comparison alongside the diary (or some other indicator) that sets the baseline for their change. Barker therefore represents layers of improbability: he was obscure, he wrote things down, and the things he wrote down, even when separated by decades and after having fallen into different hands, managed to achieve relative permanence. To add another layer, it was the Merivale family that preserved Barker's later letters to make sense not of Barker but of his correspondent, their ancestor Samuel.[4] Why Barker's diary was preserved is never clear. But given that the only surviving volume was written in Edward Leigh's *Critica Sacra,* it is possible that what someone along the way deemed worth keeping was not his diary but the book in which it was interposed. Without these chance occurrences, there would be little evidence of Barker's later life, or his early life, or an occasion to compare the two.

All that said, if these sources allow for something rare, it is also the case that Barker's change took place between his diary and his letters. His outlook was orthodox in the former, if also suggestive of some intellectual discontent, and heterodox in the latter. We need other sources to get at the intervening years between the last diary entry in 1731 and the first letter at the tail end of 1758. Here too it turns out that chance helps. There is also "something in names" that can rescue you from obscurity.

The first archival appearance Barker makes after the diary is not, on the face of it, unorthodox, but it is odd. The unmistakable name "Barker Mr Pentecost" appears among a list of subscribers to a group of sermons written by William Stephens and published posthumously in 1737. This is not the William Stephens who wrote a book accusing deists, of all people, of fomenting religious intolerance.[5] The book Barker supported was written by a vicar of St. Andrews in Plymouth who died in

1732.[6] It is not a given, however, that he subscribed to the content of the book, which was simply titled *Sermons on Several Subjects*. Publication by subscription—eighteenth-century crowdfunding—could take years from start to finish, which means it is hard to know how long before its publication Barker committed to helping bring the book into print.[7] The project may have begun shortly after (or even before) the vicar's death in 1732, right around the time Barker's diary ended. Even then, it is not a given that Barker assented to Stephens's actual religious views. There may have been some overlap in belief between Dissent and Anglicanism, but Stephens was still an Anglican priest and Barker a diehard Dissenter. There were better places for Barker to spend his money. Just as likely is that he helped publish Stephens's sermons because he was again trying to win the favors of local men in Plymouth. St. Andrews was one of the richest parishes in England, and, as Barker indicated in his last will and testament, it was in its churchyard that he wanted to be buried after a funeral performed "in as public a manner as possible."[8]

It was also in the St. Andrews churchyard that, in 1736, Barker buried his wife, Alice. Given the timing, he may have been angling with Stephens's supporters for this precious real estate. We noted earlier that he never tells us how he felt about his first wife.[9] He was willing to say in his diary that he had been in love with and was even set to marry another woman, Peggy Lace, who died in 1711. It is curious that he married Alice the very next year.[10] It is curious too that he was never moved to say anything of substance about Alice either in his diary or in hindsight in his later letters to Samuel Merivale, at which point he was living with a third woman, Jane Mills. (Whether Pentecost and Jane were married is another mystery to which we will return, although I will still refer to Alice as his *first wife* for clarity.) Alice's father, John Beer, had been mayor of Plymouth in 1717, and surely this helped Pentecost's business prospects. The details from the 1710s and 1720s are missing, but the likely benefits of the marriage may have still been reverberating in the late 1730s, at which point Barker was also identifying as a wine cooper and probably helping fulfill the Royal Navy's orders for barrels given his ties to the pursery.[11] There are indications in these years, all the same, that Barker still had to hustle for work.[12] It may well be that showing some support for an Anglican vicar was part of that process too.

Barker's career was in any case more noticeably taking off shortly after Alice's death. In September 1741, he was appointed purser of the third-rate *Royal Oak*, which would bring him into contact with, among others, Admiral Thomas Mathews.[13] Four years later, he had moved to the ninety-gun second-rate *Barfleur*, a bigger ship that would have brought larger purser commissions, which were partly calculated by ship size.

After five more years, he was appointed to the HMS *Sandwich*, a ship of the same class on which he served until receiving a commission for the similarly sized *Ocean*. "When she is launched," he wrote in old age to Merivale about the *Ocean*, "God only knows how I shall be disposed of."[14] In fact, when it did launch, Barker was reassigned at the last minute to the *Bristol*.[15] "What a difference do I find in getting into and out of a ship," a seventy-year-old Barker wrote in one of his last letters.[16] We never hear about the *Bristol* again.[17]

What else seems apparent in these intervening years is that job security was adjacent to the favors Barker was able to return to ever more powerful men. It is hard to know when exactly he met Admiral Mathews, the eventual commander of the Royal Navy's Mediterranean fleet. But the fact that he impressed a high-ranking official may speak to his competence, or to his powers of persuasion, or at the very least to the potential Mathews saw in Barker to do something for him. The two had met by 1743 at the latest. And at some point during that year Barker introduced Mathews to a third figure, William Lynch, who had served in the Spanish navy but was now willing to come over to the British side during the War of Austrian Succession. Barker never comments on these matters in his letters. The backstory emerges from one of his Zelig-like appearances during Mathews's court-martial in 1746, where the admiral was accused of mishandling the British assault on the French-Spanish fleet during the Battle of Toulon two years earlier. Barker had been on shore during the fighting, but in the trial against Mathews and several of his commanders he was called by John Ambrose, captain of the HMS *Rupert*, to testify to the credibility of another witness whom Ambrose had requested earlier in the trial, the defector from the Spanish side, William Lynch.

Barker explained on the witness stand that, after he had introduced Lynch to Mathews in 1743, the admiral put Lynch to work as an English spy. In a round of questioning by the navy's lawyers, who doubted Lynch's loyalties, he then insisted that there was nothing suspicious about the way that Lynch had left the Spanish service. Lynch, in Barker's testimony, had informed the Spanish commanders that he needed to take care of some affairs in Ireland (why is never made clear). His Spanish captain complied with the request but gave him what Barker in the trial referred to as "a sort of ticket," which he described as a surety for the payment of Lynch's wages on the condition that he return to Spain. The discussion of the nature of the "ticket" was relevant to the trial because, as Barker explained, the wages it promised indicated that Lynch was "very badly paid" by the Spanish crown, while it was being underpaid that gave Lynch incentive to join the English side. Or it gave Lynch the material incentive. When asked about Lynch's religion, with the insinuation that he was Catholic, Barker assured the judges that Lynch was Protestant and would swear an oath to the king.[18]

Barker's testimony probably helped the captain of the *Rupert*, John Ambrose, whose punishment for Toulon was not severe enough to keep him from ascending the ranks to become an admiral. There are other subtle clues that Barker was an effective witness. When a judge wondered how the purser of the *Barfleur* could have read and comprehended the "ticket" that Lynch was given by his Spanish captain—"Do you read, write, or understand Spanish," the counsel asked—Barker was confident and careful with his language: "[N]o, not well: I could see there was his Name; and understand so far, as that he was on board the Spanish Ship, because I understand a little Latin. I could read the Spanish to understand it so far." After the court recapped Barker's earlier comment about Lynch leaving the Spanish navy—"I think you say, [Lynch] lost his wages, after he had deserted the Spanish Service; and you saw it, under his Captain's Hand"—Barker's tone verged on being sharp: "I did not say he deserted the Spanish Service. I said, he left the Service." But, in any case, Barker did not just offer a careful witness's service to Ambrose; he offered it to Mathews by vouching for the credibility of Mathews's chosen spy.[19]

A further suggestion raised by these various connections is that Barker himself played a role in Mathews's spy ring. He makes an offhand comment to Merivale that at one point in the 1740s he had been "called a spy by some French and English."[20] In the same letter, he references another moment in the 1740s when he says he made improvements to a system of cipher introduced to him by someone named Don Carlos Gibert. The comments are clipped but full of possibilities, especially given Barker's knowledge of cryptology. If people had once thought he was a spy, maybe they were right to think so. He never denies the charge. And, if it is true, his knowledge of cryptology would have been a key skill to possess.

Not much else can be said about Barker and Mathews's relationship. But that the two men stayed on good terms also comes forward in the diary of another man, George Marsh, who also reveals information about yet another chapter in Barker's life.[21] On March 19, 1750, Marsh and Barker opened a wine store on Savage Gardens near Tower Hill in London, which they mainly used to supply the navy.[22] The two men met while Barker was a guest at George Marsh's brother Milbourn's wedding. In conversation there, Barker "proposed to me," wrote George Marsh, "our joining stocks and going into the wine trade and said his father was a wine cooper and that he himself perfectly understood the business, and that he was sure with his connections it would prove more advantageous than being a placeman, the income of which being very small."[23]

Selling wine was a challenging enterprise for a drunkard trying not to drink. But if forging a relationship to alcohol less mired in puritanical self-loathing made drinking easier to control, the wine business itself suggests the success of Barker's deviation from orthodoxy. Marsh, in any case, never mentions that Barker had a drinking problem, and Marsh was willing to be critical of his partner, "a very artful avaricious tho' sensible man," in other ways.[24] That comment came in March 1755, the year the wine store closed. The entry is worth reading in full for a sense of Marsh's regret and relief:

> Agreed with Mr Barker to dissolve our partnership having sold but 3 or 4 pipes [casks] of wine during it and did not get payment for the greatest part thereof, so that we lost very considerably thereby, but by the agency, which was all got by me, I cleared about £500. The dissolving this partnership therefore gave me the greatest pleasure, Mr Barker being a very artful avaricious tho' sensible man, and as he found I should every year increase my income by the agency of which he had, and was to have half, without the least trouble or interest of his, he wished much to continue it, but my very sincere worthy and learned friend Mr Joseph Hart, happily brought it to a conclusion, for whom Mr Barker had the highest esteem and veneration.[25]

Artful was not a compliment in the business world, and *avaricious* speaks for itself. Still, if the London store was not a brilliant success, Marsh must have known what he was getting into, which was a relationship in which Barker could offer the business connections. What Marsh was complaining about was the unfairness of the profit share given the uneven burden of work. But it is hard to imagine Marsh not knowing that Barker would remain active as a purser after they started their business. It was this continued involvement that helped ensure the purchase of their supplies by the Royal Navy. It is true that Barker did maintain a London address; he kept two rooms in the house that he and Marsh rented on Savage Gardens.[26] But Marsh himself elsewhere noted neutrally that Barker came to the rooms only "occasionally." It is likely that he was rarely around to do the labor, which was probably never what he was going to bring to the table. Also, £500 for five years of work was not insignificant in the 1750s, a decade in which the daily wage of a skilled tradesman was about two shillings. Barker and Marsh each made in five years, in other words, what it took five thousand workdays for a tradesman to make.[27] The slight against Barker may then have had something to do with Marsh's own ambition. His later ascent through the chain of command in the navy was, as Linda Colley has described it, remarkable. What makes it all the more ironic is that Marsh's eventual success probably happened, in part, because Barker initially brought him into contact with Thomas Mathews, who would later offer Marsh connections to the Victualling Board, of which, like Samuel Pepys a century earlier, he became commissioner before rising to the rank of a full commissioner of the navy, meeting regularly with prime ministers, and amassing a small fortune.[28]

But, as for the main thread, can anything more concrete be said about Barker's philosophical outlook during these intervening years?

There is one more episode from Barker's active years in the navy that relates, almost incredibly, to deism. In 1747, at the close of the War of Austrian Succession, Barker was onboard the HMS *Dover* when it overtook the French man-of-war *Renommée*, a heavily armed frigate that was headed from France to Saint-Domingue. The skirmish was probably not fierce—the *Renommée* had been weakened the previous day in a drawn-out battle with the HMS *Victory*.[29] Maybe in part for that reason, the atmosphere of the French surrender on the officer's deck of the *Dover*, which had not been involved in the heated conflict, was relatively cordial. What was nevertheless surprising is that the officers' deck operated like a forum for the Enlightenment public sphere.[30] "There is nothing more certain," wrote Barker, "than that there are many Deists in France." Onboard the *Renommée*, he explained to Merivale, there were "several Officers" that he "judg'd from their Contempt of their professed religion to be such." One of those officers, "a Capt in the Army, who was going to settle at Martineeq put the inclosed paper into [his] hand."[31]

What was on that piece of paper is not entirely clear. (If Barker enclosed it in his letter to Merivale from 1759, as he says, nothing survives in the archive.) Shortly after hearing the story about the *Dover*, Merivale apologizes to Barker for being remiss in translating something Barker had sent him.[32] A few days later, Merivale again complains about specific problems of translation—"the particles 'de' and 'des' that recur too often . . . perplex me much"—before quoting enough text ("Martyrs delicate, confesseurs attachez au lucre") to be identified as the *Monita secreta*, an exposé of jesuitical methods written in the mid-seventeenth century.[33] The *Monita secreta* had ostensibly nothing to do with deism, but in his letter about the *Renommée* Barker also quips that French officers were identifiable by their contempt of their religion—the same kind of contempt implied in the *Monita secreta*'s presentation of the Jesuits.

More likely than the *Monita secreta*, however, what changed hands on the ship were four obscure lines of deistic poetry. We can infer as much because, in a different letter, Barker writes in passing that, once upon a time, "a French captain gave [him] 4 Lines," before reproducing, probably by memory given the misspelling and missing punctuation, the following quatrain:

Loin de rien decider de cet Etre Supreme
Gardons en l'adorant un silence profonde:
Le Mystere est immence, et l'Esprit s'y confound
Pour dire ce qu'il est, il faut etre luy meme.[34]

With very minor variations, these same lines appear in Louis-Sébastien Mercier's science fiction novel *Dans l'an 2440* (In the year 2440), an ambitious "supreme best-seller" of the eighteenth century, eventually running through twenty-five editions before the French Revolution.[35] In it, the protagonist has a vision of Paris in the twenty-fifth century, at which point there is no longer any traditional religion, army, foreign trade, slavery, arbitrary arrest, or hereditary monarchy.[36] The utopian novel also offers an arresting scene in which the hero comes across a temple engraved with the sole tenet of the closest thing the future does have to a religion. Taking the anthropomorphism of enlightened religiosity to its logical conclusion, it reads:

Loin de rien décider sur cet Être Suprême,
Gardons, en l'adorant, un silence profond,
Sa nature est immense et l'esprit s'y confond,
Pour savoir ce qu'il est, il faut être lui-même.

"Far from determining anything about this Supreme Being," the lines can be rendered in English, "Let us maintain a profound silence as we worship it, / Its nature is immense and merged with the mind, / To know what it is, you have to be it yourself." In this imagined future, "man," in the intervening years between the eighteenth and the twenty-fifth centuries, had finally become "God."

But this is what is so striking. When Pentecost Barker took possession of these lines on the deck of a British warship, Louis-Sébastien Mercier was only seven years old. His futuristic novel would not be published until 1771, nearly a decade after Barker's death. This quatrain, which Mercier did not actually write but only appropriated, was apparently so evocative in the eighteenth century—elegant in form, radical in content—that it circulated on single sheets of paper like the password to the secret sphere of a Deist International, decades before Mercier finally put it in print. The only other thing Barker says about the lines is that they won a poet a literary prize.[37] But if the backstory is obscure, the lines clearly captured

Barker's emerging beliefs: the idea, to which we will turn, that the soul is a particle of a supreme being and the idea that the whole reason we can contemplate the divine—the whole reason we "can look from Nature to Nature's God," as Barker put it—is because all of us possess the divine in our minds already.[38] We can only imagine how potent ideas about the divine, spiritual connection, and camaraderie felt as, on the vast ocean, they traded hands between ostensibly mortal enemies.[39]

If it is needed, one final piece of evidence that Barker had come to his heterodox beliefs by the 1740s at the latest was the appearance of the name "Pentecost Barker" among the subscribers to a deistic work written by James Foster, *Discourses on All the Principal Branches of Natural Religion and Social Virtue*, published in two volumes between 1749 and 1752.[40] This was the same James Foster we encountered earlier, epitomizing the enlightened age in his argument with John Brine over human nature. Foster and Brine were recurring authors in Barker and Merivale's letters. Brine was the paradigmatic bigot, while Foster embodied the enlightened age. "I have only one vol of James Foster [Foster's *Sermons* (1733)], in which is the sermon Of Mysteries," Barker wrote Merivale.[41] "[A]nd I find there a passage which seems totally so well with our way of thinking that I must imprint it on my memory":

> [N]o doctrine, which in the least encourages immorality, can be part of a divine revelation. Doctrines of this kind can't be charg'd on Christianity, which prescribes the noblest system of morals, without making it contradict itself. Nor in the nature of the thing, can they belong to any religion that is of divine original, because of the absolute wisdom, and spotless purity of the great governor of the world. Even miracles themselves can't prove such doctrines to be true, which are necessarily false, dishonorable to the moral attributes of God, and inconsistent with the true perfection and happiness of mankind: but this point is so exceeding clear that I need not enlarge on it.

"Surely one may safely build on this Foundation," he continued, "and conclude that predestination as established by Calvin, Brine & many others is, and must be, false because inconsistent with the moral attributes of God." Furthermore: "[A] thinking man can never rest in opinions so derogatory to Almighty Wisdom, Goodness and Power. I remember when I was at Stratton [in] 1724 and Orthodox enough. Original Sin was on the Carpet, and a plain country Farmer had somewhat to say against it as inconsistent with the Mercy of God. Should I, said the Old Man, plant a Tree, in purpose of let[ting] it grow, & then cut it down & burn it?" Was the old farmer thinking of Isaiah 44:15,[42] which may have implied that he associated original sin with popery? Was this an expression of an early modern agrarian radicalism that related abstract doctrine to the mundane facts of everyday life? The "old farmer" lies on the edge of archival oblivion, but if he does nothing else, he casts light on a world in which *everyone* seemed to have an opinion about original sin. And the meaning of what he said in 1724 was, in any case, compelling enough for Barker to remember it in later life: "There is force in such short questions and truly I think one may safely say that God did never make any Man to keep him alive in Misery."[43]

Barker's subscription to Foster's later work, his *Discourses on All the Principal Branches of Natural Religion*, was, in short, a clear sign that the purser had changed by the 1740s. But worth noting too is that the sermon of Foster's that Barker quoted to Merivale ("no doctrine, which in the least encourages immorality, can be part of a divine revelation") was first published in 1733, which raises the possibility that Barker was sympathetic to Foster's ideas at the moment they first appeared in print in a book that Barker indicates he owned, even if he does not indicate exactly when he first owned it. In other words, there is no doubt that Barker had embraced heterodoxy by the 1740s. But there is also a chance that he had started to embrace or to think more favorably about it in the early 1730s. Which brings us back to the possibility that he never wrote another diary volume after 1731 because by then he had had enough of the orthodoxy by which such diaries were sustained.

It is worth looking at one last bit of evidence from these intervening years, although it comes after the swerve from orthodoxy. Barker did not leave London directly after the business venture with Marsh ended. He put this ad in the *Whitehall Evening Post* in the spring of 1755:

> Whereas the Partnership in Wine and Commission Business, which commenced between Pentecost Barker and George Marsh in the Beginning of the Year 1750, at their House in Savage Gardens, is now at an End, Barker having this Day quitted his Moiety of the House. Those Gentlemen his Friends, who were recommended by Barker to Marsh, are now desired to apply to Pentecost Barker only, and direct for him at the Rainbow Coffee-House in Cornhill and their Orders shall be duly executed.[44]

His falling out with Marsh must have stung. Here in 1755, the year of the partnership's dissolution, he was trying to set up a base of operations to do more of the grunt work that he had pawned off on Marsh, and he still could not help but point out that he had been the one to introduce Marsh to "[t]hose Gentlemen *his* Friends."

What else the ad contains is his new address: the Rainbow Coffee House in Cornhill, in the financial heart of London. This was a Huguenot hangout, and because Barker was friendly with the French Protestant community in Plymouth it makes sense for that reason alone that he would find his way there. But by 1754 at the latest the Rainbow Coffee House had also become the meeting place of the Imperial George Masonic lodge. Had Barker become a Freemason?[45] The lodge records do not go back far enough to confirm his membership. But to the extent that Freemasonry encouraged deism, fellow feeling, and open-mindedness, a lodge filled with fellow travelers would have been, as we are about to see, ideal.[46]

CHAPTER FIVE

Philalethes and Charistes

I believe I may truly say you do not sit down with more pleasure to write me than I do to write you—briefly, Charistes loves Philalethes, & Philalethes loves Charistes—voila q'il est fini.

PHILALETHES
to Charistes, August 29, 1759

Barker never directly comments on his first name, but by 1759 he was signing his letters to Samuel Merivale as if he recognized that Pentecost was an awkward fit with what he had become. A few times in their correspondence he called himself Pamphilius, after the third-century Pamphilus of Caesarea, a Beirut-born presbyter and early Christian universalist.[1] As he remained a nominal Presbyterian, he too declared: "I am a Universalist . . . one that in imitation of the Divine Being hath a Universal Love for all Mankind."[2] On a few other occasions, he referred to himself using the anagram "Peter Bentcoskar," which was also fitting, if differently.[3] There was little sense in keeping the name his parents had given him now that he had refashioned himself beyond their religiosity. But the name that stuck—and the one he consistently used to sign his letters to Merivale once he landed on it—was Philalethes. It had all the desired advantages. It started with a *P*, as did all his first names. It was hortatory ("lover of truth") but in a general sense. And it captured his religious outlook. To those in the know, Philalethes was also the name of the "Christian deist" interlocutor in a contemporary dialogue, Thomas Morgan's *The Moral Philosopher* (1738).[4] Philalethes—and on one rare occasion "Philalethes Rekrab" (*Barker* backward)—seemed a clear way to signal both his break from the past and his new intellectual confidence.[5]

Then there was "Charistes," a name that Merivale adopted to write to Barker and, eventually, to publish two articles for Joseph Priestley's *Theological Repository*.[6] The meaning of *Charistes* is less clear. It may have been an allusion to George Benson, who had written under the same pen name a handful of anti-Calvinist essays meant to be published in the *Old Whig*, a Rational Dissenter periodical from the 1730s.[7] The essays turned out to be too heretical to bring out to the public, but they were known and admired among the heterodox, and by allusion Merivale may have been paying homage. Or it may be no coincidence, either for Merivale or Benson, that *Charistes* is an anagram for *chastiser*. Merivale did not mind rebuking the orthodox, at least vicariously in his letters to Barker, who could not get enough of his friend's learned criticisms.

Barker and Merivale's correspondence—over three hundred letters written over the course of three and a half years, from December 1758 to July 1762—has remained unknown outside a few members of the Merivale family, who gave it to a public archive in Devon in 1980.[8] Even so it remained uncataloged until I made inquiries a decade ago after seeing a reference to it in an old run of a Huguenot journal.[9] The correspondence was hard to find, and I was actively looking for it. Who else has cared about Pentecost Barker?[10] Who else has cared about Samuel Merivale, a less marginal figure by virtue of being a minister and an author but one who published in an arcane theology journal under a pseudonym that confusingly was used by another Dissenter who shared his views? Neither of these men was exactly looking to be found.

That was reasonable enough. A few days before his death in 1759, Peter Baron, the longtime minister at Batter Street in Plymouth, fell unconscious in front of an emotional Barker, who wrote Merivale in distress to report that their friend was close to the end: "Those Eyes closed that used to behold me with pleasure, shut for ever here. The delightful Tongue that I have heard with inexpressible Joy—forever dumb. The Friendly hand shake I have grasp'd often expressing thereby the inward Sentiments of the Mind, dead & motionless. I cannot bear it."[11] Just as painfully, Barker was about to lose his only Plymouth confidant. When Baron died a few days later, Barker lamented: "I have no Orestes or Pylades left within the Bounds of this Corporation." But the point of saying all that was to acknowledge that Charistes, his friend in Tavistock, fifteen miles away, would continue to fill the role of confidant, much as Philalethes would hold Charistes's heretical ideas in confidence.[12] When Merivale sent his treatise questioning the immateriality of the soul to Barker, he cautioned his friend that "it must not fall under any other eye."[13] Merivale, especially, had a lot to lose.[14] He was still on the job market, and had he been a ministerial candidate at a divided congregation any number of his radical ideas could have come back to haunt him.

It may be in part for the same reason that Barker and Merivale's letters are also filled with encrypted words and symbols. Both men played around with language, but especially Barker, who in keeping with his interests in cryptology made up math enigmas, anagrams (*Peter Bentcoskar* was not the only one), and confounding rebuses that he often sent to Merivale's daughter Jenny.[15] Merivale joined Barker in using in their letters planetary symbols to represent days of the week (the sun for Sunday, the moon for Monday, etc.), a triangle to represent the Trinity, *Brine* to signify a bigot, an *X* for Christ. Some of this was just shorthand, but some of it gives the impression that both men were communicating partly in code, which is also apparent in their nicknames.[16] Created I think in part in the spirit of philosophical self-fashioning, those nicknames also functioned as disguises, and they were often aimed at getting a laugh. Sometimes Barker's second wife, Jane Mills, was "Philaletha" and Merivale's wife, Betsy, was "Charista."[17] Peter Baron was virtually always "Sophron." "Logisto" was a heterodox minister in Devonshire.[18] The "Sanctity Shepherd" was a minister with the last name Shepherd and a constant source of ire, although no one irritated Barker as much as "Pope Joan," the leader of the "Methodistical gang," the orthodox parishioners at Batter Street who advocated for a Calvinist replacement after Sophron's death.[19]

The inside jokes were also a reflection of the fact that Philalethes and Charistes liked each other, deeply. In another letter written to Merivale on the eve of Peter Baron's death, Barker explained that "Sophron" was the only ally he had in Plymouth "whose friendship is not cemented by a Selfish Principle."[20] Maybe he remembered that Richard Baxter ("honest Dick" in Barker's code) had, as Max Weber put it, "advised his flock to be deeply mistrustful, even of best friends."[21] But *Selfish Principle* was more obvious shorthand for the cynical Enlightenment view that sociability arose not from natural benevolence but as an aftereffect of one looking after oneself. This was asserted by enlighteners as a fact of nature rather than a sign of moral depravity. But removing morality from the equation hardly made distinguishing instrumental from affective relationships any easier. It is a testament to the depth of the problem that David Hume's short, loaded essay "The Middle Station in Life" (1776) found the middle class at its most valuable not because of its material benefits but because it could solve the problem of how to identify true friends. If freed from both the excessive greed found in the upper station and the desperate need found among the lower orders, middling friends would, Hume thought, seek out each other on emotional rather than transactional terms. But all that was theoretical. In practice, Barker occupied the middle class and still felt that no friend cared about him selflessly—or at least no friend other than Merivale in the final years of his life. "I believe I may truly say," he wrote after reading one of Merivale's denunciations of orthodoxy, "you do not sit down with more pleasure to write me than I do to write you—briefly, Charistes loves Philalethes, & Philalethes loves Charistes—voila q'il est fini."[22]

Love for others was also in abundant supply in Barker and Merivale's correspondence. Much of it was felt for Baron, whose grave illness and eventual death recur as themes throughout 1759.[23] Much of it was also felt for Jane—or, as her parents and friends called her, Jenny—Samuel and Elizabeth's one daughter and the oldest of their three children.[24] Walter, the youngest son, died of a lung infection when he was two and a half. John, the middle child, lived a long life. Jenny made it to her teenage years, but only briefly. With a "tender and weakly constitution from her infancy," she was, her father lamented, subject "to frequent and violent palpitations of the Heart," which her doctors thought arose from a "polypus" or tumor. Eighteenth-century medicine could already do little to remedy heart conditions. But at age twelve Jenny's condition worsened when a fever caused intermittent paralysis on her left side. A year later, "greatly emaciated by a long continued Hectic," her father recorded in his memorandum book that her "Body and Limbs swelled at last by a Dropsy."[25] That was in January 1763, two months before her fourteenth birthday, three months after Barker's death.[26]

Jenny was Samuel's "tender darling," his "sweet, tender Dove," his "precious maid." But she was more than an object of adoration. He also called her his "little friend and confidante," his "most favourite Companion, Counsellor, and Friend," his "promising genius." As Barker, the master of nicknames, put it, she was a "Cygne Noire," a black swan, a singularity. Only a few short letters from Jenny survive, but her voice can be heard in other ways, and we will come back to it in the next chapter.[27]

Much of what makes the Barker-Merivale correspondence remarkable is that it reveals two relatively obscure men writing intently about Enlightenment ideas, books, and authors. In the spirit of Immanuel Kant's motto for the Enlightenment, *sapere aude* (dare to know), Barker and Merivale were audacious in reading whatever they could get their hands on. They thought life was full of mysteries—about the afterlife, divinity, morality, the nature of being—and books offered a way to try to figure those mysteries out. But more than just exposing each other to ideas, their correspondence captures the process by which they tried to sort their own ideas out. It is telling that some of the beliefs they worked toward do not have fixed names. In a later generation, they would have consistently called themselves *Unitarians*, a word that Barker and Merivale do in fact occasionally use toward the end of their correspondence. More typically, however, they are *Rational Dissenters* or *Universalists*. In the same vein, a later generation would have adopted the isms in circulation after the French Revolution and likely used the word *socialism* where Barker and Merivale say they were drawn to "the levelling scheme."[28] Barker undoubtedly would have called himself an *abolitionist* had the word been around. Instead, when he condemns the slave trade, he folds it into the "merciless scheme," which he associated with the tyranny of religious orthodoxy.[29] What is in any case clear about their process of sorting out beliefs and seeking out new explanations is that it was not simply driven by ideas and their logical interrelationships. Barker and Merivale were in an ongoing and adaptable conversation with books, with experience, and with themselves.

Experience shapes another revelation of these letters, which is what they have to say about *Rex v. Barker* (1762).[30] In another Zelig-like moment in the courtroom (except here, as opposed to the Mathews trial, the purser made the marquee), Barker used the occasion of Sophron's death in 1759 to try to pull Batter Street along with him down his own path to enlightenment. His fellow congregants were overwhelmingly uninterested. And the dispute that followed ended up being so protracted and contentious that it landed at the Court of King's Bench during the tenure of Lord Mansfield, the English-speaking world's most important jurist and the chief justice of the British Empire's most powerful and consequential common law court. Barker did not live long enough to hear the final verdict, in which a writ of mandamus gave the traditionalists permission to take over Batter Street. But he and Merivale wrote each other about the case often. And their letters shed light on Mansfield's ruling, which on the surface looks like mandamus simply used for restitution. But, as with many things related to Pentecost Barker, the story is complicated.

⁓

The fact that in later life Barker became a Batter Street trustee, a lay parishioner delegated powers of congregational oversight, was further testament to his improving prospects in the years beyond his diary. Being a trustee nevertheless came at a tricky time. Because ministerial election in a Presbyterian chapel happened by congregational vote, finding a replacement minister for Peter Baron would have always been complicated by the sheer number of voices entitled to weigh in on the decision. But Batter Street was also so divided after Baron's death that, as Lord

Mansfield reckoned in his later opinion for *Rex v. Barker,* it was on the verge of violence.

There was a reason to dub Baron *Sophron,* a name derived from an ancient Greek word for *prudent.*[31] In the same even-tempered spirit, and despite his own heterodox views, Baron had kept the latent rifts at Batter Street from erupting, which was an accomplishment that impressed Merivale as much as it did Barker.[32] "In general," Merivale explained in an homage to Baron that doubled as a statement on a minister's ideal role, "prudence to manage people's prejudices is not less necessary than integrity to deal faithfully with them, in their most important concerns." This was the balancing act that Merivale thought all Rational Dissenter ministers had to perform with special skill. "The Truth should in no case be knowingly denied but it may not be necessary to us publickly"—by which Merivale meant from the pulpit—"to declare all that we take for Truth, when we know our Hearers cannot bear it; for to exclaim against every Error of which they are Tenacious, especially if it is not directly prejudicial to the cause of religion . . . could . . . encrease their Prejudices against us, & the Truth itself!" Ministers, Merivale continued in sharper language, should thus avoid "casting pearls before swine, lest they should be condemned by men who are stupid . . . or lest we ourselves should be torn & abused by those who are more wrathful & malignant."[33]

Merivale was prescient in more ways than one. Shortly after the outbreak of the French Revolution, reactionary mobs, well aware of the beliefs held by Merivale's young acquaintance Joseph Priestley, tried to snuff out the chemist and Unitarian in his Birmingham laboratory. Priestley escaped, but the mobs burned his lab to the ground, impelling him to flee to the United States. Even more do Merivale's words about an ideal minister prefigure Immanuel Kant's. What Merivale was saying was that some hearers were enlightened and some were not. "And surely this will warrant any of us," Merivale explained, "to make a distinction amongst men, in our applications to them, and to forbear inculcating some particular Truths, commonly inveigh'd against, till we find or make them favourably disposed for receiving them." Exactly how a minister was supposed to dispose hearers favorably to the "truth" Merivale left unanswered. But he outlined the spheres both appropriate and inappropriate to the task: "I suppose much more may be done in this way, by writing, or conversation than by Preaching."[34]

When Kant sat down a quarter century later to write his short, influential essay on the definition of *enlightenment,* his most illustrative example was a minister daring to push the limits of his own theological imagination while refraining from pushing the limits of his congregation. Kant called the separate sphere suitable for enlightening the *public,* by which he meant exactly what Merivale was talking about, even though the Tavistock minister used the word *public* with a different referent. It was Kant's terminology that was counterintuitive in his own example because a minister could easily reach a bigger public—which is to say more people—by way of a sermon at a crowded chapel than by way of an article in an arcane academic journal. For Merivale, a chapel was accordingly the sort of venue where one "publickly" and therefore cautiously spoke from the pulpit. Kant, however, consigned occupational discourse—what a minister or a tax collector or a soldier says while on the job—to the *private* realm. The thrust of what Merivale and Kant were both saying was nevertheless the same. Do not challenge congregational hearers directly when some were enlightened and some were, as Merivale put it, "stupid" and "malignant." Reserve your intellectual daring for "writing" and "conversation."[35]

Finding the balance was a preoccupation of heterodox ministers as the rift in Dissenter chapels all over England was widening, especially by midcentury. "In almost every town there is a struggle between Light and Darkness," wrote one of era's influential Dissenters, Samuel Bourn, in 1744.[36] On one side, Rational Dissenters were coming to renounce traditional doctrines. On the other, the orthodox were digging in to orthodoxy. With enlightenment so uneven, but with congregational self-determination a principle neither side wanted to give up, there was no easy way to force a shift in ideological direction. Merivale knew as much when Barker first asked him to relocate to Plymouth to become Baron's replacement. The minister may have tried to soften his rejection with a joke: "I would as soon subscribe to Pope Pius creed."[37] But he was right to believe that, amid the tension in Plymouth, no one could come in under the cover of being a moderate, preaching one way to people like Philalethes and another to Pope Joan.

By the fall of 1759, the conflict was already so out in the open that Batter Street was starting to entertain a sort of two-state solution. With "enthusiasm spreading like a cancer among us," Barker wrote, the congregants discussed replacing Baron with two different ministers: "so we have Armin[ius] in the morning and Calvin in the afternoon."[38] The prospect of that arrangement (which was pursued elsewhere in Dissenter chapels in England) nevertheless vanished.[39] The "Methodistical gang" started pushing to replace Baron with a single minister who adhered to what Barker referred to as the "Assembly catechism," meaning the Calvinist confession of faith written down by the Westminster Assembly in the 1640s and, for Barker, a signifier of everything that was wrong with orthodox Dissent. As he put it: "A man should judge for [him]self, and not take his religion from Baxter, [John] Flavel or anyone else."[40] Dissent was about *dissenting*. Or as Merivale put it: "[I]t is only by steady Dissent from established Errors and Impositions that the cause of xtian liberty and Truth is likely to prevail." This was why Merivale and Barker could, for example, admire Anglican authors but still be gravely concerned "when those who wish well to [liberty and truth] are ready to return to the National Church."[41] Even if the national church lined up perfectly with a Dissenter's beliefs, and notwithstanding the fact that religious conformity also brought practical benefits, Anglicanism imposed an intolerable orthodoxy. Arguably its most "established error" was the very notion of orthodoxy. "However well persuaded I might be in my own mind of the falsehood or pernicious tendency of any particular doctrines," wrote Merivale, "I should not think my judgment a rule for others to conform to."[42] It was in this sense that Dissent was not only "steady," to quote Merivale, but never-ending, with its only permanent feature an openness to improvement no matter how disruptive the disagreement. Indeed, Barker wrote, it was by virtue of this process that Batter Street had "subsisted since the Glorious Revolution in 1688," while now it was on course to being "shipwrecked."[43]

The reason, as Barker cryptically joked in another letter to Merivale, was that "the Pope declares herself a Calvinist." This was his reference to the "Methodistical" ringleader Barker had dubbed "Pope Joan." "If she can be 'mark'd out for Heaven,'" then "I suppose the Rest of Man & Womankind might go to H—— and be d——d as Wicked Sailors say."[44] Joan (I will assume this part of her name was real) is impossible to access outside the Barker-Merivale correspondence, which is unfortunate. Evangelicalism provided opportunities for women to become leaders, and it would be worth knowing more about Joan and her emergence as the voice of Plymouth's evangelical Presbyterians.[45] But in Barker's journal she is virtually always depicted unfavorably. By itself, that may say something about the gendered terms of the tension Barker felt with her. "I remember a man, an old Quaker," he wrote Merivale in a pointed reference to Joan, "who after my Mother's death said, said [*sic*] to my father Gregory, Thou will marry again, but above all women take care of a religious shrew. Scolding in Scripture Language is the bitterest, most venomous, and biting scolding of all Scoldings."[46] Barker rarely invokes stereotypes like the "scold" in his letters. But if anyone offered an occasion to pile on the insults, it was Joan, a woman in whom he found, as he wrote elsewhere, that "the ego is ever in her mouth." And yet, even here Barker could show some compassion. As relentlessly as he pushed for John Hanmer to replace Sophron, Barker admitted that Hanmer had made a mistake in not catering to Joan's needs. Those needs may have been out of sync with Rational Dissent, but they still arose from what

Barker thought was the wellspring of true religiosity: conscience. Hanmer had "never once either before [or after] Sophrons death made any visit to J[oan]," he rued to Merivale. For that matter, Barker showed some goodwill toward Joan in arranging for a face-to-face meeting in the effort to give "her an opportunity to discharge a part of what had long lain upon her mind."[47] By then, Hanmer had been appointed minister and was now preaching at Batter Street. That mostly unwanted appointment may have doomed the meeting to be fraught. In any case, it was.

"I am so full of a long confab with Pope Joan yesterday that to ease my stomach I must give some vent to it," Barker started a long letter to Merivale.[48] From the moment he and Joan sat down to talk, she "began with vilifying and abasing poor H[anmer]" before proposing her alternative choices for minister, all of whom Barker described as "Mad Men": "To this nothing was said but she went on incessantly for an hour and a half to declare her faith in the Trinity, original sin, [and] Calvinism." Joan then brought up "her father's dependence on Christ for salvation without works," which was almost too much for Barker, who "had great difficulty to forbear saying that [her father's] works were such as to need some screen or other." But rather than telling her that her father's behavior left something to be desired, he shifted course and asked her to locate the Trinity in the Bible, after which he cited his beloved James Foster's dictum that "where mystery begins religion ends." Barker's antitrinitarian challenge was incendiary enough, but the reference to Foster "put her into fury," during which "she raved [that Foster] was no more than a stage player and people went to hear him for diversion as they did to the Playhouse." Even Joan could admit that Foster was an impressive performer. But that was the insult. What is more, Foster had once said (so Joan claimed) that, if Christ "had not come, God would have found out another way, and we were not [therefore] at all obliged to Christ." In private, Barker agreed with exactly this heretical view, but as he sat with Joan he kept quiet and endured the invective.[49] "I will hear no Arminian no Arian etc.," she continued; "you are no trustees"; "you will answer it another day a counsel at law says so"; "I have been a mind to put your letters [which letters is unclear] in print." The temperature cooled slightly when Barker assumed (so he says) a calm voice, which at least made Joan "perceive I could be less zealous than she was." But this also gave her an opportunity to give him "a paper," now lost but apparently included in his letter to Merivale. The paper had been handed to him by Joan "to convert" him, Barker explained. Here Barker admitted that he had no on-the-spot rebuttal.[50] Maybe he was at a loss because he feared outing himself as a deist. In any case, he asked Merivale to answer the paper himself "in a few, very few, words," before promising his judicious friend that "no one creature living shall know it but myself."

But the main point is that the meeting got nowhere. "Sophron foresaw that Pope Joan would be a disturber of the peace of our Israel. The plot against Mr H[anmer] was laid many years ago," Barker would later tell Merivale.[51] Now Barker's meeting with Joan in the spring of 1760 had ensured that the congregation was not going to sort it out on their own. It was time to call in the lawyers.

A century and a half old by the 1760s, the writ of mandamus was typically a form of restoring figures of some authority to positions of which they had been deprived or from which they had been ejected without due process. A precedent-setting case had occurred in, of all places, Plymouth over a set of incidents from the era of Mansfield's illustrious predecessor on the Court of King's Bench, Edward Coke. In 1615, Coke had to render a judgment on the case of James Bagg, a powerful Plymouth merchant who had lent the town corporation a substantial sum of money and then felt entitled to start publicly hurling insults at his political competition. Bagg called one Plymouth mayor a "cozening knave." Toward another, Coke later wrote, Bagg turned "the hinder part of his body in an inhuman and uncivil manner and scoffingly, contemptuously, and uncivilly, with a loud voice, said . . . 'come and kiss,'" before threatening to make the mayor's "neck crack."[52] There was plenty of incentive for the town's leaders to remove Bagg from public office. But the legal grounds for doing so were thin. Coke therefore issued a writ of mandamus to restore Bagg to the corporation and, in effect, to override Plymouth's ruling elites.

On the face of it, restitution of an occupational position was also the reason that Mansfield drew on mandamus a century and a half later when the court was again confronted with a Plymouth case. The position in question in the 1760s was not a secular public office but a ministerial vacancy at a Presbyterian chapel. But Mansfield found the distinction irrelevant. The choice he had to make was whether someone had wrongly been kept from any position. As he explained in his ruling: "[W]rits of mandamus have been granted, to admit lecturers, clerks, sextons, and scavengers, etc. to restore an alderman to precedency, an attorney to practice in an Inferior Court etc." There was no precedent for excluding the clergy, including Dissenters. "Since the Act of Toleration, [mandamus] ought to be extended to protect an endowed pastor of Protestant Dissenters; from analogy and the reason of the thing."[53]

In the aftermath of Barker's meeting with Joan, the Batter Street dispute had gotten only more intractable, especially after the orthodox parishioners settled on Christopher Mends as their candidate for the election that Barker was still at pains to keep from occurring. Whether anyone other than a rationalist would have ever been acceptable to Barker is doubtful. But in his eyes Mends was as bad as it could get—he was a Calvinist with no formal training who followed the Methodist George Whitfield. Still, the actions Barker took to withhold the election clearly defied the custom by which an entire Presbyterian congregation was supposed to choose a new minister. One problem, then, was that he spearheaded an effort that broke with procedure. The other was that the man he had picked instead of Mends, John Hanmer, was clearly out of step ideologically with most of the congregation. The court recognized as much. Barker himself seemed to recognize as much. Nowhere in his letters does he make the case that he had the votes on his side. He may blame Joan for the being the "great incendiary."[54] But what she incited was already majority opinion.

To Lord Mansfield, what mattered turned out not to be Hanmer himself. The issue was the more fundamental prevention of an election, which Mansfield saw as an extension of the congregation's right to self-rule. The Court of King's Bench accordingly worried that, if it failed to intervene, "the congregation may be tempted to resist violence by force [leading to a] breach of the public peace, to the reproach of Government, and the scandal of religion." But was this the fair assumption to make about Dissent? Was congregational self-determination Dissent's defining principle? Or was the heart of the matter, as Barker thought, the individual right to dissent? In a less divisive chapel, those two principles should have overlapped—all congregants, theoretically, would see eye to eye enough for the election of a minister to capture the general will of the congregation. If for whatever reason general opinion happened to conflict with an errant minister, any election for a replacement would itself embody both the spirit of dissenting—dissenting from errant ministerial opinion—and the use of an election to resolve the problem. But, if that was the theory, what complicated Batter Street from Barker's point of view and presumably from the perspective of other heterodox parishioners was Mends's orthodoxy. How could such a dogmatic minister ever encourage the spirit of individual dissenting? More fundamentally, how could what Barker disparagingly called *orthodoxy* and what he ideally meant by *Dissent* ever go hand in hand? Mansfield's writ, in other words, gave a Dissenter congregation the right to choose a minister whose position, if held consistently, would have undermined the freedom of conscience that Barker saw as the core meaning of his religious outlook.[55] One legal historian of the United States has recently called *Rex v. Barker* "the leading case regarding mandamus and one frequently cited by early national American lawyers and judges as the quintessential summation of what mandamus was."[56] The reason for the claim is that in Barker' case mandamus upheld the rights of voluntary associations, of which Batter Street, like any Dissenter congregation, was an example. That seems a fair assessment of the legacy of the ruling. But if *Rex v. Barker* can be read as a tolerant judicial decision by virtue of upholding the rights of a religion that existed outside the national church, the ruling also did its part to help preserve the timeworn spirit of Calvinist intolerance. The Batter Street association may have been voluntary. But within that association, at least with Mends at the helm, there was an orthodox expectation that everyone would fall in line.

So why did Barker not just go elsewhere to practice his religion? He was obviously not required to suffer through orthodoxy. Simply put, leaving a chapel was easier said than done. "People are generally wedded to their Houses [of worship] and seats they have been accustomed to," Merivale commented about the case, "and perhaps would rather abandon a Minister they had some regard for, and accept a strange preacher of strange doctrines, than change their places."[57] That was true for Barker. He not only possessed the basic privileges at Batter Street, like a prominent pew; he was also a figure of authority. And he was not just a trustee; he was the leader of the three trustees. It also mattered that Baron had been one of his closest friends (and for years his next-door neighbor).[58] It mattered too that the battle with Joan was a test of his resolve as a proponent of rational religion.

Barker nevertheless did eventually give up the fight. He died before hearing the final ruling, but he knew what was coming, and by July 1762 he told Merivale: "I shall oppose no longer. Mon parti est pris. I know what I have to do, i.e., to sit down in sorrow the inch of time I have to burn out, and lament that so good a house [Batter Street] should be for the use of Enthusiasts, Tritheists, Antinomians, and solifidians, and that I have lived long enough to see law enforced without a statute, a private agreement broke thro by unlawful public authority."[59] The secular law had entered a domain where Barker thought it did not belong. The court was ostensibly protecting the principle of religious diversity inherent in the category of Dissent, but from Barker's close-up view it was effectively ensuring that the congregation would quash dissenting from its own orthodoxy. The chapel that the nation's highest common law court sought to preserve would in Barker's estimation fall to ruin.

It is hard not to wonder whether something good for Barker nevertheless came from all this. His correspondence with Merivale had been initiated, after all, to determine whether the minister in Tavistock was interested in getting involved in Plymouth: "You would I have for a pastor, preferable to any one man in the world, and no wonder when our souls seem so near akin."[60] Even if nothing came of that specific plan, the friendship it cemented arguably grew to be worth as least as much as a replacement minister. In conversation with Merivale, Barker could say almost anything. Maybe the forum turned out to be unexpected—a correspondence rather than a congregation. But the intellectual and religious freedom it allowed seemed, in the end, to capture far better what Barker took to be the essence of Dissent: the practice of looking for the truth wherever it might be found.

Samuel Merivale—whose origins were as humble as Barker's—is intriguing in his own right. He was born in Northampton in 1715 to a stocking-weaver father who died when Samuel was eighteen and a mother—the sister of John Brine—who was still alive in the 1760s and still steadfast in her beliefs. He also had to contend with an overbearing uncle, although John Brine may have served an unexpected purpose in focusing his critical energy. It was by the early age of fourteen that he felt emboldened, as he later wrote, to leave "the Principles of Calvin . . . for those of Arminius, or Baxter at least."[61] That decision was no doubt all the harder given that he had the option to attend Brine's Independent Academy in London tuition free, but instead he felt the pull of Northampton's liberal Dissenter Academy, which was founded and overseen by Philip Doddridge, not an avowed anti-Calvinists but an open-minded figure who stressed, above all, "free inquiry" in the process of education.[62]

By the early 1730s, Merivale had secured a job as a preacher for a Presbyterian congregation in Lincolnshire. His salary was low, and his finances were further strained by the debts the family had inherited after his father's death. His first courtship—of the daughter of a wealthy Lincolnshire merchant—was probably undertaken to get the family back on financial track. But in any case the effort failed, and he took a job three hundred miles to the southwest in Tavistock, a Devonshire market town of around two thousand inhabitants at the time, where in 1744 he was ordained a minister through an examination process presided over by Peter "Sophron" Baron.[63] The position came with 140 congregants and a bigger salary. It also brought Merivale into contact with the daughter of another well-to-do family, his future wife, Elizabeth "Betsy" Hillow, a woman he at first found "disfigured with the Small Pox," or so he wrote a friend. But she had "a great deal of natural good Sense, which, especially since I have been acquainted with her, she has improved by reading."[64] The courtship was still uncertain as Merivale could not get out from underneath the family debt, which left his future father-in-law unimpressed.[65] In what seems like something of a panic, he briefly entertained moving once again across the country, this time to preach to a wealthy Dissenter congregation in Birmingham, by then a city of over thirty thousand people. But he stayed in Devon when he realized that the higher cost of living in a bigger, growing city would have eaten up the larger salary. Betsy's father eventually relented, and the young couple married in August 1748.[66] Jane, or Jenny, was born on cue nine months later, followed by John in three years and Walter in another three.

It was during the 1740s that Merivale started occasionally traveling fifteen miles south to Plymouth to preach at Batter Street as a guest of Baron's. It was also then that he met Barker, although when exactly they realized they were kindred spirits is harder to say.[67] By the time their correspondence begins in 1758, neither seemed to have any hesitation about expressing heretical ideas. (There is a surviving fragment of a letter that Barker sent to Merivale in 1746 that only superficially touches on a few financial matters.) Yet, even if they were philosophically on the same page by 1758, they could differ on the details. "We think alike on most points," Barker once put it both to affirm their sympathies and to acknowledge their differences.[68]

Merivale believed, correctly, that Barker was "a much readier writer."[69] Barker sent off, on average, two letters for every one of Merivale's.[70] Barker, also by his admission, liked to improvise. "As you know my rambling way of writing," he told Merivale, "your goodness will excuse my want of Method."[71] This too was on the nose. When an idea came to Barker, he was ready to think it through while writing it down and shortly before putting it in the post to his friend. And before Merivale had a chance to respond he would often send off a follow-up letter with more thoughts on the same matter. Merivale was, for his part, a more careful writer and reader. Barker may have been the one to come across some of the books they read together, but he seems on a couple of occasions to have loaned books to Merivale before reading them thoroughly. Merivale, no doubt in part because of his careful ministerial training, virtually never commented on anything he had not apparently first read carefully.

A case in point is Voltaire's *Candide*, which Barker loaned to Merivale in 1759, the year the short novel was published. Merivale already admired Voltaire. So did Barker. But *Candide*'s cynicism was challenging. As Merivale put it, *Candide*, a book first published anonymously, "has afforded me so little pleasure that I would not willingly consider is as the production of so agreeable a writer as Voltaire did not the public voice so unanimously attribute it to him." It was as if Voltaire was overtaken by the "very spirit of Gulliver," added Merivale, who could no more get Voltaire's point than he could "what that strange mortal [Jonathan] Swift aimed at in his Gulliver's Travels." There were admittedly "some strokes of just satire," and "here and there one meets with something humorous." For that matter there was "a Good Lesson of Industry & Contentment [which] is indeed inculcated at last; but there was surely no need of going so far to fetch it." Voltaire, Merivale continued, also made no effort to "establish any just Principles of Religion, he seems rather laboring to overthrow them. The notion that all is intended for the best, is made a perfect joke of from the Beginning to the End; and the Writer, by his Representation of Things appears to favor either Martin's Scheme of Manicheism or that of the Dervish Towards the Conclusion . . . which supposes human affairs quite beneath the Notice of the Deity."[72]

Barker did not think *Candide* was Voltaire's best book either. "It is not to be named at the same time with Zadig." Voltaire may well ridicule the "German Pride" of Leibniz, Barker added, but he also believed that "the French Pride equals or even exceeds it in many cases." Yet that is all Barker says before adding this telling line: "I know nothing of Martin, who wrote of Manicheism."[73] Barker had picked up on the phrase "Martin's Scheme of Manicheism" from Merivale's letter as if the reference was to an actual Manichaean author. But Merivale was simply talking about the Manichaean character in the book named Martin, who is not an incidental character, although one Barker apparently missed or had not yet come across before sending Merivale the book.

Other times Barker and Merivale both seem to read thoroughly but still differently. Consider the way they approached *Code de la nature; ou, Le véritable esprit de ses loix de tout temps négligé ou méconnu* (1755), a book once thought to be authored by Diderot but now attributed to an obscure French tax collector, Etienne-Gabriel Morelly.[74] This was a profoundly radical Enlightenment work: philosophically materialist and protosocialist with, writes one recent historian, its "system of communal property . . . predicated on a rejection of the idea of original sin."[75] More radically than Rousseau in his *Discourse on Inequality,* which was published the same year, the *Code* maintained that eliminating private property would take the wind out of the sails of the Augustinian view of human nature.[76] Jansenist authors like Abbé Noël Antoine Pluche thought, on the other hand, that amour propre and its corollary, avarice, were natural and universal.[77] But writing against Pluche, among others, Morelly maintained that, by virtue of amour propre being a "pernicious consequence" of private property, it was instead the case that self-love—and by implication economic self-interest—were socially conditioned and avoidable traits. Karl Marx made the passing comment in *Capital* that "primitive accumulation plays approximately the same role in political economy as original sin does in theology."[78] For Morelly, the reasoning was more than analogical. Original sin was born directly through the outcome of primitive accumulation, the outcome being the eventual creation of private property.

Barker sent Merivale the book. And when Merivale read it (with great interest), he immediately seized on the *Code's* "levelling scheme," which he seemed to endorse: "If ever the World is brought to such a state of universal Righteousness & Peace, Love & Joy, as we seem taught to expect under the Millennium, one necessary pre-requisite must be the Throwing down of Distinctions between Man & Man and the enjoying of all things in Common."[79] Barker admitted that he too was interested in the leveling scheme, but what had made him send the book to Merivale was a short passage about religion that he would quote and requote throughout his letters, even more than the four lines from the French captain:

> Criez tant qu'il vous plaira, imposteurs ou fanatiques, qui avez interêt de nous persuader des chiméres; vos vains raisonnemens ne pourront jamais étouffer cette vérité aussi évidente que le premier axiome de mathématique. Si la Suprême Puissance est unie dans un Etre à une infini sagesse, elle ne punit point, elle perfectionne ou anéantit. Choisissez.[80]

"Shout as much as you like, impostors or fanatics, who have an interest in persuading us of chimeras," the passage reads in English. "Your vain reasonings can never stifle this truth, which is as obvious as the first axiom of mathematics. If the Supreme Power is united in a Being with infinite wisdom, it does not punish, it perfects or annihilates. Choose."

The fact that Barker chose to highlight a passage from Morelly about religion illustrates his difference from Merivale from another angle.[81] He may have read selectively, but he was shrewd in finding passages that supported his metaphysics. The notion of perfectibility squared, for example, with his anthro-optimism, much as the word *anéantit* resonates with an idea Barker and Merivale both passingly entertain as more humane than eternal suffering in hell—the idea that the souls of the wicked might simply be annihilated by the Supreme Being in the afterlife.[82] Barker also elsewhere invokes images like *imposteurs, fanatiques,* and *chiméres,* keywords of the materialist radical Enlightenment.[83] Not least, he consistently believed that the Supreme Being never uses the threat of punishment to engender fear. It was up to believers to confront the true or the false on their own. In Barker's mind, everyone possessed a capacity that, as a younger man, he had himself exercised when he swerved from orthodoxy: the agency to choose.

Code de la nature was published in 1755, *Candide* in 1759. Those dates are telling. The books Barker and Merivale generally discuss in detail had been recently published. This is not to say that the two men do not also name-check other authors and texts. But any detailed sense of what they thought about many texts that they were not in the process of carefully reading is often unclear. In another sense, stray references indicate that they kept up with the latest books by reading the periodical press, particularly the *London Magazine*, the *Gentleman's Magazine*, the *Monthly Review*, and the *Critical Review*. These periodicals had vague political or cultural associations—the *Monthly Review* and the *London Magazine* were slightly Whig in outlook, while the *Gentleman's Magazine* and the *Critical Review* leaned High Church and Tory. But Barker and Merivale give little hint of caring about political party associations. They needed book reviews to cut through the mass of information, and despite their both being Whigs (like virtually all Dissenters) they turned to periodicals without, by all appearances, much political discrimination.[84]

Barker and Merivale did not read indiscriminately, however. Even when they briefly mention authors or their ideas, it is obvious whether they are for or against them. They often simply invoke an author's name, without commentary, to lend a statement support or to smear it as uncredible. But even here much is missing. Their brief, passing mentions so often fail to impart the dynamic process of reader response that is clearly on display when they do spend more time with a text.[85] A different mystery altogether is that some authors who should have appeared in their letters do not. It is hard to explain why they never read Adam Smith's *Theory of Moral Sentiments* considering its publication date, not to mention the subjects it takes up and Barker and Merivale's interest in Scottish Enlightenment authors like Hutcheson and Hume. Considering that they later read Rousseau's *Julie*, it is surprising that they never talk about Rousseau's *Discourse on Inequality*.[86] If in fact they had encountered these books, it is just as hard to imagine that they would not have written about them. All this also raises a further possibility that some of the relevant letters were simply lost.

Another feature of their correspondence is that they sometimes devote words to an author by way of transcription rather than commentary.

Easier than sending books back and forth in the mail was copying out operative passages, which also served the purpose of committing those passages to memory. Much of the time, Merivale and Barker seemed to feel that comment on their transcriptions was unnecessary. Again, this is a missed opportunity because when they do follow their transcriptions with commentary—something that they also do on occasion—the commentary is always revealing. Merivale, for example, begins a long paragraph in one of his letters by writing: "[While] looking over [John] Locke's Familiar Letters the other day, I met with a passage that I thought would please you. Tis a letter to that good natured and truly catholic Divine [Philipp van] Limborch."[87] He then proceeds to transcribe a chunk of a letter from Locke to Limborch from October 4, 1698, which he follows with Limborch's response from December 9 of the same year.[88] The passage from Locke turns on an idiosyncratic distinction between "evangelicals" and "papists," which he described as two overarching classes of people. By *evangelical,* Locke explains that he means anyone guided by conscience, while *papists* are people prone to error because they let themselves be directed by the arguments of others. Limborch responded that, in truth, any congregation harbors both kinds of people. Even in Roman Catholic congregations some believers are guided by conscience to the displeasure of their coreligionists, he admits, before concluding that he therefore loves *evangelicals*—a word that in their repurposed terms simply means anyone guided by conscience, no matter what community they are a part of.

Merivale got the gist of all this. But as he expanded on it he made clear his more specific concerns. By his own admission less charitable than Limborch, Merivale homed in on papists among evangelicals rather than evangelicals among papists. He wanted, in other words, to appropriate the word *papist* for a Protestant context. His concern was that "every bigot is a papist." In other words, there were still too many papists among their Dissenter coreligionists—which was not at all to say too many closet Catholics but rather to say too many dogmatic Calvinists. (This is a striking turnaround from the typical use of *papist* to mean Catholic-leaning and *evangelical* to mean the hotter sort of Protestant.) But there is something else to notice. Although Merivale and Barker typically used the word *Brine* to signify "bigot," Merivale was using the evangelical/papist conceit in the Limborch-Locke exchange not only to lend his own views authority but also to rescue heresy. As he writes Barker, he was willing to "let an evangelic xtian be ever so great a Heretic," by which he meant that conscience should lead one happily into heresy when necessary. He continued: "A sincere Lover of & Inquirer after truth, tho called a Deist or Atheist by those who take all their opinions on Trust, & would thrust them down the throats of others[,] is certainly a much better xtian than they."[89]

Comments like this point to another thread in the Barker and Merivale letters. They regularly use Enlightenment authorities to make a case against "Tritheism, Antinomianism, and the other shocking isms that are growing up amongst us Dissenters."[90] It is hard to overstate this. Their general concern with religion may say something about the imbrication of Christianity and the Enlightenment—as should be unmistakable by this point, neither of these men was against the spirit of religion. But they make constant use of Enlightenment authors to assail Christian *orthodoxy*. And when all was said and done, they hoped Christianity would itself be a subordinate category to a more universalist mode of religiosity. As Barker writes Merivale in one of his very last letters: "[A] great noise is made about Deism whereas rightly considered, every Christian must be a Deist first, believe in one eternal God, and I think he must also be a Unitarian or believe in contradictions."[91]

When it came to the errors of orthodoxy, Barker and Merivale not surprisingly had plenty of particular things to say. They often call *tritheism*, or belief in the Trinity, the ultimate contradiction. How, for example, does it make sense that two numbers, "3" and "1," are the same? they ask rhetorically. By the same token, there was something equally contradictory about imagining that there could be three eternal gods who had created the universe. "There cannot be 3 Equals," as Barker once put it. "There must be an inferiority."[92] The Trinity was just as unacceptable because it was polytheistic, hence the insult built into *tritheism*. Polytheism, in turn, made the Trinity a sort of blasphemy, although the charge of blasphemy was itself used idiosyncratically to mean a breach of the reasonable rather than of the sacred. "The Catholicks do actually call [Mary] the Mother of God," Barker put it, "in which there is something horrible as if God could be born—and this alone is sufficient to root up a certain Doctrine." Not least, Barker and Merivale occasionally point out that in one way or another the Trinity is inconsistent with the Bible. When Jesus prays in the garden, Barker wrote sneeringly, "did x pray to himself?"[93]

Antinomian was Barker and Merivale's word for *predestinarian*, and, as with *tritheism*, it was used as a subtle insult. In its typical theological sense, *antinomian* refers to someone who uses his or her assurance of spiritual election as license to ignore the moral law. Antinomianism was, in other words, normally seen only as the worst-case scenario of predestinarianism. But Barker and Merivale's insult was that *any* predestinarian was antinomian, which was to say that any predestinarian was indifferent to moral conduct. Recall that, when Barker held his tongue as Pope Joan invoked her predestinarian father, what he *really* wanted to say—what he later says to Merivale—was that Joan's morally flawed father was an all-too-predictable antinomian outcome of predestination. Calvinists often argued that, on the contrary, giving too much salvific weight to moral conduct caused the same kind of delusional self-inflation Barker discerned in the elect. This was a theological charge Barker well knew. But he threw it back at the Calvinists. "Surely it is owing to Self Love," he writes, "that a Man comes to what he calls full assurance of his own Safety."[94]

There is little mystery where Barker and Merivale stood on original sin, but since we have seen one unqualified condemnation after another, here we might consider a curious—but ultimately telling—moment in the correspondence when Barker was willing to admit to at least one consequence of Adam's fall, namely, death. This happens in a debate with an orthodox man whom Barker simply calls "R." Barker was forced into conversation while waiting for Merivale to send him a copy of John Taylor's heterodox *The Scripture Doctrine of Original Sin* (1740), "certainly the best treatise that ever was wrote on the subject," opined Merivale, who had used the book tactically.[95] In fact, the reason that Barker had not received the book before this moment was that Merivale had lent it to a unnamed friend in the attempt to offer her "an antidote to Wesley's Treatise on the Subject," the latter of which Merivale explained "had been recommended to her by a Methodist, and which I found she was inclin'd to take for Gospel."[96] Even without Taylor's book fresh in his mind, however, Barker told Merivale that he felt good about being able to avoid a detailed argument about original sin with R, who was, Barker admitted, "bookish" and would, Barker worried, be a formidable opponent: "[R wanted to] put into my hands [a book] about Original Sin. I am grown savvy of late. I answered Mr Lock[e] had satisfied me as to that Point. In the day thou eatest therefore thou shall surely Dye. This said I is all I fear from Adam's Fall—Death temporal."[97]

Consistently maligned in Barker and Merivale's letters was also, as we have seen, solifideism. And again the reason is not hard to find. Pinning salvation to faith alone made moral conduct irrelevant. All this raises another general point. In the typical discursive oppositions of Christian theology, so much of what Barker and Merivale believed is simply the negation of what they no longer believed. Against solifideism and antinomianism, they laid stress on moral conduct. Against the Trinity, they thought that a supreme being was wholly singular. Against original sin, they had an optimistic view of human nature and agency.

But some of what Barker and Merivale believed stood outside these dialectical relationships. For example, they do not always use the word *particle* as a perfect stand-in for *soul*. On one occasion, when he tries to capture the notion of the particle, Merivale describes it as "materialist" and as a "ray or emanation of the Deity himself." He gave Barker credit for the concept, which he thought had the advantage of giving "us a high Idea of our own original Dignity and Excellence, and may serve (as you [Barker] have often justly observed) to animate us to an answerably noble conduct." But, more pessimistic about human nature than Barker, he worried that the particle did not square with the examples in our behavior of "degeneracy." On the one hand, Merivale reasoned: "I acknowledge the idea of the absolute Infinity and immensity of the godhead seems to swallow up everything in it; and to exclude the possibility of any other real distinct and separate existence." Here he was imagining, alternatively, that everything in the universe was part "of one stupendous whole," with the result that the particle was absorbed in God. But, on the other hand, even if he could flesh out Barker's idea in these terms, he was not necessarily convinced. "Such imaginations" he called "rash and presumptuous": "[I] think it's better to acknowledge my utter ignorance of these matters than pretend to decide upon them one way or another."[98]

To make matters more obscure but also more intriguing, Merivale wrote a manuscript to entertain the prospect that what he called the *soul*—a word that, unlike Barker, he did not eschew—is material. The manuscript does not survive. But Merivale sent it to Barker and to Barker only, and he and Barker reference it in their letters.[99] In one of those passing references, Merivale admitted that he did not *necessarily* believe in what the manuscript puts forward, namely, the soul's materiality. He tells Barker that attacking the traditional view was a lot easier than defending a new theory of the soul altogether. It is always easier to challenge, he writes, than to create a system of thought. Like a virologist who makes a virus stronger in the lab to test out a vaccine, he seems to have wanted to give the materialist argument a gain of function to bolster the counterargument. This was not uncommon in theology. Recall Benjamin Franklin's comment about the counterarguments in the Boyle Lectures being more convincing than the refutations. In the same vein, atheism spread in mid-seventeenth-century France, it has been argued, not because dogmatic atheists gained ground but because the atheistic arguments leveled up by theologians in search of countermeasures escaped from the laboratory.[100] But in Merivale's case, all he does is strengthen the virus. He never offers the antidote. Why increase the gain of function for its own sake? What is intriguing is that the answer to that question is never made clear.

Barker was, in any case, convinced of the merits of his own view of the particle, which he often described as a particle of *Nous*, the Greek word used by Plato and the Neoplatonists to signify the cosmic intelligence.[101] All this suggests what was also the case. Barker did not exactly have an orthodox view of heaven and hell. He did believe in an afterlife, which he thought was one of Christianity's great concepts. But he never makes clear what he thought the afterlife was like. The subject comes up, for example, in a letter in which he thinks through the calculus of punishment and reward. He recounts hearing a parable in Turkey about "a man [who] meets a woman with fire in one hand and water in the other": "He asked her what she was about to do with it? Answer: I am going to drown hell and burn paradise [so] that people may attend to the affairs of this world."[102] Whether or not he knew her name, Barker was invoking the story of the Sufi Rabia al-Adawiyya, one of the major female voices of Islam, who famously used this same allegory to say that fear of punishment or the promise of reward diverts attention from Allah. Barker, or the person from whom he heard the story during one of his trips to Turkey, was, it seems, in the same spirit calling too much concern about the afterlife a distraction from the affairs of this world.[103] And Barker, to whose remarkable repertoire of ideas we can add elements of Sufism, wrote it all down approvingly.

Dismissing hell nevertheless raised the question of what happens to bad particles. Should there be no consequences for having lived an evil life? Here Barker and Merivale wondered aloud about the possibilities. They pondered after reading Samuel Bourn's *A Letter to the Rev. Samuel Chandler, D.D., concerning the Christian Doctrine of Future Punishment* (1759) whether corrupt souls were simply annihilated in the afterlife. The particle would in this case never experience gratifying reunion with *Nous*, hence the punishment. But the great advantage is that particles would be mercifully spared perpetual torment.

Barker raised another possibility, which was that, by the time we all die, we will have already been through hell. In one of the most arresting images in any of his letters, he tells Merivale that one has to contemplate the "sinless beings as such no doubt there may be in many of the numberless worlds." If these beings out there in the universe were "to come into our World in a Fleet of Ships, or by some method or way that we can form no ideas of," they would know right away why we had been "kept here in such misery." Just think, he continued, about all the miseries the species endures. Some are humanmade ("wars," "inquisitions," "whips," "hatred," "envy," "malice," "strifes," "robbery," "murder"), some are made worse by the limits of human understanding ("earthquakes," "fevers," "small pox," "pestilences"), and some Barker names because they obviously hit close to home ("gouts," "drunkenness," "lawsuits").[104] As benign sinless aliens would be kind enough to point out, these things by themselves added up to suffering enough. What religion needs hell when earth is hell already?

Still, none of this solved the problem of how to ensure good behavior—a solution that would also theoretically minimize the this-worldly hellishness. Here Barker was at his most optimistic. He thought the guarantee of good conduct was rational understanding of *Nous,* which was tantamount to understanding love and goodness. The particle would recognize itself in the process of grasping the divine because the particle was itself a piece of the thing it was trying to understand. The underlying question was no different from the animating question of the entire liberal tradition. How can autonomous people cohere into a stable society? Not unlike Rousseau's hope that individuals might autonomously align with the general will if they could discern in the generality their own freedom, Barker's hope was that, if only particles could understand where they came from and where they would one day return, moral conduct would naturally follow.

There is an obvious social and political subtext here, and we will come back to it in later chapters, but, staying for now on the subject of the divine, did Barker and Merivale see *Nous* as God in the Judeo-Christian sense? I think they did, but only generally. All the religions they had encountered presumed that something in the universe had at least been responsible for creation. But after comparison and cross-referencing, the common features of this Supreme Being came down to rudimentary and minimalist qualities like benevolence, rationality, and goodness, which were qualities also shared, as Barker and Merivale saw it, by human beings. The specificity of God was otherwise absent.[105]

Take, for example, a letter from 1759 in which Barker was in one sense at pains to say that he believed in God. "That God is—is as sure as that I am," he wrote after reading and referencing the Newtonian theologian Samuel Clarke. After laying down that baseline belief, however, he spends the duration of the letter describing the proper-name figure from the Bible, *God,* in ways that hardly look biblical. Still thinking about Clarke, but now referencing, at once, John Petvin (1691–1745), the author of the Neoplatonist *Letters concerning Mind* (1750), the deist William Wollaston, and the deistic *Letters Writ by a Turkish Spy,* he writes: "Petvin says—something is, therefore something has always been, viz., there must have been ever a cause preceding something—Now what can he mean, by cause, but God. Wollaston's reasoning is to the same purpose I met with . . . in the Turkish Spy. This cause must be the Nous of the Ancients—and ~~must be~~ (I forget the Greek word) the Intelligence. And I should think it impossible for any Man to say cooly—that the world came by chance, or was form'd as we see it—without an Intelligent Being, after all, I can't make anything of Necessity, unless I express it thus—there must Necessarily be such a Being, or what we see could not have been."[106] Barker was searching through the possibilities. Something like God existed and had always existed. If there was any necessary truth, this was it. "But who can say How He is," Barker concluded, asking a question he never firmly answered.[107]

What about Jesus? Both committed antitrinitarians, Barker and Merivale saw Jesus as a man. They both also valued the Bible as a book in which they thought Jesus had important things to say. But they also both rarely talk about Jesus. Barker in particular thought Jesus had been put to bad use by the orthodox. The God of deism, unlike the trinitarian God of Calvin, was the sort of being anyone could understand, whether in Africa, America, Asia, or Europe. But the focus on Jesus lent itself to exclusion. In 1760, Barker told Merivale he had gotten into an argument with an orthodox man "years ago." The unnamed man told Barker "that had not X interposed, the whole race of mankind must have perished for ever." Barker shot back with biblical quotations: "I stunned him with a few plain texts, indeed: God so loved &c that He sent &c." Barker underlined *sent* to signal what he and Merivale both knew, which is to say that God could not *send* himself and hence, from another angle, that the Trinity was an absurd idea. But the man was not stunned into silence. Instead: "[T]his bigot [brought up] Whitfield to convert me, which [I] protected against, and said bluntly I pretended to have seen as much of the World as W[hitefield] & could teach him as much as he could me."[108]

It was not just that constant talk about Jesus could miss the point of universalism. The problem was also what all that talk was meant to impart. In early 1760, Barker told Merivale that he thought there were two kinds of Christians and, accordingly, two versions of Jesus: "I will be a xtian with you and [John] Balguy, and Dr. [James] Foster, and my cousin [i.e., brother-in-law, Peter] Cock . . . but I will not I cannot with [Calvinists] etc etc etc too many of them. How fine and how beautiful are the sermons of X on the Mount! Why don't [the orthodox] preach from them? But they run to Paul's Epistles. . . . Transub[stantiation] Confession Absolution etc etc makes Deists in France. The Δ [Trinity] and Satisfaction [predestinarianism] makes em [deists] in England. But tho I am censur'd for the Rational, nothing but Reason will make reasonable xtians."[109] Barker's language is typically rambling and truncated, but his point is clear enough. There was both a reasonable Christianity and an absurd Christianity. The former ran straight from the Sermon on the Mount to deism, the latter straight from Paul (and the Augustinian tradition) to orthodoxy.

Countless, if not all, of Barker and Merivale's comments on divine nature imply their thoughts on human nature. In one broad sense, they thought human nature could improve. This was the implication of the idea that by way of our common rationality we can all come to better resemble the divine intelligence. In another sense, Barker in particular suggested that where understanding of *Nous* was at its most profound was where there was ultimately very little difference between human and divine nature, a notion he found expressed profoundly in the four lines handed to him by the French captain in which knowledge of the self and the divine were tantamount to the same thing.

A notch or two below this level of abstraction, Barker and Merivale also read authors who tried to get at the details of human nature. Both, for example, register their interest (without much elaboration) in David Hartley's associationist ideas, to which Merivale introduced Barker. But the other vexing question is, Where exactly in the self does the capacity for making moral actions come from? What was the psychological mechanism of doing the right thing? Among the numerous eighteenth-century authors who tackled this subject, Barker and Merivale were especially taken by what Francis Hutcheson (1694–1746) and John Balguy (1686–1748) had to say.

We met Hutcheson earlier as Adam Smith's college professor, sitting as the angel on one of Smith's shoulders opposite Bernard Mandeville, or "mandevil" as he was commonly known. Hutcheson was, as one historian of Enlightenment Scotland writes, "one of the most ambitious, admired and innovative philosophy teachers in the English-speaking world in the early eighteenth century."[110] Barker and Merivale admired him in particular, as did others, because of his counter to the anthropessimism of Mandeville, in whose thought anything that looked like morality was only a function of self-love and interest. Hutcheson countered that the "Author of Nature" had supplied human beings with a "moral sense" that transcended interest and drew all people to admire and enact benevolent actions.

If Hutcheson worried about the artifice of morality in Mandeville, however, John Balguy worried about the arbitrariness of morality in Hutcheson. Balguy is now largely neglected. But that Barker and Merivale were so taken by this rationalist Anglican minister—and ultimately sided with him over the former Reformed minister Hutcheson—is telling of Balguy's resonance at the time. In two works that tackled Hutcheson, *The Foundation of Moral Goodness* (1728) and *The Second Part of the Foundation of Moral Goodness* (1729), Balguy could agree that it might appear as if we act according to moral instinct. But more mature moral thinking depends on our rational capacity to see the absolute good or bad in actions. If, as Hutcheson thought, we depend on a moral sense implanted by God, then we were ultimately relying on a sort of unthinking instinct that Balguy believed wrongly denied moral agency. Agency, he thought, depended precisely on our ability to recognize the reasonableness and rightness of any action under consideration. Barker and Merivale agreed. They saw Balguy's argument (which they also associated with Richard Price and Henry Grove) as consistent with their stress on moral conduct and consistent with the notion that the human capacity to reason was not a reduction but a reflection of *Nous*.[111]

Barker and Merivale make other passing comments about Balguy and Hutcheson to the same effect. But to see how the abstractions of moral philosophy were put in conversation with the moral theater of the broader world, we should turn to one of Barker's most loaded letters and a tangible example of human depravity.

As we saw, Barker condemned slavery in his diary but seemed to need to be confronted with it before broaching it in any detail. The same holds true for the letters: he condemned slavery to Merivale (whose responses on the subject have unfortunately been lost) but only after encountering a negative review of the early abolitionist pamphlet *Two Dialogues on the Man-Trade* that was published in the *Monthly Review* in 1760 under the pseudonym "J. Philmore." The *Two Dialogues* was not a widely selling or circulating pamphlet, but it contained what has been described as "the most radical antislavery doctrine . . . found in any publication that appeared before the French Revolution."[112] In a passage that even later Quaker abolitionists like Anthony Benezet did not reprint, Philmore wrote: "[A]ll the black men now in our [British] plantations, who are by unjust force deprived of their liberty, and held in slavery, as they have none upon earth to appeal to, may lawfully repel that force with force, and to recover their liberty, destroy their oppressors." Indeed, he continued, it was "the duty of others, white as well as blacks, to assist those miserable creatures, if they can, in their attempts to deliver themselves out of slavery, and to rescue them out of the hands of their cruel tyrants."[113] Beyond the moral obligation for individuals, Philmore thought even more radically that there was justification for any nation in the world to declare war on England for its dominant role in the slave trade.[114]

Barker offers no evidence that he read this radical pamphlet, but he read a critical review of it in which a proslavery and anonymous reviewer insisted that the slave trade should continue. Without its economic benefits, Philmore's critic wrote, "we were never any more to see an ounce of tobacco or sugar in Great Britain." Even more, "the European inhabitants" living in the empire would "become slaves" to the "three hundred thousand emancipated slaves." Such retribution would not be driven by universal human emotions, however. The reviewer made the racist argument that "idleness, perfidy, and barbarity, are the genuine characteristics of all the Africans, [and] are more particularly exemplified in the inhabitants of that part of Guinea called the Slave-coast": "Neither reason, justice, nor religion, can vindicate the giving liberty to a people, who, it is morally certain, would employ that liberty in the destruction of those who gave it. . . . [T]hese truly pitiable creatures might by degree be brought to consider their American bondage only as a happy deliverance from African barbarity."[115]

Barker found slavery as easy to renounce as any part of the theological "merciless scheme" with which he ultimately associated it. And after reading this proslavery attack on Philmore, he thought it was "blasphemy to say that God, an infinitely good Being, would create Millions of intellig[ent] Creatures of whom he knew the far greatest part (according to some) must be forever wretched": "Cui bono?"[116] The parenthetical "according to some" was revealingly vague. It might refer to slavery's defenders, a reference that fits the immediate context. It might also refer to orthodox theologians, whose Calvinist doctrines compounded the punishment of the body by throwing into the fire untold millions of heathen souls. But however thorough Barker's condemnation of slavery, it was complicated by a note written by Philmore's reviewer. That note, printed in the side margin of the *Monthly Review*, reads matter-of-factly: "[B]efore the slave-trade commenced, it was customary for the negroes, who were perpetually at war with one another, to murder all their prisoners, after having made them undergo the most excruciating torments."[117] Barker admitted that here he could not "understand how to explain moral fitness to my satisfaction." What he had in mind was both the slave trade and broader, abstract philosophical questions "that would puzzle the strongest Brain as to many points in Hutcheson's Enquiry," which is to say Hutcheson's *Inquiry into the Original of Our Ideas of Beauty and Virtue* (1726). Setting Hutcheson against the hostile footnote, Barker asked: "What notion of a moral sense can the Negro's in Africa have? You see by a Note in February's [*Monthly*] *Review* that before the Slave Trade, whatever Prisoners were taken in War, were after excruciating Torment put to Death."[118]

Barker accepted the note's veracity for long enough to set the example of human atrocity it described against his reading of Hutcheson and

Balguy. Already he was growing convinced of Balguy's counterargument that actions were themselves inherently good or bad and could be rationally understood as such without the addition of a moral sense. That made it all the easier to believe that a Hutchesonian moral sense was lacking in anybody who enslaved or tortured other people. Barker writes: "[W]as it [morally] fit that because one side [tortured and murdered Africans], so should the other?" How "can it be reconciled with the right Reason that the Divine Being should permit this from Age to Age?" These questions were largely rhetorical. Barker knew, as he writes in the same letter, that a supreme being who was tolerant of such atrocities "never was nor never can be." The God in which Barker had come to believe would have to see such actions as a breach of morality, which would then be understood by all rational beings as wrong, as Balguy suggested. When Barker then returns to the question of morality—"is there moral Fitness in Acts like these?"—the answer is therefore clear. "It cannot be. To say that these numberless miserable bring the misery on themselves"—which was the implication of the marginal note in the review—"will not solve the matter. Suppose them as wicked as possible. For had they not been made, they could not have been thus wicked."[119]

Something else is worth noting here. Barker thought slavery was immoral, but the note he encountered in the review was meant by Philmore's critic to weaken precisely such a moral aversion. In effect, this proslavery note was asking the reader to reconsider a fundamental moral question. How wrong was it to do something to presumably wicked people? Original sin may have never been invoked by Philmore's critical reviewer. But the argument looks familiar. There was an Augustinian tradition, as we saw earlier, that maintained that slavery was against the law of nature before the Fall but not after, which was effectively to say that moral depravity justifies enslavement. A similar rational underpins the note in the review of Philmore. But the crucial difference is that, in the note, the depravity is delimited. While the doctrine of original sin was supposed to be universal in scope, in other words, the depravity in the note was pronounced only in Africans. What is discernible in this conjuncture between an abolitionist pamphlet and its proslavery critic is therefore both a profound change and a profound continuity. The change is from sin to race as a justification for enslavement. The continuity is the use of depravity, even if now in a racist guise, against humanitarian redress.

To be clear, Barker was not buying the critical reviewer's argument. But if it at the very least encouraged readers to entertain a racist argument, it is no accident that, in his next letter and nowhere else in any of his surviving writings, Barker invokes skin color. His comment is made in passing, and the letter in which it appears is typically rambling. Between reporting to Merivale that "Mrs Barker" cut herself with a broken glass and that he had just read a review of Herman Boerhaave's lectures (in which Barker says he was pleased to hear that the "Divine Particle is in the Brain"), he inserts this non sequitur: "[T]he Man after Gods own heart cannot be wash'd clean, no no, as soon may you wash an Ethiopian white. I remember a sign in this Town 3 year ago. The[y] labour in vain, rubbing scrubbing a Negro to no purpose."[120]

The trope Barker was invoking—the futility of washing an Ethiopian white as a metaphor for helplessness in the face of original sin—pervades English religious writing, particularly in the Reformed tradition.[121] Its theological purpose was to reaffirm original sin as a condition of humankind as a whole. But in another sense it leaned in the racist direction of the note in the review of Philmore. The trope did not just say that human beings trying to redeem themselves was as futile as trying to change skin color; it suggested that, the darker the skin, the deeper the sin.[122] Why, then, would Barker invoke a formulation in which a racist trope *affirms* original sin, a doctrine he detested? As elsewhere in his letters, he was here being sardonic. He was always looking for new ways to repudiate religious orthodoxy or call out the orthodox as ignorant. And here he was not only assailing original sin but also grimly mocking a racist metaphor used to defend what he saw as a bankrupt theological concept. His second sentence about "a sign in this Town" is in the same vein sarcastic, like the repeated "no no." By his own admission, he shifted abruptly from one topic to the next throughout his letters. But nothing runs more consistently through his freely associative prose than his pronouncements about the universality of his love for humankind.

Here, then, we have yet another striking moment buried in the dense writings of an obscure ship's purser. Barker was not just renouncing theological orthodoxy and in the same breath condemning the slave trade. He was pushing back against the conceit of using dark skin to symbolize sin.[123] Yet it is significant too that, only days after reading the review of Philmore, he was encouraged to think about race, not to mention the presumption of moral inferiority in the service of slavery. In microcosmic form, we can see in Barker's life his repudiation of slavery, whatever its justification, but also the impression that racialized thinking was leaving on Britons more generally.

There is a further point, one that also connects divine and human nature. When Barker expresses what he sometimes calls the "Pamphilian scheme"—his shorthand for his universalist religiosity—he makes clear, almost despite himself, that universalism in religion was as much about the here and now as it was about the hereafter. "I am a Universalist . . .

that in imitation of the Divine Being hath a Universal Love *for all Mankind,*" he claimed on one occasion.[124] On another, he invokes the image of precious metals as a metaphor for the value of his relationship with Merivale. But then he moves from the metaphoric to the literal and calls to mind actual mines in the ground in Mexico and South America. He expresses an abstract trope, in other words, but then expresses fellow feeling with the flesh-and-blood subjects of the trope: "Rest we content and esteem ourselves richer having discovered a mine that will produce more secret pleasure, than if we had the mines of Peru and Mexico, and a million of rational Indians condemned to dig up heaps of gold and large bags of Pitts large diamonds." As if to drive home the point that not just theology but "love of mankind" was the broader meaning of the "Pamphilian scheme"—the scheme so-named for Pamphilus of Caesarea—Barker signs this same letter about mines "Pamphilus Philalethes."[125]

Barker can admittedly joke about the issue of universal love, or he does so at least once. But he also does so at the expense of Britain's on-again, off-again enemy. While extolling his love of humanity to Merivale, he adds the caveat: "[I]f I have a Distast or Aversion to any part of the Globe's inhabitants it is the treacherous French."[126] But if the joke landed, it was because both men knew the happier reality. Despite decades of French-British animosity, Barker had made lasting and profound connections with philosophes, with the Huguenot community in Plymouth, and with French soldiers on the high seas. The reality was that Barker could love *even the French*. About others, the love seemed unqualified. Charistes loved Philalethes, Philalethes loved Charistes, and Philalethes and Charistes seemed to love everyone else.

But about one person, in particular, the love as it came from both Barker and Merivale was supercharged. And she too has a story to tell.

CHAPTER SIX

The Cygne Noire

We must get entirely clear of all the notions drawn from the wild traditions of original sin on which priests have erected their tremendous structures of imposition to persuade us that we are naturally inclined to evil.

MARY WOLLSTONECRAFT,
The Origin and Progress of the French Revolution (1794)

Set against most people in their society, Philalethes and Charistes were not exactly typical. They spent time thinking about weighty subjects, learning ancient languages, writing each other long letters, tackling the contradictions of religious orthodoxy. Literacy rates may have been comparatively high in the early modern British Isles, but in 1690, the year Barker was born, probably only half of all men and fewer women could read. Among those who could, it is safe to assume that the majority were not radical in their beliefs. Even so, there is nothing categorically surprising about Samuel Merivale. He was a heretical minister, trained in the progressive Northampton Academy, one of the closest institutions eighteenth-century Britain had to an experimental college, and much of what preoccupied him was consistent with a curiosity cultivated by that training. That Barker was a layman with an abbreviated education makes his preoccupations more unusual, but being a religious seeker was not inconsistent with the ethos of Dissent. Jenny Merivale was another story. She had opinions about these weighty subjects when she was a preteen and, for a moment, when she was a teenager.

It is hard enough to find the kinds of sources that offer access to the intellectual history of obscure people like Barker. It is even harder to discover what children at the time thought in detail about anything, let alone philosophy and theology. If their beliefs did not already emulate their parents, the circumstances in which any writings they may have produced were likely to survive were rare.[1] One uncommon fragment of childhood belief comes from the prolific hymn writer and Dissenter educator Isaac Watts. At the mere age of seven, Watts had already learned how to channel original sin into spiritually suitable self-disparagement. Even here, however, it is difficult to imagine the remarkable poem having survived (thanks to parents no doubt proud of their child for being both clever and suitably ashamed) without the brag-worthy acrostic:

I am a vile polluted lump of earth,
So I've continued ever since my birth,
Although Jehovah grace does daily give me,
As sure this monster Satan will deceive me,
Come therefore, Lord from Satan's claws relieve me.

Wash me in thy blood, O Christ,
And grace divine impart,
Then search and try the corners of my heart,
That I in all things may be fit to do
Service to thee, and sing thy praises too.[2]

Jenny's father managed to preserve at least one of her poems in a letter to Barker and probably for the same reason: it was clever enough to brag about. She had sent Barker a rebus puzzle that used visual symbols to suggest the name "Martha Woodman" (the puzzle does not exist, and there is no explanation of Martha Woodman's identity). Barker thought he had figured out the hidden name, but he guessed incorrectly, so Jenny's father asked "whether she could not answer her enigma in almost the same words as it was proposed without the trouble of seeking new Rhimes." He continued: "As soon as she understood my meaning she began as follows":

The three strok'd M, shuns Light & dwells in **M**ines;
Art conquers Strength & Nature's Work refines;
Ha! Is ye sound oft us'd to express surprise
Wood chiefly fuel to this Realm supplies;
Man was created last & placed in Paradise
Hence Martha Woodman as I apprehend
Must be the Name & Surname of your Friend.[3]

Samuel noted other signs of his daughter's precocity. As he struggled with translation, he marveled at her ease with both Greek and Latin. As her poem indicates, she was equally adept at playing language games.

In the summer of 1759, Samuel received an obscure letter addressed to Jenny in the post. "Had I not known there was no French Priest in Town," he later wrote Barker, "I should have actually sent her to enquire for M. Valmerie, as [the return address] had much the look of a French Name." Samuel gave Jenny the letter, informing her that she had received it from someone with that name, but Jenny insisted that she did not recognize the sender: "I told her I believed she did, tho she might not know the name. . . . I bid her look again on the superscription, & she immediately told me 'twas for me; & made it out as plain as a Pikestaff that twas my own name in Disguise."[4] Barker, the cryptologist, had sent the letter using an anagram for *Merivale* (*Valmerie*), and he had addressed it to Jenny knowing that she would easily crack the code.

All these examples occurred when Jenny was ten years old, at which point she already had "a shelf of Books (consisting of 30 or 40)," including at least one quarto volume sent to her by Barker. ("My Jenny's eyes sparkled at the sight of what you [were] so kind to send to her," Merivale related to his friend in Plymouth. "You have gain'd her heart forever.")[5] But there was more to Jenny than her precociousness. Isaac Watts may have felt the redemptive power of Christ when he contemplated original sin as a seven-year-old. Jenny encountered the doctrine and felt its sting.

On one level, that should not be surprising. Why would her aversion to orthodoxy not have been cultivated by her parents, just as Watts's feelings of depravity were surely cultivated by his? There is a vivid letter from Jenny's father that further reveals how this process may have worked. The letter was written after Barker accused a minister of preaching an orthodox sermon that left him "disgusted." Merivale knew the minister in question and was surprised to hear of his orthodoxy because of "the delicacy of his taste in many respects (shown particularly in the choice of his books)." But Merivale trusted Barker's assessment, so, when Jenny heard the same man sermonize, Merivale asked to hear her own impressions. After he and his daughter talked, he recapped their conversation in a letter he sent back to Barker using dialogue to convey their conversation but without indicating by name who is speaking. Here are Merivale's words from that letter, verbatim, but with my insertion of names for clarification:

> SAMUEL [*to Barker*]: I asked my little darling (who sometimes attends to what she hears) how she liked last Sunday's Performance. The answer was, she did not know what [the minister] was talking about.
>
> SAMUEL [*from here on speaking to Jenny*]: But you knew what he was talking about the other Sunday?

JENNY: Yes.

SAMUEL: Did you like him better then?

JENNY: No.

SAMUEL: Why did you not like him?

JENNY: Because he talked of such frightful things. Many of the folks were crying, and some of them groaning almost all the time.

SAMUEL: Did you not cry too?

JENNY: No.

SAMUEL: Why? Did you not believe what he said?

JENNY: I don't know. I never heard such things before.

SAMUEL: How could you bear to hear that vast numbers of people should suffer such agonies of Body and Mind, and that forever; and not cry at the Thoughts [*sic*] of it? Was not you afraid for yourself, if you could be unconcerned for others?

JENNY: No.

SAMUEL: Why so?

JENNY: Because I hope I shall never go to Hell.

SAMUEL: And what reason have you to hope so?

JENNY: O Papa, he said towards the end of the sermon that he hoped none of those that heard him would ever feel what he had been describing.

SAMUEL: Did he so?

JENNY: And yet he and many others believe that not one in a thousand shall escape, or can possibly escape those punishments, let them do what they will to avoid it, and that God made men on purpose to damn the far greater part of them.

SAMUEL: What do you think of that, my Dear? Must not we all be in the greatest danger of eternal misery upon this supposition? And have not we reason enough to fear it?

JENNY: O Dear!

SAMUEL: That can never be true I'm sure. Could you take pleasure in the thought of most of your fellow creatures being exposed, unavoidably exposed to such torments forever?

JENNY: No sure.

SAMUEL: And could no good-natured man think of it without pain?

JENNY: No certainly.

SAMUEL: God has more goodness and mercy in his nature than the best of us can pretend to.

JENNY: Yes.

SAMUEL: How then can we believe that he produces creatures into being on purpose to make them miserable?

JENNY: No that can't be.

SAMUEL: But those that are wicked must be miserable so long as they remain so. Don't you believe that?

JENNY: Yes. But then it is their own fault, if they will be wicked: God does not force them to be so.

SAMUEL: Very right my dear. But would not you wish that even wicked people might become good and happy rather than continue bad and miserable?

JENNY: Yes.

SAMUEL: And don't you think God is more desirous they should repent and be saved than that they should be hardened in their wickedness and be ruined forever?

JENNY: Yes sure: or else how can he be good, and love goodness, and hate wickedness?

SAMUEL: Yet those that live and die in wickedness will surely be miserable after they are dead, for God will certainly make a far greater difference hereafter than he does here between good and bad men.

JENNY: Very true Papa, but may'nt bad men repent when they come to suffer for their sins hereafter as well as they do sometimes here?

SAMUEL: I should think they may, my dear; and if they do, a good and merciful God will surely show compassion to them. But this is certain that the wicked and impenitent can never be happy. However, let nothing tempt you to think hardly of your maker. He is the kindest and best of fathers and loves us all better than we love ourselves. If he punishes any of his creatures it's not for his pleasure but for their profit; at least it's for the good of the creation in general, and we may hope will issue at last in the good of the sufferers themselves. Think thus of God my dear, and you must needs love him. But those that look upon him as a cruel tyrant instead of a tender parent can never love him nor think of him with pleasure.

SAMUEL [*now to Barker again*]: The dear creature's countenance brightened and sparkled at this discourse. She said it was charming and much better than what she had heard the Sunday before and was going on when her mother entered and put an end to the conference.[6]

This was almost a Rational Dissenter catechism. The core ideas are here—the primacy of moral conduct, the rational God, the implicitly optimistic view of human nature, the God of orthodoxy cast as wrathful.

And in keeping with the veneration of conscience, it is by way of a Socratic dialogue rather than by rote memorization that Jenny reaches the right conclusion. The image of parishioners "crying" and "groaning" under the weight of Calvinist ideas is no less interesting for being filled with emotion, much as Jenny seems to have been when she contemplated the implications of orthodoxy or, for that matter, when her "countenance brightened and sparkled" after her father's intervention. It is intriguing in a different way altogether that, when Jenny asks whether souls can repent in the afterlife, her father seems to go along with the idea that God might show the penitent mercy, even after death. Barker and Merivale condemn the concept of purgatory as exploitative when they address it directly.[7] But if Merivale was here trying to placate his daughter with a parallel notion, that alone might indicate how distraught she was on hearing a fire-and-brimstone preacher.

Clearly Jenny's father did his part to shape her views. For that matter, he exercised his influence in relation to more than religion. Very few letters from Jenny survive, and the few that do were written to her father while he was away for several months trying to settle his wife's family's estate. But even in those few letters the paternal influence is palpable. Samuel noted and celebrated, for example, the occasion of Jenny's first successful attempt at correspondence all on her own: "Your momma and I are much pleased with the first letter you have ever wrote without help, short as it is; And hope you will repeat your attempts of this kind at proper seasons." The same letter gave him the occasion to implore her nevertheless to write expressively. "You have nothing to do," he continued, "but to sit down, and think what you would say to us if present, and then let your pen speak it instead of your tongue. Make but a beginning, take time before you, and one thing will draw on another insensibly."[8] Other passing comments in his letters to Jenny express the same didacticism. "Eat not too much fruit; pass not all your time in idleness," he told her before sending her the second volume of Hume's *History of England* (1754–61).[9] In another of her letters, she indicates that she was reading Swift's *Gulliver's Travels* alongside Virgil.[10] In another of his we learn that, like Barker, she had committed parts of Pope's *Essay on Man* to memory.[11]

But despite all these signs of paternal influence, Jenny was more than an echo. Apart from the fact that plenty of children, then as now, become more activated than their parents are by a worldview the parents first nurture, there was another facet of experience that may have had a bearing on her philosophical outlook: her chronically poor health. Whatever the underlying cause (her father thought it was a tumor), she had frequent heart palpitations. Even before suffering paralysis on her left side she was also regularly stricken with debilitating fevers. Barker did not just refer to her as the "Cygne Noire." He also occasionally called her "my little Phoenix" when she returned, as she almost always did, from the brink of death. When Philalethes and Charistes constantly say to each other that the worst part about original sin is that it assumes a God who wants people, including children, to be born for the sake of suffering, how could they not be thinking in part about Jenny? We know Jenny heard that argument too—Merivale makes that clear in their dialogue ("How . . . can we believe that [God] produces creatures into being on purpose to make them miserable?"). But she knew viscerally what it could mean to conceive of someone as born to suffer. And if the message of orthodoxy was that this was just the way it is, she was not buying it. We are rarely given anything close to a full story behind the passing references Samuel makes to her. But the context we have developed so far points to her acuity about doctrine when he writes that a visiting preacher "offended the poor little Heart so highly, by his notions of original sin."[12]

Yet it is still hard to know what exactly "offended . . . so highly" meant? Did Jenny come home in tears? Was she enraged? Was she filled with learned rebuttals? What exactly was she hearing and feeling in original sin?

~

If part of what Jenny felt was that children were original sin's most unjust victims, she was not alone. Few subjects were more theologically vexing than early death. In such situations, the only basis on which to judge whether young souls were on the right path was the evidence of their behavior, however limited in supply. The problem, as the orthodox saw it, is that, wherever behavior took on saving power, it threatened the centrality of faith, if it did not also threaten belief in God's infinite foreknowledge. Calvin himself struggled with the issue, but he avoided ceding salvific potency to good deeds by arguing that the deceased children of the elect were moral dependents of their parents and therefore likely to be saved by a sort of spiritual genetics.[13] Whether the argument was convincing is debatable. New England Puritans, some of Calvin's most devoted followers, baptized their children almost immediately after birth, which at the very least suggests lingering attachment to the un-Calvinist notion that baptism could help wash away sin.[14]

Zoom ahead in New England to the later eighteenth century, and thanks in part to Daniel Webster's anonymously written *A Winter Evening's Conversation upon the Doctrine of Original Sin* (1757), the unjustness of infant mortality had become as divisive as any issue confronting Reformed congregations across the Atlantic.[15] But, in fact, there were signs of theological tension around infant and childhood mortality decades earlier in England. This is one of the things that made Richard Baxter waver on original sin. Unlike Calvin, however, Baxter took an obvious step away from orthodoxy by arguing that depravity had to exist in unequal portions in infants and adults: "The State of an Infant as a meer Child of Adam, is not the worst that an Infant is capable of on earth." Sounding more like a moral empiricist than an innatist, he concluded that human nature in an infant was therefore "not in the utmost degree of its depravation": "Custom in actual Sin may make [our nature] worse in the adult."[16]

Here was yet another emotional pressure bearing down on original sin. But Philalethes, Charistes, and very possibly the Cygne Noire took the argument further. By criticizing original sin for unacceptably suggesting that people were born to suffer, they were not just asserting the primacy of moral conduct. They were making a statement about their belief in a supreme being who could not possibly be such a cruel tyrant. From another angle, all Merivale and Barker had to do was look at Jenny to see what could be imagined and accomplished when people were given the intellectual freedom that they thought Calvinism denied. As Jenny's health continued to decline, trying to keep her spirits up became, in the same vein, all the more pressing. A watershed moment was the death of her mother, Betsy, who succumbed to illness on March 30, 1761. The letters that Samuel sent to Barker around this time do not survive. But Samuel's distress reverberates in Barker's responses.

Betsy Merivale and Jane Barker are, it is worth saying before going further, only silhouetted in the letters of their husbands. This is not to say that either of the two women were locked in unhappy relationships. There is something suggestive in how regularly Samuel and Pentecost wish each other's wives the best as they sign off their letters. Suggestive too is a warm, if fleeting, scene that Pentecost offers of Jane lying in bed at two in the morning, asking her husband about what he was perusing by the fire. He reads her a page from David Hartley on "vibration, medullary particles, and molecules" before she jokes that "she could make no more of it than she could . . . of a sermon of Mr what d'ye call 'em's."[17] More suggestive still is the possibility that "the Barkers" were never legally married—and therefore lived together in a relationship, one might infer, more for emotional needs and desires than for the various instrumental reasons that so often drove couples into formal union. Pentecost does admittedly refer to her variously as "Jane Barker," "Mrs Barker," and "Mrs. B." But after his death Merivale pointed to the other possibility.

In a letter to Jenny, he wrote that their late friend in Plymouth "left the Income of all he has to his Dear Wife Jane Barker (or as some call her Jane Mills, which seems to intimate she [was] no legal wife)."[18]

Betsy Merivale appears more often in her husband's letters but typically when she is ill, which was always cause for Samuel's concern. We admittedly never hear from Jenny herself about how affected she was by her mother's death. But we can imagine. Samuel recounts a wrenching scene (Betsy would eventually recover from this episode) during which "my tender little maid [Jenny was] very anxious about her poor Mamma [and] would keep almost constantly with her, and did all in her power to assist and comfort her": "Then she found yesterday morning that the doctor thought it not proper for [Betsy] to rise, she burst out into tears afresh, but got into a private corner to give them vent, and her heart was too full to permit her to speak to me when I parted with her."[19]

It is hard not to wonder why Jenny needed to cry by herself in a corner. Somewhere in the equation may lie the discipline implied by her mastery of Latin and Greek, not to mention the fatherly advice. Or maybe the same scene indicates that she had the self-possession to protect her mother from the distressing effects of her own distress. Samuel, it is worth saying, never openly chides her for being too expressive. On the contrary, even if every one of her letters to her father had survived, there is reason to believe they would still conceal as much as they reveal. After Betsy's death, for example, Samuel poured out his grief to his daughter: "We have sustained indeed a loss that is irreparable; a loss which I still deeply regret and ever shall, and of which I know you are not insensible. But oh! How much more insupportable would it be to me, had not Providence left me two such dear pledges [Jenny and her younger brother] of my past felicity; for whose sake chiefly life is valuable to me; for whom I seem to bear the affection of a double parent, and towards whom I would if possible discharge a double parents duty." Jenny apparently could not muster the same emotion in writing. Days later, her father addressed her in third-person pronouns: "I should be glad of longer letters [that] throw aside all Constraint, when either writing or talking to her Papa; and with the utmost Freedom pour forth all the Thoughts, Inclinations and Emotions, Joys or Sorrows of her little Heart into his Bosom, who regards her not merely as the Child of his Love, but as his most favourite Companion, Counsellor, and Friend."[20]

Early in 1762, Jenny felt stomach pains for two days, followed by a hectic fever. This was months after her mother's death and maybe too a testament to the ripple effects of bereavement. A doctor was called in and drew "8 or 9 ounces of gluey blood" before pronouncing it to be in a "highly inflammatory state."[21] Whatever was happening in her body, the illness left Jenny's left side paralyzed. The happier years of her "promising genius, her good and amiable Dispositions, her entertaining and endearing Converse,"[22] made it all the harder for those who loved her to bear that her particle was now trapped in what Barker once described as the "prison" of the body.[23] In the very few letters Barker and Merivale wrote in 1762, we can hear their shared relief that Jenny was seeming to improve, although Merivale was still terrified of losing his "greatest earthly comfort."[24] Barker died before Jenny did, so we never learn about her death in the Barker-Merivale correspondence. We instead have to turn to Samuel's memorandum book, where an entry records that she died a year after her paralysis.

That entry, as we noted in passing earlier, says more in material form than it does in content. Samuel hardly ever has to scratch out a word in his short memorandum book. But he scratches out several words in his long entry on Jenny, which is also the most detailed entry he writes: "Jane [Jenny] Merivale died ~~four~~ Jan. 27, 1763 about 10 in the morning, after ~~a~~ a long & complicated disorder; having been of a tender & ~~we~~akly constitution from her infancy; subject to frequent & violent palpitations of Heart (occasioned as some thought by a Polypus) losing the use of ~~her~~ left side about a year before her Death in a fever; ~~& g~~ greatly emaciated by a long continued hectic; & her Body & Limbs swelled at last by a dropsy." The most affecting part of the entry is that, after the final period that follows "dropsy," he starts a new sentence with the word "She" but goes no further.[25] The incomplete sentence lies on the page of his journal like a life cut short.

In forcing Barker and Merivale to contemplate the future state, death made them think about what was essentially human and what was inessentially human. The body, for example, was in the end unimportant. What mattered were thought and feeling. "When the mind is set free from its Prison the Body," Barker wrote, "we may expect such a Flow or spring tide of rational pleasures as we now can find no words to express."[26] Thinking in these terms—imagining a human essence surviving the body—is not wildly different from more common Christian views of the soul. But the stress on rationality also suggests something leveling.[27] Like the *Nous* of which it was a piece, the particle possessed a transcendent intelligence. And like any utopian horizon, the future state in which the particle would be reunited with the *Nous* to some degree shaped and reflected life on earth. "So long as a future state is admitted," Merivale once wrote Barker, "there is room left for adjusting all present appearances of inequality."[28] The particle seemed to point, that is, to a future state that signaled how to make life on earth better.

Jenny was born a decade before Mary Wollstonecraft, roughly two decades after Catherine Macauley, and six years after the education reformer Anna Letitia Barbauld. Given her gift for languages and the encouragement she got from her open-minded father and their friend Pentecost, and given too her uncanny ability to solve puzzles at the age of ten, it is hard not to wonder how as an adult she might have tried like others of her generation to solve the puzzle of patriarchy. Here it is worth thinking about Wollstonecraft's essays from the 1790s, at which point Jenny, had she lived, would have been in her forties. In the backlash against the French Revolution, original sin was reaffirmed by traditionalists as theological grounds for embracing the authority of throne and altar. No one would make that case quite like Joseph de Maistre, the author for whom original sin explained "everything," particularly the need to submit to kings, the sacred church, brazen force, and tradition.[29] Wollstonecraft set her sights on Edmund Burke, who held constitutions in higher regard than did Maistre and for that matter felt tempered sympathy for the Americans in 1776. Republicans like Tom Paine used the American Revolution to renounce monarchy and what Paine saw as its theological underpinning. ("It unanswerably follows," wrote Paine in *Common Sense*, "that original sin and hereditary succession are parallels. Dishonourable rank! Inglorious connection! Yet the most subtle sophist cannot produce a juster simile.")[30] Burke, however, thought that American adherence to the ideals of the ancient English constitution was a salutary form of looking back rather than forward. Nothing had fundamentally changed in his mind when, after the storming of the Bastille, he followed from afar the revolutionaries' rationalist effort to make a radical break from the past. By 1790, he was expressly locating the danger posed to political stability in the overweening confidence in the species, which he was convinced would in the coming violence bear out the position that people require governance, as he put it, by "a power out of themselves."[31]

Among the many ways in which Wollstonecraft fired back at Burke was by exposing his deep assumptions. The accumulation of tradition that he cast as a power out of ourselves was for Wollstonecraft, writing in *A Vindication of the Rights of Woman* (1792), a constellation of "moss-covered opinions" that over time "assume the disproportioned form of prejudices."[32] Two years later, she suggested that the deepest of those opinions—the ultimate form of prejudgment—was the determination of our nature from the moment we are born. For her, a crucial piece of the puzzle was obvious: "We must get entirely clear of all the notions drawn from the wild traditions of original sin on which priests have erected their tremendous structures of imposition to persuade us that we are naturally inclined to evil." With its plural ending, "wild traditions" made "original sin" more broadly cultural. But the other myths Wollstonecraft cited—"Pandora's box," the "theft of Prometheus," and "fables too tedious to enumerate"—all amounted to the same thing.[33] They made a disparaging object lesson out of the presumed depravity of human nature.

At the beginning of the modern age of revolutions, it had become intuitive to British radicals that such an assumption was ready-made for the restoration of tyranny. In the image of "wild traditions," in other words, Wollstonecraft was also offering a capstone lesson in Enlightenment political thought, a subject to which we are turning next. But Jenny Merivale offers a lesson of her own. The aversion that she felt toward original sin—an aversion nurtured by camaraderie with her beloved father and the avuncular Pentecost Barker—was pointing to the conclusion that, even if her congenital heart condition meant that she had been born in suffering, she was not born *to* suffer. She deserved better. Not because she was the singular "Cygne Noire." She may have been worthy of all the praise that radiates from these two older men. But by all indications she was headed toward a broad view of the world in which, fundamentally, she was no different from anyone else.

CHAPTER SEVEN

The Politics of Fear

A tyrannical captain that I sail'd under would maintain that Fear had more Influence over Mankind than Love. I was wont to tell him, That I could not judge for others, but as to myself I assumed that Love was predominant in me, and that I would do ten times more for a man I loved than for One I feared.

PENTECOST BARKER
to Samuel Merivale, January 1, 1759

Despite everything that has been said, the view that all people are created equal can *follow* from original sin, at least if the doctrine asserts that all people, without exception, are equally bad. The system of checks and balances built into the American constitution may have rested on a politically hopeful belief that selfishness could in its reliability be harnessed as its own countervailing force, but underlying that belief was still the anthropologically pessimistic conviction that people are reliably selfish. Such anthropological faith of course rested not on doctrinal original sin but on a secular notion of selfishness naturalized as interest. But if a secular pessimism about human nature could underpin politically ambitious experiments in self-rule, there is no necessary reason that a spiritual pessimism could not do the same.

To some degree it did before the end of the seventeenth century. Martin Luther may have urged the princes of Europe to smite the peasants behind the rebellions of the 1520s, but he was antiauthoritarian when it came to the politics of the pope in a way that supported his belief that contamination by inherited sin equalizes spiritual authority. "Whoever crawls out of baptism," he put it, "can boast that he has already been consecrated a priest, bishop, and pope."[1] Calvin, directly to the point, thought: "[I]t is because of the vice and defectiveness of men that it is safer and more acceptable for a plurality to govern."[2] In the same vein, the "resistance theorists" whom Calvin inspired were committed to Augustinian theology as they theorized defiance of "tyrants."[3] So for that matter were the Jansenists, whose criticisms of the Gallican church were taken to threaten the authority of the king.[4] With more success, it was the Augustinian English Puritans who pushed for a measure of self-determination in the revolutionary mid-seventeenth century, while the loyal supporters of Charles I were drawn to Arminianism as that religious philosophy was first being smeared as "Pelagian."[5]

Why, then, did Wollstonecraft and Paine so easily conflate original sin with tyrannical rule, as have countless others since? When "the human being is defined by original sin," writes one recent political philosopher, "authoritarianism—in the form of dictatorship, say—becomes *necessary* as the *only* means that might save beings from themselves."[6] "Liberalism," writes another, "was, *at bottom*, the theological position known as Pelagianism."[7] There may be some deep reasons for these affinities. Certainly, there are plenty of prominent examples found long before the eighteenth century to lend them support. Paul came closer than any author in the Bible to formulating original sin while insisting that "every person be in subjection to the governing authorities" (Rom. 13:1). Augustine, who did formulate it, thought being free meant happily carrying out the will of one's master.[8] When Luther wrote on political—as opposed to ecclesiastical—authority, he insisted that Christ demanded submission to the prince, while his politically radical counterparts framed original sin as everything from an artifact of belief in a fictive devil to a form of property appropriation.[9] But my point is only this: these more familiar affinities were not *necessarily* the case.

This is not to make a trivial qualification. Noting exceptions to what now feel like political-theological axioms gets at the operative concept, which is to say political "exceptionality," according to which sovereigns have a capacity to act like no other figure in society. Famously, this was the core concept for Carl Schmitt, who a century ago opened his *Political Theology* (1922) with a line that almost made the rest of the text unnecessary: "Sovereign is he who decides on the exception."[10] Yet, as we have noted, Schmitt's concept of the political in these terms was nothing new. "We did not have to wait for Schmitt to learn that the sovereign is the one who decides exceptionally and performatively about the exception, the one who keeps or grants himself the right to suspend rights or law; nor did we need him to know that this politico-juridical concept, like all the others, secularizes a theological heritage," wrote Jacques Derrida in one of his lucid final essays.[11] In fact, it is debatable whether Schmitt really secularized a theological heritage. When he wrote that "the denial of original sin destroys all social order," the whole point was to stress the ongoing importance of theology to politics.[12] But what he drew from this heritage was in any case precisely, as Derrida writes, sovereignty deciding "exceptionally . . . about the exception." That kind of sovereignty was precisely the capricious authority that Wollstonecraft and Paine found justified by original sin and, years earlier, Pentecost Barker expressly associated with original sin, tyranny, and fear. As Barker wrote Merivale in one of his first letters, smearing together the God of Calvin and the commander of a ship: "A tyrannical captain that I sail'd under would maintain that Fear had more Influence over Mankind than Love. I was wont to tell him, That I could not judge for others, but as to myself I assumed that Love was predominant in me, and that I would do ten times more for a man I loved than for One I feared."[13]

The rationale that original sin demanded fear of the divine was not esoteric. "Since the fall of Adam all men who are propagated according to nature are born in sin. That is, they are without *fear* of God," Martin Luther and his cohorts wrote in the Augsburg Confession, a landmark document of the Reformation.[14] Fear was in this defining early Protestant sense the express feeling God demanded. And because one of the consequences of being born in sin was that fear of the divine was detrimentally missing from one's psyche, key to salvation was getting the fear back. But the captain analogy was not just pointing out the austerity of the orthodox view of divine authority. Barker was talking about earthly tyrants, like the tyrannical captain himself, whom in another letter Barker called "the greatest idolizer of men in power that ever I met with."[15] Here it is worth recalling Barker's metaphor of physical restraint in relation to the magisterial Protestant reformers. Sometimes it is cast as the "shackles" of Luther and Calvin, sometimes the "fetters." Sometimes Barker simply uses the word *whips* to convey raw capricious power. But the metaphor always resonates with a notion of earthly authority. As Barker put it in relation to his former captain: "[T]here can be no merit nor praise due to one who is restrain'd from Evil by Fear, more than to a Dog or Monkey kept under from Fear of the whip."[16]

Christopher Hill, the venerable historian of the seventeenth century, once wrote that "any man is an intellectual to some extent, even though he does not occupy the social position of intellectual; just as any man can fry an egg, though few are professional cooks."[17] Barker had lived his long life as, variously, an alcoholic, a Calvinist, a deist, a vegetarian, a barrel maker, a naval officer, and a suicidal hypochondriac. He had seen battles at sea in his service in the Mediterranean, from Iberia to Turkey, and through the same military service had found the opportunity to enrich his outlook through cultural encounters. His position was backed up by a heroic amount of reading, not to mention by the benefits of proximity that come with being a contemporary witness to the past. There is a good chance he was even a spy. With all his perspectives and varied experience somewhere in the mix, he could fry an egg and then some. Like much that he has to say, the allegory that he forged in an argument with his commanding officer on the sea-lanes of the British Empire is accordingly worth drawing out.

Like any emotion, fear can change in meaning depending on its object. It can also play a secondary role in the thinking of some Enlightenment authors who find much to fear, for example, when social contracts are broken or when institutions fail. But no enlightener—even the most dismal secular anthro-pessimist—charts a path from fear to irrationally accepted authority, let alone to regular supernatural intervention. The fear Barker was invoking was what he saw, shrewdly, as the ethos of orthodoxy. This was the fear that underpinned the "merciless scheme" writ large. It was a primordial, organizing emotion, and, as Barker surely knew, it was the very first emotion that Genesis records Adam and Eve feeling after the Fall.[18] Not least, fear was the emotion demanded equally by a Calvinist God and an earthly tyrant.

Just as crucially, Barker was also pinning fear to the doctrine of original sin. To go back to the point about exceptions, it is important that these politically tyrannical associations of fear do not automatically follow from the notion of original sin as a *universalist* doctrine. This is not at all to say that Barker, Wollstonecraft, Paine, and others were wrong to associate original sin with authoritarianism. On the contrary, they were making what in the eighteenth century had become an axiomatic association. But the reasons that the association hardened into an axiom go beyond the logic of theology. The political meaning of original sin has its own history, which I want to consider here as we take a brief but crucial detour from Barker and enter the realm of more abstract political thought.

My argument, put simply, is that, as Enlightenment culture was taking shape at the end of the seventeenth century, original sin was given what turned out to be an influential authoritarian twist—an all-important allowance for *exceptions*—that customized it to the political theology of fear. And the cultural success of this interpretive twist did as much as anything to put it at odds with Enlightenment thought. Not least, it was in the sphere of political thought (as opposed to economic thought, the less straightforward subject of our next chapter) that the Enlightenment and original sin were so often at their most antithetical.

The origins of Enlightenment political thought are commonly traced to John Locke, who wrote his *Two Treatises of Government* in dialogue with Robert Filmer's *Patriarcha,* which was published in 1680 but written and first circulated in manuscript in the 1630s. Filmer argued that a society is an extended family whose authority originates with the first patriarch, Adam, and descends to the world's kings, eventually percolating down to the fathers of the lowliest families. Locke's counterargument (which was published in 1689 but written nearly a decade earlier) was that civil society depends not on biblical tradition but on the contractual arrangements people make with one another to protect the fruits of their labor. Filmer believed that the Fall had deleterious effects. So did Locke. To assume as much at the time was routine in England, whether one was Whig, Tory, High Church, or Dissenter. Filmer for that matter also stresses the impracticality of self-rule and its inevitable degeneration into anarchy. But *Patriarcha* does not stake its claims on original sin.[19] What matters more than being born into sin is being born into familism, with the father at the top of the chain of authority. Filmer never mentions original sin. And he invokes the Fall only on an occasion in the opening paragraph where he admonishes Catholic and Protestant resistance theorists alike for having lost sight of the fact "that the desire of liberty was the cause of the fall of Adam."[20] That by itself is incongruous. Adam is Filmer's paragon of authority by virtue of being the patriarch. But in relation to the Fall the patriarch's failings are a cautionary tale.

One critic of Filmer's to grasp this incongruity was John Milton. In a thinly veiled reference to *Patriarcha* while it was still only in manuscript circulation, the republican Milton has the archangel Michael proclaim in *Paradise Lost* that whatever reverence Adam deserved in the garden of Eden was forfeited after the Fall: "Adam, thou knowst heaven his, and all the earth . . . / But this pre-eminence thou' hast *lost,* brought down / To dwell on even ground now with thy sons."[21] The other critic of Filmer's who discerned the same incongruity, if not contradiction, was Locke himself. In the *First Treatise,* Locke pointed out that God compelled Adam to *labor* for his living. He gave Adam not a "scepter" but a "spade": "'Twould be hard to imagine that God, in the same Breath, should make [Adam] Universal Monarch over all Mankind, and a day labourer for his Life; turn him out of Paradice, to till the Ground . . . and at the same time, advance him to a Throne, and all the Priviledges and

Ease of Absolute Power."[22] Of course, the way in which Locke in turn relocates political legitimacy to the state of nature does its part to diminish the political force of scripture. But there is a case to be made—it can be made with the example just given—that his puritanism was still residual in the early 1680s.[23] Even in the more abstract and well-known *Second Treatise*, his case rests on the reliability of bad behavior. What makes the state of nature give way to civil society is, after all, the inevitable fear of "inconveniences," his euphemism for the anxiety people feel over losing their hard-earned property to theft.[24] That is hardly a rosy view of the species—to say that by nature we constantly threaten to steal each other's stuff.

In no obvious sense, then, does the Filmer-Locke exchange line up with the view of original sin as axiomatically authoritarian. The better claimant than Filmer to being the architect of original sin in its modern exceptional political sense was Louis XIV's personal pastor and political mouthpiece Jacques-Bénigne Bossuet, who formulated his political theory not in the decades before the crises of the midcentury years, as did Filmer, but, significantly, in the decades after.

From the vantage of the late seventeenth century, the alignments of politics and theology ran in several directions. Augustinians could be found, as easily as could Pelagians, among the rebellious or those otherwise threatening to the status quo. In the Fronde, a chaotic rebellion in mid-seventeenth-century France during which "the monarchy was shaken to its core," Bossuet wrote that "the remedies from all sides were more dangerous than the evils [of war] themselves."[25] One thing he meant by this is that any remedy other than monarchy was dangerous. But he was also saying that the plural alternatives, each more deleterious than the last, came from across the theological spectrum. The Fronde occurred, for example, against the backdrop of the English Civil War, which threatened any European monarch but hit close to home for Louis XIV, a man whose aunt had been married to Charles I before being made a widow by popular regicide. On the one hand, war in England culminated in a godly revolution that demonstrated the antimonarchical potential of Calvinism. On the other hand, it opened up a radical—and, as Christopher Hill expressly saw it, a theologically Pelagian—revolution within the otherwise Augustinian Puritan revolution.[26] Revolutionaries within the revolution like Gerrard Winstanley could not have been much clearer about their distaste for original sin.[27] Maybe few bothered to read such fringe writers, like the equally Pelagian Muggletonians. But the Quakers were more visible, and they too doubted the imputation of Adam's sin to the rest of humanity, if they did not reject the doctrine outright.[28] So did the Levellers, who for a brief moment in the late 1640s looked as if they might seize political power through the influence they wielded in the New Model Army. In one sense, the Levellers enlisted the Fall to explain the rise of tyranny: recognizing the problem posed to democracy by the tendency people exhibit to work against their own political interests, they thought the Fall and its corruption of reason had made people gullible to political manipulation. But Leveller writers offset that cynicism with the hopeful claim that human nature can nevertheless be repaired through the recovery of "divinely implanted reason."[29] Underneath it all, in other words, we are fixable. And the access codes to a better nature can be retrieved and reactivated through thoughtful participation in politics.

How preoccupied Bossuet was by all the details of these experiments in political thought is hard to say. The turmoil of the midcentury years constituted a set of events, he wrote during a later moment of reflection, "of which I would like to be able to be eternally silent."[30] But here, and not for the only time, he sounded disingenuous. Any shrewd observer could notice the connections between English and French radicalism.[31] When the Ormée revolutionaries seized Bordeaux and asserted their sovereignty, they used Edward Sexby's French translation of Leveller writings to begin drafting a constitution.[32] Some Leveller ideas were also detectable in the "Mazarinades," the thousands of pamphlets that addressed government policy during the Fronde.[33] But we do not need to search for circumstantial evidence. Bossuet breaks his "eternal silence" when he speaks very directly about the details of the English Civil War in his printed funeral oration for Charles I's French wife, a text that among other things indicates how well he knew the names and reputed beliefs of radical English sectarians.[34]

The Fronde began to subside as Louis XIV was chastened by the English regicide, yet another indicator of events being linked across the Channel. Only weeks after Charles I's beheading in January 1649, the French crown gave in to some of the opposition's demands by restoring the venal system. Louis would also work in the medium- and long-term toward domesticating the nobility while taking the practical step of building a vast new palace at Versailles, safely outside Paris. But it is also telling that it was Bossuet's theoretical approach that gained ground among royalists throughout the post-Fronde years.[35] In the theoretical realm, French kings already had a sophisticated defender in Jean Bodin, who shortly after the St. Bartholomew's Day Massacre in 1572 had argued that in monarchical states the king's authority should be absolute.[36] Bodin had made his case after empirically investigating the origins of sovereignty, which meant reading widely in the histories of ancient and modern states and then deriving a generalized taxonomy of legal forms, a "science" of politics in Bodin's own characterization.[37] (As a further illustration that the affinity between original sin and authoritarianism was not yet axiomatic, Bodin was also no Augustinian.[38] His "Colloquium heptaplomeres de rerum sublimium arcanis abditis," a manuscript dialogue, written in the 1580s, between a Catholic, a Jew, a Lutheran, a Calvinist, a Muslim, a skeptic, and a philosophical naturalist, gives the refutation of original sin, convincingly, to the majority of interlocutors. What is more, he was making a case against emerging Calvinist—which is to say anything but Pelagian—resistance theory.) A century later and after the Fronde, however, several rationalist arguments—the most important from Hobbes and Spinoza—had emerged to challenge the religious basis for authority altogether. In this changed context, studying the politics of the past in Bodin's comparatively empirical manner could be viewed as succumbing to rationalism via another route. Bossuet took a different course. He eschewed any empirically inflected political analysis and instead produced his *Discourse on Universal History* (1681), a book that affirmed the Judeo-Christian tradition, as written in Holy Scripture, as the only history that mattered.

The underlying rationale—that the Bible was itself the proof of its universality—was obviously circular, and it undeniably made for bad history by Enlightenment standards. With his usual anti-Semitism, Voltaire wrote that Bossuet exemplified the flaw of so many of his predecessors with his "so-called *Universal History*, which is only that of four or five peoples, and above all of the small Jewish nation, either ignored or justly despised by the rest of the world." It is as if "a Cornish writer were to say that nothing happened in the Roman Empire," he added, "except in view of the province of Wales."[39] But Bossuet was practicing bad historiographic form by standards that had settled into place long before Voltaire. Bodin's sixteenth century had already witnessed what the historian Sanjay Subrahmanyam has described as "the rise to prominence of the innovative form of 'world history' . . . history-writing on a world scale," which occurred against the backdrop of "various kinds of nonlocal history (themselves often with 'universal' pretensions)."[40] By these terms, Bodin had already been writing world history decades before Bossuet was born. Whatever his biases, that is, he had endeavored to account for detailed and varied experience across time and space wherever the past informed his effort to understand politics.[41] Bossuet, on the other hand, signaled by his title the very different atavistic thing that he was doing. He was taking the Judeo-Christian perspective as constitutive of the entire universe. And again the rationale goes back to original sin. The epistemological effects of the Fall made human reason inadequate. The Bible, on the other hand, was "a perfect book," one that conveyed to God's people, Bossuet insisted, the history of their origins, religion, social organization, manners, and philosophy and, in so doing, framed the universe.[42]

Here Bossuet was incongruous for other reasons: a Roman Catholic venerating the Bible to such a degree sounded Lutheran.[43] But this and some of the other ways in which he looked like his enemies—contemporaries also wondered whether he was a closet Jansenist—signal the bishop's tactic. To his fellow Augustinian opponents, he could say that the right lesson had to be drawn from the text and the doctrines that both he and they could agree were authoritative. When Protestants (like Pierre Jurieu) educed a spirit of independence and private judgment from the Bible, for example, they had the right book in mind, but neglecting the church's history of expertise in interpreting scripture they had drawn the wrong lesson from it. When Jansenists turned to original sin, they seized on the operative doctrine but read it the wrong way. As Dale Van Kley writes, the Jansenist "exaltation of God and demotion of everything else was one of its original political sins, implicitly demoting sacral kingship."[44] Bossuet could be more particular in his responses to his rationalist opponents: Leibniz defended Christianity but as an irenicist (Bossuet countered that Catholic doctrine had to be preserved in its particularity); Hobbes defended the right kind of government but as an amoral materialist (Bossuet countered that bad behavior was never morally innocent). But underpinning all Bossuet's responses lay the same theme. Original sin had done unfixable damage to human reason. Any exercise of that reason was therefore doomed to be as flawed as the human beings who exercised it. And any political system that failed to take this feature of human nature into account was doomed to degenerate into chaos.

How, then, did the political-theological solution work? How could original sin retain its universalist reach while also serving to justify the politically crucial *exception*? From one side of his mouth Bossuet in fact sounded a lot like his Jansenist enemies in saying that everyone suffers from original sin—"nul ne s'en exempte," he wrote in a lengthy meditation on the doctrine from his *Élévations sur les mystères* (1731). The book of Ecclesiastes, which he quoted there, even spelled this out in allusively political terms: "[A] heavy yoke is upon the sons of Adam . . . from him that weareth purple and a crown, unto him that is clothed with a linen frock."[45] But from the other side of his mouth he insisted that, while in a technical sense no one can be exempt from original sin by virtue of his or her descent from Adam, God had given effective exemption to kings through the divine bestowal of "particular grace." This was the case Bossuet spelled out in *Politics Drawn from Holy Scripture*, a book not published until 1709, but one whose theme was already contained in the first six chapters (or "books"), which were written thirty years earlier, widely known among political theorists, and conveyed in many of the high-profile sermons Bossuet was already preaching in the 1670s.

Despite his professed aversion to rationalism, Bossuet's case for exemption did rest, in one sense, on an argument, this one against yet another rationalist, the Cartesian Nicholas Malebranche.[46] A providentialist but also a generalist, Malebranche thought God had designed a cosmic system that could largely run itself. If that was so, Bossuet thought it was only a short and dangerous step to believing that people could be self-maintaining. His political theology, in contrast, required an actively involved deity whose constant and specific interventions could explain both the soap opera–like details of monarchical politics and the reason that kings possessed the sovereignty denied to everyone else. As he would come to argue, the way in which God exempted kings was by perpetually paying attention and perpetually and particularly intervening.[47] God ordained "in all nations," writes Patrick Riley in an insightful analysis of Bossuet's politics, "les familles particulières who ought to govern those nations, and, still more *en particulier*, the precise persons within those families who will help a ruling house 'to rise, to sustain itself, or to fall.'"[48] And, crucially, God displayed a pattern in his providence. Aberrations like the revolt of the Maccabees notwithstanding, the Bible (thought Bossuet) consistently showed that kings were so exceptional and so favored by the divine that the recurrence of their exceptionality yielded a political axiom: God prefers kings.

"John Locke and Jacques-Bénigne Bossuet did not . . . meet in controversy as Filmer did, posthumously, with Locke," wrote the historian J. H. Burns at the end of a sweeping survey of early modern political theory. But Burns finished the thought by acknowledging that "there is, it can be said, an implicit dialectic in which the thesis advanced by Bossuet, particularly in his *Politique tireé des propres paroles de l'Ecriture sainte*, is met and challenged in Locke's *Two Treatises of Government*."[49] Burns located the contrast in Locke's view that absolutism led to slavery, as opposed to Bossuet's view that it led to sacred, paternal order.[50] We could modify these terms. There is an "implicit dialectic" apparent in the changing political meaning of original sin.

Locke seemed, for example, to move steadily, if subtly, away from Augustinian doctrine in the 1680s and 1690s. He had admittedly entertained an anti-innatist psychology before this moment.[51] But in *An*

Essay concerning Human Understanding (1690), which was written in 1685 during his exile in Holland as he was hiding from James II's agents and encountering waves of Huguenot refugees fleeing France after the revocation of the Edict of Nantes, he crystallized his epistemology in a way that made original sin unsustainable in any remotely orthodox sense. If the slate is wiped clean at the beginning of each individual life, and if morality therefore emerges as a thing shaped by environment rather than as a thing fixed in nature or revealed in the Bible, what sense does it make to continue talking about Adam's sin as an inherited condition?[52] In *Some Thoughts concerning Education* (1693), he affirmed more expressly that good and evil are an outcome of upbringing, not inborn depravity.[53] In his *Reasonableness of Christianity* (1695), he wryly noted that, if Adam's sin "meant the corruption of human nature in his posterity, it is strange that the New Testament should not anywhere take notice of it."[54] Even in some of these later works there can be residual Puritan pessimism. But if Locke continued to find resonance in the Fall—Barker rightly noted that Locke connected the Fall to mortality—then his later caveats and skeptical comments are arguably even more suggestive of an aversion to the political uses to which original sin was now being put and by more authors than just Bossuet.[55]

Given that seventeenth-century liberals and republicans had used the Fall *against* Filmer's *Patriarcha*, Bossuet's special allowance for kings was particularly useful as a work-around. It is hard not to wonder whether part of the reason Filmer never found his way to a similar argument is that the midcentury crises that influenced Bossuet had not yet occurred. For that matter, the reigning monarch under whom Filmer loyally wrote, Charles I, was put off by the Augustinian influence in Protestantism.[56] But there nevertheless is a subtle theological shift in other English political writing during the Exclusion Crisis, a tense moment from 1679 to 1681 during which "Whigs" and "Tories" emerged as oppositional political parties around the issue of whether the future king James II should be excluded from the throne because of his reputed Catholicism. Amid the threat of another civil war, some royalist authors seemed more tuned in to original sin as a basis for obedience and tuned in too to the way in which prominent Dissenters who were allied with the Whig proponents of exclusion were now deviating from their characteristic Augustinianism, a development that on its own may have invited royalists to revisit original sin in, compared to the 1630s, a more favorable mood.[57]

The Tory propagandist Roger L'Estrange warned his readers in a passing comment from 1681 that Dissenters had come to believe that "there is no Original sin in us; only Adam's first sin was Original Sin."[58] It was an exaggeration to say that this heterodox belief was held by *all* Dissenters.

But the claim still implies an emerging belief that renouncing original sin *would* threaten the traditional political order, which the Tories were trying to uphold.[59] L'Estrange was also not writing pure fiction in this case. One Puritan Whig who at least partly fits the characterization was the widely read Richard Baxter. Where his Puritan forebears had not ventured to question the pillars of Reformed orthodoxy, Baxter, writing in the mid-1670s, tied original sin not only to the problem of infant mortality but also to the paradox that Adam and Eve were allowed to exercise earth-shattering agency in the act of disobeying God even as their actions in doing so foreclosed the salvific agency of everybody else.[60]

More redolent of the Bossuetian argument was the subtext of John Dryden's *Absalom and Achitophel* (1681), a satiric retelling of the story of King David with obvious contemporary political allusions. Rather than making a simple patriarchal argument, Dryden pinned the dynastic succession to both familism and Adam's sin. "How could heavenly justice damn us all," he asked, "Who ne'er consented to our father's fall?" Absent such surrender to sin, the world would be turned upside down:

> Then kings are slaves to those whom they command
> And tenants to their people's pleasure stand.
> Add, that the pow'r property allow'd
> Is mischievously seated in the crowd.[61]

There is no direct evidence that Dryden had read Bossuet when he wrote his poem.[62] But when Dryden shortly afterward sat down to write his refutation of Spinozism in the *Religio Laici* (1682), he had thoroughly absorbed Bossuet's *Universal History*.[63]

James II ascended to the throne in early 1685, and a failed rebellion months later led him to execute the Duke of Monmouth ("Absalom") along with hundreds of rebels. Monmouth's rebellion also led several prominent members of the Anglican clergy to deliver a series of sermons justifying James's succession and the punishments meted out to the insurrectionists. These so-called Monmouth sermons occasioned "the final flowering of divine right royalism in," what Mark Goldie calls, "its *pre*-Revolution form."[64] Most of the sermons, that is, were familist in the mold of Filmer. But what is interesting is that, as Goldie also notes, some divines moderated their enthusiasm for James with "a deeply Augustinian sense that all princes were fallible mortals."[65] (As a Catholic king of a thoroughly Protestant nation, James II was nothing for even diehard Anglicans to get too excited about.) Even more intriguing is the errant Monmouth sermonizer Daniel Whitby, who condemned Monmouth and the rebellion when he rose to the pulpit in James's defense but nevertheless averred that political authority arose from individual consent, a stance that was out of step enough with Tory ideology to earn him the nickname "Whigby."[66] When the dust from both Monmouth's rebellion and the Revolution of 1688 had settled, Whitby would own up to being a contract theorist and Latitudinarian. And then, almost on cue, in 1690 he would write (but not publish) one of the seventeenth century's most thorough and explicit theological repudiations of original sin, a work long considered ground zero for the Enlightenment's theological assault on the doctrine.[67] That assessment seems fair but incomplete. Whitby was just as much a part of the first wave of the Enlightenment's own political theology, in which, despite Bossuet's insistence, the denial of original sin had not destroyed all social order. On the contrary, rejecting original sin was now coinciding with a leap of anthropological faith in which it seemed possible that, as nascent liberal thought promised, people could keep themselves in line even when unrestrained by the old external forms of authority.

Something happened to original sin at the end of the seventeenth century. Before this moment, the doctrine was compatible with a notion of human equality by virtue of the universality of depravity. But in Bossuet's hands, above all others, the doctrine was politically reframed to privilege kings while leaving everyone else cast as depraved. The distinction made a crucial difference. With kings understood as exceptional, the mere invocation of original sin could function as political shorthand for the belief that self-rule was doomed to failure.

But original sin and self-rule would also come to seem antithetical for another reason. The Bossuetian tradition was not only about the exception. It was also linked to the *classical spirit*, to use the term we associated earlier in this book with Ferdinand Brunetière, the fin de siècle literary critic whom Carl Becker dubbed the leader of the Bossuet cult. The Bossuetian tradition, to put it another way, was also about the willfully and *aestheticized* irrational.

In the 1740s, Pentecost Barker spent some time in the south of France, where he met and "had some serious Discourse with an Italian Abbé who had a little Chapel on the Road between [Nice] and Villa Franca." No doubt enlivened by the prospect of conversation with a philosophical adversary, he started talking about religion with the cleric, who "loved English Men, having been here with the Savoyard Minister when the Hanoverian Succession was settled." It is not clear what all he and the abbé talked about, but at some point in the conversation he admitted that, "in a Sea Life, I had done many things amiss that I avoided on-shore." The abbé "deem'd it a sort of Confession," and that gave him an opening in which Barker soon realized that the man "was fond of making me a Good Catholick, and put a Treatise of Bossuet Bishop of Meaux's into my hand for that purpose."[68]

Bossuet has long been seen to possess such power. Edward Gibbon dubbed him "a master of all weapons of controversy" and then gave him credit for a misguided youthful conversion to Catholicism. Bossuet assumes, "with consummate art," wrote Gibbon, "the tone of candor and simplicity; and the ten-horned monster is transformed, at his magic touch, into the milk-white hind, who must be loved as soon as she is seen": "To my present feelings it seems incredible that I should ever believe that I believed in transubstantiation. But my conqueror oppressed me. . . . [E]very objection was resolved into omnipotence; and after repeating at St. Mary's the Athanasian creed, I humbly acquiesced in the mystery of the real presence."[69] With none of Gibbon's regrets, Ferdinand Brunetière wrote about Bossuet in the manner of the devout: "[H]e is the guide and he is the master, he is the conductor of souls, he is the director of spirit, I would gladly say the director of studies, he is the thinker whose lessons have not ceased and will never cease to be current, to be alive."[70] Even those who have found Bossuet's arguments specious recognize the power of the prose. Voltaire considered his style "brilliant."[71] Cassirer described the *Universal History* as "sublime."[72] Carl Becker called him "eloquent" (*Beredte*).[73] In more recent years, the historian of political thought Patrick Riley marveled, if ruefully, at "the sheer magnificence of Bossuet's prose, always of a marmoreal splendor."[74]

Bossuet's sermons on original sin were among his most compelling. The images can be arresting and evocative. Adam committed not just the "homicide" of the human race but the "parricide of himself." Or there is the grotesque. Adam killed all his children "and slew them not in the cradle but in their mother's womb even before their birth." Or there is the totalizing language. Adam's sin "spread through the human race the concupiscence that produces all crimes."[75] Or there is the weaving together of text and exegesis in crisp, compressed, rapid-fire language: "'All the thoughts of man are inclined to evil at all times.' Weigh these words: All the thoughts, and these: At all times. We don't do all evil, but we are inclined to it; the only thing missing is the opportunity . . . : man left to himself would avoid no evil. Add these words: 'The wickedness of men was great on earth,' and these: 'My spirit shall not abide in man, because he is flesh.'"[76]

More remarkable still are passages that manage to convey the misery of the human condition in the language of happiness. As Bossuet writes in another gloss on Genesis, God made humans perfect while also giving us the ability to preserve our perfection for posterity. All we had to do was maintain our gratefulness to God for encapsulating in Adam all the happiness of those who would eventually constitute the human race. Things of course changed with the original sin. But this too was part of the relationship of equivalence with Adam that granted us our happiness. "Look at all that's contained in Adam," Bossuet writes, "look at our being and well-being, our happiness and our unhappiness. God sees us *only* in Adam, in whom he made all of us."[77] This is to say, through the logic of the word *only* ("ne . . . que"), that God also never sees us without seeing us in Adam. We always already reflect Adam's catastrophic decision alongside the other woeful tendencies wrought and explained by the Fall. In case that seems unfair, Bossuet finishes his explanation in verb tenses that make linear time and the cause-and-effect relationship that underpins blame as irrelevant as empirical history: "[W]hatever Adam does we do with him. We are enveloped in him. We are one in the same with him morally. If Adam obeys, we obey in him. If he sins, we sin in him. God will treat the whole human race as Adam—as this one man in whom he puts everything, and everything deserved."[78]

Convincing someone to accept these "wild traditions," in Wollstonecraft's phrase, did not just require a willingness to embrace mysticism. It required taking the blame for someone else's actions. Adam and Eve were the only ones who had committed the crime. "Why should all mankind / For one man's fault, be condemned, / If guiltless," asks God rhetorically in *Paradise Lost*, before answering the question with original sin's major premise: because all are corrupt with "both mind and will depraved."[79] In Bossuet's authoritarian terms, original sin was an even harder sell to anyone coming to define their political outlook on default assumptions of innocence, like those associated with habeas corpus, a notion powerfully articulated by radicals and constitutionalists in the mid-seventeenth century.[80] But it was this very hard sell that explains the stirring eloquence.[81] Jonathan Edward's co-option of Lockean psychology may have been ingenious in content, but it was turgid in form. John Wesley's defense of original sin, published like Edwards's in 1757, was comparatively naive philosophically, but it is filled with the lyrical prose of the sort we saw at the beginning of this book (in, e.g., Wesley's funeral sermon for John Fletcher). There is a reason that the unnamed woman to whom Merivale loaned his copy of John Taylor's "antidote" against original sin had first been given a copy of Wesley by an evangelical Methodist. Wesley's power to persuade lay in the language. The Italian abbé presumably wanted to give Barker a copy of Bossuet for the same reason. It was less the raw argument that seduced than it was the prose.[82]

Becker's use of the word *cult* to refer to Bossuet's modernist followers may operate on another level if, like more than a few cult leaders, Bossuet was disingenuous. The bishop's piety can seem elusive—or at the very least instrumentalist—when set in the context of the ambitious regime he worked for. Louis XIV poured money into the Académie des Sciences and spent decades and a fortune building a royal palace at Versailles that doubled as a showpiece of modern technology.[83] Even if the Bourbon regime benefited from sacred veneration of the throne and altar, there was nothing fundamentally irrational about its aims. Louis XIV's France could just as easily be characterized as a science state.[84] And it would only further reflect the crown's hegemonic ambition that it enlisted a brilliant "irrationalist" like Bossuet to speak to those more compelled by the sacred than by the secular. "I adore your Justice, Lord, however impenetrable to my sense and my reason. As long as I see the sacred rules, I love them and abide by them," Bossuet wrote mellifluously while serving a king he called "a new Constantine" for an express reason: "[V]ous avez exterminé les hérétiques."[85] Bossuet, in other words, seemed all too aware of the *modernity* of the authoritarian regime he was defending, however atavistically. If "*new* Constantine" alone does not reflect that perspective, consider a sermon preached after the revocation of the Edicts of Nantes in 1685, which expelled France's religious minority and was filled with the tragedy that tends to attend massive, forced deportations. Here Bossuet celebrated precisely the modernity of the moment, a modernity running along an authoritarian track. His regime had, after all, succeeded where others had failed:

> [O]ur fathers [in the early church] did not see, as we do, an inveterate heresy suddenly fall; the misguided flocks returning in droves, and our churches not big enough to receive them; their false shepherds abandoning them, without even waiting for an order, and happy to use their banishment as an excuse; everything calm in such a great movement; *the universe astonished to see in so new an event the most assured mark, as well as the most beautiful use of authority.*[86]

I emphasize the last clause because it virtually says it all. Successfully exterminating a religious minority was a new event in Bossuet's universe, a universe, as always for the bishop, whose viability rested on the Judeo-Christian tradition. What is more, this event marked both a defining moment for authority—because authority had long since needed to rid itself of any who did not believe the underpinning political theology—and the "most beautiful use" of authority, "le plus bel usage" in the original—because all this had been made possible, in part, by aestheticizing the irrational. It is no wonder that Bossuet was so exemplary to later reactionaries. Disingenuous or not, he sought to undermine self-rule in the same breath in which he eschewed the culture of fact. And it was his aestheticized, authoritarian irrationalism, as much as the language of the exception, that captured what would become the axiomatic political associations of original sin.[87]

Nearly a century after Bossuet's death, as the Bourbon monarchy the bishop defended was collapsing, Edmund Burke, "the Bossuet of politics" according to an admiring early biographer, wrote in his own stirring prose that what made a tragedy out of the "empire of light and reason" was that it threatened to dissolve "all the pleasing illusions which made power gentle and obedience liberal, which harmonized the different shades of life, and which, by a bland assimilation, incorporated into politics the sentiments which beautify and soften private society."[88] Legitimizing fear, harmonizing inequality, persuading people, in graceful prose, to accept a capricious regime—these recurring political and cultural accomplishments were ready-made for "pleasing illusions." But that enlighteners were not persuaded is telling. It was here in the discourse of political theology that the contrast between the Enlightenment and a notion of original sin designed to preclude self-rule was most apparent. And it was here that fear—the emotion that Barker highlighted and dreaded—did the work necessary to sustain such authority. "Fear is a bridle necessary to men because of their pride and their natural indocility," Bossuet minced no words to say in his *Politics Drawn from Holy Scripture*. "The people must thus fear the prince; but if the prince fears the people, all is lost."[89]

It was also here in the context of political theology, to return to the early historiography, that the Enlightenment once seemed especially coherent—and coherent for the very reason that it denied original sin. As original sin became axiomatically linked to tyranny and authoritarianism, renouncing this theological doctrine became a comparatively radical political act. It meant assailing at once the politics of fear, religious intolerance, and irrationalism. Again, it is no accident that Cassirer and Becker had their eyes on original sin as fascism was spreading across the same map on which liberal democracies were failing.

We might go further but in a slightly different direction. If secular depravity is substituted for original sin, there is a parallel between what Bossuet was trying to accomplish and what the proslavery critic of the abolitionist J. Philmore was working toward in the book review that

Barker read in 1761 (the critic never signs his name, so we have to refer to him simply as *Philmore's critic*). As we saw in chapter 6, Philmore's critic was defending slavery by imputing characteristics to Africans—but to Africans only—that would not seem out of place in the bleakest Augustinian gloss on human nature. At the same time, he was conspicuously not invoking original sin, even in the sense in which it had once been used to justify slavery. For earlier writers who ascribed original sin this power, the crucial major premise was that human depravity was *universal*, a condition of humankind that held everywhere in the postlapsarian world. Philmore's critic was instead making *exceptions*. He was expressly ascribing depravity only to Africans to justify, specifically, the continuance of the Atlantic slave trade. And he was implicitly tempering his anthro-pessimism for Europeans, who possessed, he assumed, the right to rule—to rule with what Barker called "fear of the whip"—for the very reason of their relative exemption. Europeans could legitimate themselves as slavers, in the mind of Philmore's critic, because, put simply, they possessed their own particular grace through race.

However, if Philmore's critic was looking for a racial basis for the same thing Bossuet was after, namely, exceptions, the other thing that he suggests is that race is an awkward fit with the earlier use of original sin to justify enslavement. Race was virtually ready-made to undermine the universality on which original sin theologically depends. Not for nothing were so many architects of racism at the time drawn to heretical polygenesis. We can go one step further. Philmore's critic rests his case not on a universalist theological depravity but on a new, invidious secular depravity. As a theological doctrine, original sin did him no favors, particularly in an era in which religious orthodoxy was losing credibility. For that matter, even depravity in a broad secular sense did him no favors without racialized exceptions. But once racialized to allow for exactly what Bossuet was after—a profoundly asymmetrical arrangement of power—depravity became a potent tool.

This brings us back to something mentioned at the beginning of this book. With respect to original sin, Enlightenment historiography got messier after the Nazi seizure of power, even more so after the war. We have tried to follow both the obvious and the not-so-obvious facets of the relationship between the Enlightenment and original sin. To turn now more fully to the not so obvious, we need to consider where the anthro-pessimism characteristic of this theological doctrine not only survived but had already started to flourish within the Enlightenment. Where that happens—where some of the implications of original sin persist but with no morality or theology—anthro-optimism remains as threatened as it had been in the confessional era by the fetters of Luther and Calvin. Witness not only the new secular views of human nature that were so serviceable to racism but also the subject to which we turn next: the role secular anthro-pessimism played in a new view of the economy, in which the proper object of Barker's keyword, *love,* was far less obvious to enlighteners than the brazen political objects of fear.

CHAPTER EIGHT

The Economy of Love

Fear does more than love with most, as to obedience, so I heard from a tyrannical commander. But I know it would not with me, and I conclude that multitudes are of the same opinion.

PENTECOST BARKER
to Samuel Merivale, May 10, 1762

Whether it was in population, trade, industry, agriculture, or the specialization of labor, the eighteenth-century economy throughout much of Europe experienced growth. This was obviously true for the economic success story of the period, Great Britain, which began its industrial revolution during the century's final decades. But it was even true of France, the economic failure of the century to the extent that financial problems led to the collapse of the powerful Bourbon regime. What caused this economic turnaround from a seventeenth century ridden with crisis is varied. Somewhere in the equation lie the labor savings generated from protoindustrial organization and new technologies, the profits Europe made from its vast slave trade, the availability of coal as a cheap fuel, and the use of the state's muscle to protect merchants in the ever-expanding empires. It is hard to pass over a list like this without thinking about human suffering and lingering consequences—racial inequality, the displacement of the workforce by machines, climate change. But it is no less axiomatic for historians to assume that, the ironies notwithstanding, much of the broader optimism felt in eighteenth-century Europe came from all this economic growth.[1]

But what also impelled economic change at the time were shifts in attitude that can be tied to original sin. If part of what made growth possible was a new view of growth itself—not just in material accumulation but in the desire to accumulate—then acquisitiveness, a long-standing marker of human depravity, had to be morally reconsidered. Where the middle class was involved in the growth—which is to say everywhere—there was just as crucially a need for people to acquire credit, which meant taking on debt, the latter an economic reality long intertwined in a metaphoric relationship with sin. Most eighteenth-century political economists were also coming to hold a labor theory of value, a questionable concept given that labor had traditionally been viewed as a woeful consequence of the Fall. Not least, the new economy benefited from a shift in emotional self-perception from, at its core, self-loathing to self-love.

The theology of original sin generally inhibited these developments. But when it comes to the *psychology* of original sin, the story is not so simple. Political economists were by and large different from the most anthro-optimistic enlighteners, who abandoned original sin in every possible sense in the effort to affirm human dignity, universal rights, equality, agency, selfless love, and so on. Political economists instead built their case against original sin by retooling Augustinianism for economic purpose. In their thinking, original sin was the object of both rejection and appropriation. The rejection occurred where political economy turned away from the Augustinian moral gloss in which self-regard or one of its variants was an overarching trait of human depravity. The appropriation occurred where political economy nevertheless retained the underlying assumption about the universality of that self-regard, if anything making the concept of man more reductionist or more "one-dimensional" in Herbert Marcuse's phrase.

The economist Albert Hirschman said as much in a now classic account of eighteenth-century economic thought when (nodding to Marcuse) he noted that political economy's rebranding of selfishness as self-interest—a motive force presumed capable of bridling more socially destabilizing emotions—was expected to create "a less multifaceted, less unpredictable, and more 'one-dimensional' human personality."[2] Writing around the same time as Hirschman, the historian Joyce Appleby found that, marveling at Dutch success, economic pamphlet authors in late seventeenth-century England redefined the economy as "impervious to social engineering and political interference" by reframing people as predictable and rational: "As long as human beings appeared, as they did in Shakespearean literature, as creatures riven by reason and passion or, as in Reformation writings, as struggling between their 'fallen' and 'redeemable' natures, they offered no firm basis for constructing a natural social order."[3] For that matter, Michel Foucault made the adjacent case in the late 1970s that political economy triumphed through the force of its assertion that people have "a nature specific to the objects and operations of governmentality," a nature that, to secure its own power, political economy put itself in a supreme position to respect.[4] These are writers of great ideological variety agreeing, in essence, that *homo economicus* is just *homo augustinius* without the guilt.[5] And their insight is worth exploring further in relation to our larger story. The same process by which early modern Augustinian assumptions and habits came to be fit for economic purpose can be found in other modes of social discipline born in religious anxiety about self-control. Here too a pattern of change and continuity recurs. Economic discipline both mirrored and undermined facets of original sin.

Or to put it differently, economic discipline preserved an Augustinian habitus but made it more natural and compelling as it gave anthropessimism a secular footing. *Habitus*, as Pierre Bourdieu defined it, is more than a collection of habits. It is "embodied history, internalized as a second nature and so forgotten as history." It "is the active presence of the whole past of which it is the product."[6] Similarly, what I mean by *Augustinian habitus* is a second-nature mode of behavior that is "forgotten as history" all the more deeply where the relationship between capitalism and original sin is noted for the moral rupture rather than the psychological continuity. The ruptures, to be sure, are an important part of the story. But so are the continuities, which form the basis of what comes to feel second nature for having been so long established.[7]

One part of this habitus is, as I have already suggested, reflected in the way in which *selfishness* embodied both moral change and psychological continuity: selfishness emerged as psychologically natural (the continuity) where economic theorizing supported the case that relentlessly pursuing material desires should no longer be seen in stark moral terms (the change). The same pattern also underpins spiritual *watchfulness*, which so often made problematic its own underlying religiosity as it anticipated the ocularity of commercial society captured so memorably in Adam Smith's "impartial spectator." Something similar holds for behavior that developed around *sin* and *debt*. As the meaning of debt changed, so did the meaning of what debt metaphorically signified, which is to say sin. On the one hand, where debts could easily be repaid, and where credit permitted the accumulation of new wealth, sin came to be seen as ever more remissible. On the other hand, where indebtedness was persistent and chastening in its effects, its regulating features started to parallel those that drew on the burden of sinful inheritance. Not of least importance in the secularized Augustinian habitus was industrious *work*. Labor had traditionally been regarded as punishment for the Fall, but over the eighteenth century it was recast as the fundamental source of economic value. How, in one sense, could the "labor theory of value" not raise questions about the consequentialness of the Fall itself? Yet, in another sense, if Max Weber was right that Augustinian Protestantism fueled a capitalist spirit that eventually made life indistinguishable from work, was labor not also part of the feedback loop in which reflexive materialism and acquisitiveness helped form a "steel hard casing" around the will?[8] Labor was not just conflated with life. In becoming an ethos, it took on the deterministic force that previous generations had uniquely felt in aspects of their religion.

None of this is to lose sight of Barker's own keyword, *love*. The significance of that loaded word in relation to the economy only deepens because of what we have already noted: its ambiguity. Where, after all, was the love supposed to be aimed? At the self, like crass anthro-pessimistic amour propre? Or at other people, so that individuals come to love the "greater whole," as Rousseau put it in his *Discourse on Political Economy* (1758), "with that exquisite feeling that every isolated man has only for himself"?[9] Barker in late life felt as Rousseau did. The better sea captain implied in his allegory—not the captain he served under and argued with but the one he wished he had served under and probably would not have argued with—acts as a proxy for the other. "Love was predominant in me," Barker writes, as we have seen, before adding that he would "do ten times more for a man I loved than for One I feared." Merivale too had an aversion to what he called "that sordid scheme of morals which supposes all the obligations to virtue to arise from a regard to our own interest" and which further supposed that "there is no such thing in human nature as a principle of generous & disinterested benevolence."[10] For anthro-optimists like Barker and Merivale, there was an economy—in the sense of being a resource allocation—of love. They—and particularly Barker—imagined that love's object could be sublimated, from the self to the other. It is in this sense that the "ten times more" in Barker's formulation is telling. He was resting a paradigm shift on a multiple. In his emotional pin factory, he was saying he would ramp up production for a better captain, just as for a better God he would be more productive in accumulating good deeds, an effort that contemporaries instinctively signaled in theological shorthand through the economic metaphor of works. But, as Merivale's comment suggests, not every enlightener was so sanguine about human nature. The "sordid scheme" was a reference not to Calvin but to the "selfish principle" typified by Bernard Mandeville and other secular anthro-pessimists whose economy of love allocated all emotional resources to the self.[11]

Alongside its elusiveness in meaning, *love* is also revealing in its elusiveness as a feeling. A common and recurring assumption of the secular Augustinian habitus was that holding oneself in the highest regard would produce a social knock-on effect: far from leading to chaos, self-love would bring mutual benefits to an economically interdependent society. But insofar as the anthro-pessimism underpinning this view also justifies an economy that runs on endless social judgment, tireless work, perpetual debt, and an unswerving belief in the inevitability of selfishness, it is hard to see how evenly the love was ever likely to be distributed. Here too, then, there is an economy of love or, rather, an economizing of love, an emotion that in its selfless variety has consistently been rationed alongside all the remarkable *growth.*

~

The religious admonition to fear that Barker associated with Luther and Calvin was so often prescribed with a dose of loathing—for the self. "Hatred of self" remains "with the penalty of sin . . . until we enter the kingdom of Heaven," wrote Luther in the *Ninety-Five Theses.*[12] Our fallen state should encourage "hatred and displeasure with ourselves," wrote Calvin in the *Institutes.*[13] Lesser authorities echoed the same advice—the Puritan minister Ralph Josselin confided to his diary, "I desire to loathe myself," as he sought a better way to absorb the weight of Christ's sacrifice.[14] The seventeenth-century Harvard tutor Michael Wigglesworth told his diary in almost the same words, "I desire to abhor myself," as he was irrepressibly drawn to "destroying [him]self daly" while fantasizing about his students.[15] For that matter, when in early life Barker pinned the essence of Christianity to self-denial, he did so because of his hatred of *homo corruptus,* the self embodied.

The examples can be multiplied by, at least, the number of extant spiritual diaries written in the Augustinian tradition. As "technologies of the self," godly diaries were undertaken to bear witness to sin, and they therefore offered endless occasion to record personal failure and the subsequent self-beratement.[16] But when it came to willful self-loathing, these diaries did not hold a monopoly. Blaise Pascal drew on his Jansenist faith to conclude in his *Pensées* (1670): "Le moi est haïssable." The reasons he offered were myriad but coalesced around a familiar theme: "All Jesus did was teach men that they loved themselves . . . [and would be sanctified] by hating themselves and following him through his misery and death on the Cross"; "the true and only virtue is therefore to hate ourselves, for our concupiscence makes us hateful"; "we must love God alone and hate ourselves alone"; and so on.[17]

Expressions of self-hatred were not without self-harm. The lay Puritan diarist Nehemiah Wallington tried nearly a dozen times to murder the self he hated.[18] Barker too was led to the brink of suicide when he was in the throes of Calvinist religiosity. But self-loathing was always intended to serve a higher spiritual purpose. As an extension of original sin, it was a reminder to resist the corporeal self and to embrace the depravity that gave Christ's sacrifice greater meaning. Just as importantly, it helped elevate Christianity above other religions. Recall the sermon in which a young Barker heard a young Peter Baron extol Christianity because it was thought to be uniquely capable of "lay[ing] down a very satisfactory acct of the Depravation of Mankind . . . [so] that we may see how vile We are, that we may be able to acquiesce in God's Afflictive Dealings and under a sense of our sad State be qualified for Grace and Mercy."[19] Or again turn to Pascal: "[N]o other religion has proposed that we should hate ourselves. No other religion therefore can please those who do hate themselves."[20]

But the encouragement that original sin gave to self-loathing also helped ensure that it was in tension with Enlightenment thought, which took positive self-regard as a baseline trait. Alongside Barker's terms—fear as emblematic of the ancien régime, love as a keyword of *éclaircissement*—loathing can be added as the mode of self-regard that operated as both cause and effect in a dynamic relationship with fear: loathing encouraged fear as reliably as fear encouraged loathing. And given that it was an extension of original sin, the prescription for self-loathing that runs through Augustinian religiosity also indicates how much Augustinianism was, morally speaking, an impediment to political economy.

Saying as much may appear on first glance to conflict with rather than complement the thesis Max Weber influentially put forward in *The Protestant Ethic and the Spirit of Capitalism* (1904–5), according to which Protestantism was economically significant where it could be traced to the effects of the Augustinian Protestant reformers, namely, Martin Luther and, more importantly for Weber, Jean Calvin. But the relationship of what I am arguing here to Weber's thesis is more complicated. For Weber, capitalism represented less a departure from preexisting forms of economic behavior than an intensification of those forms to the point at which they became ends in and of themselves. This characterization was in part a way for Weber to capture capitalism's irrationality, which is to say its absence of obvious rationales. What is the purpose of acquiring only for the sake of acquiring, of making money and then not spending it, and so on?[21]

In Weber's view, modern capitalism also became a deterministic force in life by replacing the determinisms of the theology that inadvertently gave it a boost. The most profound of these older determinisms for Weber was the doctrine of predestination, which made people who had turned away from the comforting practices of the late medieval church anxious and desperate to find any assurance of their salvation. Out of that desperation came the practice of examining mundane life for signs of spiritual election. And since work was such a regular feature of the mundane, godly people began to scrutinize their work, in particular, to see whether it signaled spiritual election (when it was profitable) or reprobation (when it was not). Hence the way in which Calvinism gave rise to a work *ethos*, by which Weber meant a force infused with enough deep meaning for it to do the thing that he normally reserved for religion: to generate an organizing principle for life.

If Calvinism encouraged capitalist behavior, and if a key doctrine on which Calvinism rested was, as Weber well knew, original sin, then it is hard to see how Weber's thesis is consistent with the view that original sin was an impediment to early capitalist development. But the causal relationship between the material and the cultural in the seventeenth century did not necessarily flow in the same direction in the eighteenth. And here, if he is considered in a broader sense, Weber offers a lasting insight. In his dynamic view of causality, the material and the cultural are bound together by ever-adapting elective affinities, the dynamic of which sometimes encourages economic forces and agents to align themselves with certain spiritual views and habits and at other times encourages cultural forces and agents to align themselves with certain worldly views and habits. Weber's specific historical investigation was, by his own admission, focused on one chapter of the dynamic relationship between material and cultural causes and motives. He tuned in to the story in the century and a half after the Reformation, a long moment in which he thought religious culture exerted enough force to shape worldly behavior. The economic phenomenon that Puritanism helped him explain, for example, was the *restrained* behavior characteristic of the middle class, restraint being the cultural habit whose relative oddness in the long-term history of the economy Weber thought cried out for something beyond a materialist explanation.

By virtue of the same logic of elective affinities, one can, however, tune in to a different moment in the past and discover that the powerful causes and motives were instead economic.[22] Certainly these motives and causes are evident in Barker's milieu. By the mid-eighteenth century, as Dissenter fortunes grew in ways that more moderate and godly generations would have found excessive, the pressure that the accumulation of wealth put on traditional morality arguably helped tip the causal balance toward the material.[23] And when that happened—when, in essence, the economy traded places with religion as a causal and motive force—original sin became a problem. Among other things, it was then seen to possess inhibiting economic meaning in highlighting the alleged danger of *excess*. As Albert Hirschman put it, "*lust* for money" had long been seen in the Augustinian tradition as a "principal sin of fallen man."[24] If massive accumulation of wealth was a glaring indicator of such underlying lust, then original sin presented, at once, a moral explanation for the religious traditionalists and a moral problem for the economic modernizers. By the same token, if the Fall could be attenuated in theological and moral significance or renounced altogether, then the religious stigma against material excess would theoretically fade.

It is not accidental that, in the long wake of the Reformation, so many unusually prosperous congregations had in one way or another turned against Augustinian theology. Already by the mid-seventeenth century, Dutch merchants were drawn to Arminianism at a time when that religious philosophy was starting to signal a retreat from the strenuous view of original sin.[25] On the other side of the equation, less prosperous Dutch were drawn to the strict Calvinism of Francis Gomarus.[26] Express and systematic challenges to original sin still brought condemnation, even in tolerant Holland. The historian Karen Hollewand has noted that, while nothing Hobbes, Spinoza, or Descartes ever wrote when living in the Netherlands's most liberal province got them expelled, when Hadriaan Beverland confronted original sin head-on in his *Peccatum originale* (1678), he was sent packing.[27] Taken on its own, Beverland's expulsion offers yet more evidence of how crucial original sin was to a broad Christian orthodoxy and how daring it was to attack it. But his case also suggests that, if he had the audacity to confront original sin, pressure against the doctrine was increasing and increasing in part because of a new moral legitimacy lent by a prosperous bourgeoisie moving steadily away from Augustinian theology.

In the absence of a detailed study of Dutch economic theology, one can only speculate. But a pattern suggesting the same elective affinities emerges more clearly during the next century. In British Unitarian and Quaker communities, where Pelagianism was firmly ensconced, the accumulation of wealth was becoming conspicuous. Quakers were prominent in banking. Unitarians and other Rational Dissenters dominated industry. While the records that permit quantifying Dissenter wealth do not appear until 1851, by the mid-nineteenth century, and by a process that had long since been under way, fortunes had accumulated to such a degree that there were, remarkably, ten times as many Unitarians among the Dissenter millionaires and half millionaires of Britain as demographically there should have been and an even more astonishing fifty times as many Quakers.[28] Equally suggestive is that, like Gomarists in the Dutch Republic, the evangelical Methodists were disproportionately poor in the same British surveys.[29] The pattern is impressionistically mirrored in

New England, where Unitarian congregations were a who's who of the elite.[30] It may not only be logical to say that where original sin declined accumulation could then proceed beyond its primitive limits. The elective affinity between, broadly speaking, Pelagianism and the unfettered accumulation of wealth also seems empirically borne out in those rare instances where evidence is available.

The point is again twofold. On the one hand, the theological decline of original sin helped middle-class religiosity become something no longer middling but rather a facilitator of conspicuous wealth. On the other hand, self-regard of a type long seen as vain and sinful was not extinguished; it was de-moralized and then venerated. The view that self-regard—even vain self-regard—was a fact of life—a view long regretfully driven home for moral reasons by doctrinaire Augustinians—was now being articulated more happily by political economists in ways that could not help but undermine Augustinianism as *theology*. There was hardly a better case against Augustinian morality, in other words, than the naturalization of Augustinian psychology.

~

The same dual meaning can be found in spiritual watchfulness, the habit of methodically examining the self and the outside world that the pious adopted to stay on spiritual course. The force of spiritual watchfulness is evident throughout the Reformed world, and it should be said that it was not only consequential in an economic sense. It underpinned the "disciplinary revolution" that helped small Calvinist regions in Europe preserve their political autonomy as they found ways for power to perform through "technologies of observation," as one sociologist puts it, rather than through the normal forms of coercion.[31] Watching was nevertheless especially individualistic—and especially serviceable to the economy—in England, where at the end of the reign of Queen Elizabeth I Puritan ministers who were unable to rely on external forms of discipline and oversight like the Calvinist consistory took the bold step of authorizing the laity to watch themselves.[32] Of all the technologies employed for this purpose, nothing is more illuminating than the kind of artifact Pentecost Barker produced in early life: a spiritual diary.

We have seen how spiritual diaries were meant to keep one on a godly path, a role they performed for countless pious people. But these diaries arose from a religiosity that rested godliness on prescribed self-loathing. Using a diary to watch the self was never supposed to offer moral improvement as a pathway to unholy self-esteem. Just the opposite. Self-esteem easily entailed a forgetfulness of human depravity that could then lead to complacency or, just as bad, to the salvific overvaluation of moral conduct, like that felt by John Fletcher, as we saw at the beginning of this book, before his spiritual rebirth. Again, this is why spiritual diarists are so self-persecutory. "Never was so great a sinner . . . as this miserable Pentecost Barker" was an improbable claim. The point of making it anyway was to maintain a soteriological awareness of the chasm between the human and the divine.

But diaries did not always go to plan. Watching could also encourage an interiority that directed itself *against* Calvinism. This could happen in one sense because the diary could validate the self that lay, unavoidably, at the heart of self-writing. Early Puritan divines were aware of this problem and accordingly advised the laity to write on a daily basis but then to discard their diaries after they had served their spiritual purpose.[33] Barker in early life reflects this same purpose, which ideally was to ignore any audience other than God and the diarist. Recall that, virtually disregarding his diary's formal appearance, he wrote his entries on the blank pages interwoven in another book. But muting the self in self-writing was often easier said than done. Already by the mid-seventeenth century, there were handfuls of diarists in the Puritan tradition who were decorating their journals with frontispieces and tables of contents. By the eighteenth century, some spiritual diaries were published with the author's consent. The self that the diary was supposed to suppress started in these cases to look like an author.[34]

In another sense, the intense self-consciousness encouraged and displayed by diary keeping also exposed the troubling consequences of original sin. As diarists monitored the depths of their interiority, they could always find shortcomings in their thoughts and behavior and therefore the occasion to do better. That regular discovery only deepened the need to watch even further. Yet, in these feedback loops of self-reflection, diarists might well also discover that they had an emotional aversion to theological doctrine, particularly original sin. That pattern is arguably already discernible by the end of the seventeenth century.[35] By the mid-eighteenth century, it was in any case far clearer that the biggest opponents of Calvinism were, like Barker and Merivale, former Calvinists, or, as nineteenth-century orthodox writers disparagingly called these people, *Calvinophobes*.[36] It is no mystery that Calvinism produced its own gravediggers. Calvinophobia partly derived from Calvinist doubts about maintaining self-control that had been worrisome enough in the earlier years of the Reformation to lead to radical solutions, like methodically keeping a written account of one's interior life through which one might stay on spiritual course or might just as well grow skeptical about the way in which that course was drawn out.

To put this in terms of the larger argument, much as was true of selfishness once it was spiritually decriminalized, the Augustinian habit of methodically watching the self could whittle away at orthodoxy. And just as in the case of the cultural acceptance of self-regard, there is an anthro-pessimism that so often survives this process. Skepticism about the prospect of self-control continued to operate through the transformation of watching into habits designed for a liberal society that prided itself, no less than many Protestant communities, on its ostensible *lack* of external controls.[37] What is more, these religious and secular cultures both prided themselves on the economizing that helped make the obvious external forms of authority unnecessary.

Here the classic trope for authority fading from view in a nominally freer environment is *panopticism,* a word that for Michel Foucault captured not the true disappearance of authority but rather its ostensible disappearance via, among other things, its internalization in the self. Foucault's term owes to the panopticon, Jeremy Bentham's late Enlightenment prison design that made such effective use of the threat of observation that the watchtower imagined for the center of the circular prison could dispense with the usual complement of prison guards.[38] For Foucault, this bypass of obvious power insidiously prefigured the modern surveillance state, in which simply knowing about the likelihood of being surveilled has the effect of disciplining behavior. But it is worth noting that Bentham, no less than the underfunded experimental Calvinists who first authorized spiritual diaries, was trying to save money. He was proud to announce at the beginning of his *Panopticon* (1787) that, with his new and improved prison, "a watchman need cost nothing."[39]

More redolent of residual watching in the economy is, in any case, what Adam Smith captured with the metaphor of the spectator. If Puritan watchfulness internalized the expectations of the godly community, spectating internalized the expectations of commercial society. Human agency, argued Smith in *The Theory of Moral Sentiments,* was guided to the right moral and economic actions by virtue of how intently people watch themselves through the eyes of the impartial spectator, an amalgam of outside perceptions that lives inside us (in "the breast," Smith put it), drawing us toward social approval and away from disapproval. There are, of course, actual people in the world paying attention to how we act and often expressly congratulating or condemning us. But the spectator operates more effectively by being a second-nature distillation of what we imagine other people like and dislike. The spectator is surveillance conducted as intimately as possible, from the inside out—after the outside comes in by way of our existence as socially impressionable beings. On the one hand, there is unmistakable optimism in what the regulation of our agency by the spectator promises: a sense of personal freedom, a secular basis for moral conduct, economic prosperity, and all in the absence of external forms of authority that for so long had been thought indispensable. On the other hand, the ingenuous approach to self-discipline still rested on skepticism about the prospect of self-control, at least if the self went unaided by something as relentless as the spectator.

None of this is to say that Smith was in any appreciable sense religious.[40] Nor is it to deny the importance of the language of Stoicism and Epicureanism that he adopts to articulate his position, language used by the Scottish Enlightenment as a whole under the influence of Cicero's *De finibus bonorum et malorum*, a refreshing alternative for Scottish enlighteners to both Calvin and Aristotle. Nor, for that matter, is any of this to deny that Smith was shrewdly describing the social emulation that was already present in his commercial society. The innovation that his ocular trope evinces, nevertheless, is another facet of the Augustinian habitus overcoming its intended moral purpose—in a word, changing—through its secular continuity. And in no obvious sense is an eternal social audience alternating between applause and boos an escape from the judgmentalism that made the watchful God of Calvin so chastening.

"Metaphors are far more than mere words," writes one biblical scholar. "How we talk about sin . . . influences what we will do about it."[41] If so, then sin in the Judeo-Christian tradition has been economically inflected for a long time. Its primary metaphor shifted from *burden* to *debt* (as the primary metaphor for virtue became *credit*) some twenty-five-hundred years ago.[42]

How people have read into these metaphors over the centuries has varied, but certainly the Augustinian Protestant reformers have consistently seen in the logic of sin *as* debt a dangerous potential to elevate moral conduct in the salvific equation: much as people can pay down their debts through hard work, or so the dangerous argument went, sinners could remit their sins through *works*, the loaded economic trope for good deeds. For more works-based theologians in the earliest centuries of Christianity, in fact, a common way of conceptualizing the remission of sin as credit had been to imagine that "Christ's life of obedience had funded a 'treasury of merits' that was later supplemented by the work of saints."[43] This was precisely the danger Martin Luther discerned in taking the metaphor too far, at which point the rich could perfunctorily augment their treasury of merits through the purchase of proxies for good deeds and then draw down that treasury to pay off their sins. Nowhere did this notion of sins in one accounting column and good deeds in the other turn works into cash payments more infuriatingly for Luther than through the sale of indulgences.

That said, every metaphor has both a *tenor,* the thing the metaphor describes, and a *vehicle,* the term that carries the weight of the comparison.[44] In the early modern era, there was nothing new in using economic tropes to capture religious concepts: sin had long been *like* debt, and virtue had long been *like* credit. What was changing was the meaning of *debt* and *credit,* the vehicles. And changing along with them was the weight of the metaphors themselves. The rise and development of fiscal states, for example, meant that national wealth and power were coming to rest as never before on perpetual debt, as long as that debt could be serviced.[45] The same held true for the softer power of the middle class, whose expansion was unthinkable without credit, the other side of the same coin. In Britain, where interest rates had come down to manageable levels by midcentury, more and more commentary comes from opinion makers stressing that "reasonable" credit was, as one Bristol merchant put it, "as necessary to a Trading Nation, as Spirits are to the Circulation of the Blood in the Body natural."[46]

In one sense, the credit economy could clearly be heralded as a success. Take the same Unitarian congregations in which wealth and the rejection of original sin went hand in hand. Particularly in the industrial towns in the north of England, where Unitarians were likely to be former Calvinist Dissenters rather than disaffected Anglicans (denominational Unitarianism was fed by both Anglicanism and Dissent), the families that rose to prominence had come from middling stock and achieved success in protoindustrial pursuits precisely because they had been able to take on debt and manage it. And in relation to theology remitting sins had become easier amid the transition away from Calvinism. Sin no longer hung around one's neck like an inherited burden—it hardly needs to be repeated that Unitarians renounced *original* sin. But, even further, the idea of perfectibility that pervades Unitarianism rests on something very much like Pentecost Barker's notion that, the more rational and loving one might become, the easier it would be to avoid sin altogether. Debt management and sin management in this sense emerged in tandem.

That was certainly true for Barker. During those intervening years between his diary and his letters, his career prospects improved as he moved toward his heterodox view of sin. But the same relationship between sin and debt is just as suggestive in the outlook of other Rational Dissenters. Take the Unitarian minister Richard Price's "sinking fund," a government investment intended to be financed by taxpayers, permitted to accumulate through the power of compounding interest, and only after many years and massive accumulation used to pay down the national debt. The idea, borrowed from Robert Walpole, was built on overweening confidence not only in the power of compounding but also on the way in which "the good [Richard] Price," as Karl Marx wrote, "was bedazzled beyond reason by the enormous quantities resulting from geometrical progression of numbers."[47] (Marx seized on a claim Price initially made in a note: that "a penny, put out to 5 per cent compound interest at our Saviour's birth, would by this time [1771], have increased to more than would be contained in 150 millions of globes, each equal to the earth in magnitude and solid gold.")[48] The sinking fund was eventually implemented by William Pitt in 1786, at a time in which confidence rested on the optimistic belief that peace would persist along with "a continual surplus of revenue over expenditure"—this was during a hopeful moment after the American Revolution but before anyone realized that a decades-long war with France was a few short years away.[49] But the sinking fund did not just rest on the expectation of peace. It mirrored Price's attitudes about moral conduct. Unmanaged debt, to be clear, was for Price a bad thing. He wanted the national debt paid down, among other things to avoid what he thought could be despotic consequences.[50] A host of traditional sins, for that matter, remained bad in and of themselves—it had not suddenly become acceptable for Unitarians to commit murder. But much as debt could now be handled through rational calculation, sin could be managed through rational understanding.[51] Changing views of sin and debt were not just emerging in tandem. They were mutually reinforcing.

Yet hardly anyone was as lucky as the wealthy Unitarians, who, at their wealthiest, represented a fraction of the population of an already demographically marginal denomination. Far more common were Britain's tradesmen, one out of every four of whom during Price's era found their way at least once in their lives to debtors' prison. Here debt was not a key to growth but a trademark of economic precarity, which, in turn, was fundamentally tied to one's sense of self-value. That was glaringly the case when debtors were jailed and lost their worth both emotionally and economically. But it was more broadly a possibility where incarceration loomed as a threat, the bodies of men and women themselves becoming objectified under these conditions, as the historian Tawny Paul writes, as "debt collateral."[52] Here, too, a social parallel could be drawn to what Barker maligned as the "dominion of sin" under which orthodoxy encouraged its believers perpetually to live.[53] Original sin had served to bind one to faith in Christ as the only redeemer—again, Barker's images of Luther's and Calvin's "shackles" and "fetters" resonate in both earthly and spiritual terms. In parallel, the dominion of debt in the eighteenth-century economy had bound countless people to faith in credit as their sole source of financial redemption.

The connection runs deeper. Being perpetually in debt was not just metaphorically related to original sin. Debt, or drowning in it, augured dismal spiritual prospects. This is exactly how Barker understood it during his diary-keeping years, thanks in no small part to the message driven home by his ministers, whom we have seen many times in this book tie prosperity to election and, by association, tie dwindling economic prospects to reprobation. What is more, Barker thought the pious were free from financial obligations in a way that suggested not only their spiritual election but also their greater ease in leading moral lives. "Neither Mr [George] Trosse nor Mr [John] Bunyan were in debt," Barker once complained in his godly diary, before anguishing that his indebtedness "hangs as a dead weight continually on me, sinks me even to deaths door."[54]

And again, as with watching and spectating or *homo augustinius* and *homo economicus*, the meanings are multiple. For those who accumulated fortunes, easily managing debt or being free from it altogether may have taken the sting out of sin. But for those who could not get out from underneath their debt, the effect was in more than one way imprisoning. Even further, the places where selfishness did not just survive but gathered strength as an anthropological major premise during the enlightened age are also the places where debt survived as a marker of a kind of depravity. Here there may be a parallel in the way in which Martin Heidegger borrowed from Augustinianism but with no apparent interest in redemption. Heidegger regularly invoked the concept of *Schulden*, a German word meaning both "debt" and "sin" and a vestige of his early absorption in Augustinian theology. The philosopher Simon Critchley puts it this way. In Heidegger's pessimistic terms, "life is a series of repayments on a loan that you didn't agree to, with ever-increasing interest, and which will cost you your life—it's a death-pledge, mort-gage."[55] In the shadow original sin cast over commercial society, one could say too that life brings inherited debt for a sin one did not commit. But at least for Luther a supplication went forth. As the *Luther Bibel* (1545) translated the pivotal line from the "Lord's Prayer," smearing together the tenor and the vehicle: "[F]orgive us our sins [*Sünden*], for we also forgive all who are indebted [*schuldig*] to us."[56] Heidegger was no devotee of enlightened political economy, but in Critchley's gloss he captures the overlap between anthro-pessimism and a condition of perpetual debt in which prayers for forgiveness—whether for *Schulden* or for *Sünden*—hardly need to be sent forward.[57]

The poet John Milton, like Richard Baxter, stood poised between Puritanism and Enlightenment. But it is telling that, if Pentecost Barker regarded "Honest Dick" Baxter as an Old Dissenter of lasting integrity (Barker uses the word *honest* in relation to John Bunyan too), he saw Milton—and was enlivened by what he saw—as far more iconoclastic. On one occasion, when he wanted to justify having arrived at his notion of the particle by way of conscience, he quoted Milton as a legitimating authority. "I argue not / Against Heav'n's hand or will, nor bate a jot / of heart or hope, but still bear up and steer / Right Onward."[58] In the same vein, Barker and Merivale were convinced, as were many others, that Milton was a Unitarian.[59] The letter of Barker's that starts his conversation with Merivale on the subject does not survive. But Merivale's response, a lengthy defense of this view of Milton, does.[60] Barker wrote back with simple agreement: "[T]hat Milton should be a Unitarian is surely facile to believe."[61]

There is another, more subtle unorthodox notion implied in *Paradise Lost,* and it revolves around Eve's readiness to get started with the less-than-Edenic life that she anticipates before the Fall. Even before she leaves paradise, that is, she longs to work. Her heroism in the poem is debatable. But one of the most careful scholars has noted that Milton "accords Eve important areas of initiative and autonomy that further qualify patriarchal assumptions." For example, she asked penetrating questions about the cosmos and divine grace. She writes the first autobiographical narrative, "with the implications autobiography carries of coming to self-awareness, probing one's own subjectivity, interpreting own's own experience, and so becoming an author." And, not least, she "proposed the proto-capitalist idea of the division of labor to help meet the problem of the garden's burgeoning growth."[62] Like the characters in *Candide* once they desist with their aimless behavior, or like John Laurence, the pastor we met earlier in this book precociously and bucolically using the phrase *enlightened age,* Eve wants to cultivate her garden. What sets her apart is that she wants to do so even when her garden is Eden. For her, paradoxically, Eden is not paradise until it accommodates a condition of the Fall.

There is a rabbinical interpretation of the Fall that says that agricultural work was required from the moment of human creation while the kind of labor the Fall made necessary was instead the study of the Torah.[63] That almost sounds like Milton's Eve, but she was created in a religious tradition that looked on physically arduous work, the labors of childbirth, and virtually any activity that required more effort than taking Eden's handouts as woes packaged into inherited sin (Gen. 3:16).[64] There is therefore something theologically destabilizing about Eve's valorization of labor. She takes the sting out of the punishment for the Fall. This is not to say that idleness is then recommended as labor's alternative—that recommendation is virtually never uttered in the corpus of mainstream early modern opinion making. Nor is it to deny that labor could play an important spiritual role, one modeled on the way in which Christ made toil part of his effort to save fallen humanity.[65] But where hard work was seen as having the laudable effect of redirecting the mind and the body to the reality of human depravity, the rationale was precisely that work was a *burden*. As Matthew Henry put it in his influential and widely read biblical commentary: "[L]abour is our duty, which we must faithfully perform: we are bound to work, not as creatures only, but as criminals; it is part of our sentence, which idleness daringly defies. . . . [U]neasiness and weariness with labour are our just punishment, which we must patiently submit to, and not complain of, since they are less than our iniquity deserves."[66] The cultural distance between work as part of Adam's sin and work as parsed by Adam Smith—for whom labor was the "cause of the greatest publick prosperity"—is vast.[67]

There is something else destabilizing about Milton's Eve being the character who foretells a new view of labor. Early modern glosses on original sin always blame Adam for the Fall. The standard formulation is *Adam's sin*, not *Eve's sin*. But in no sense was this not sexist. On the scales of patriarchal logic, the decisions that register were made by the husband. Eve may have given into temptation first, but she is not even given the agency to take the blame for her mistake. Adam is. Milton's Eve is therefore already a departure from convention by virtue of getting so much airtime. But, what is more, her valuation of work resonates with the hopefulness of the poem. The *paradise* of *Paradise Lost* may on one level refer to the republican experiment that ended with the restoration of the status quo in 1660. In another sense, however, a different kind of paradise lies on the horizon as Adam and Eve walk away from Eden with the benefits of their apparent free will. Richard Baxter, as we noted, lamented the way in which orthodox views of original sin empowered the first human couple to exercise agency in such a consequential act that they closed off the agency of everybody else. One could look at Eve's outlook as if it expresses the same theological dissatisfaction that Baxter felt, in which case it is possible to see in the fulfilling work that Eve and her children (i.e., humankind) will carry on after Eden the same agency she displayed when she ate the forbidden fruit.

If this reading has merit, one could view Milton as, put simply, valorizing labor, in which case he was not alone among the fallen Augustinians. John Locke captured the same underpinning economic logic in a letter on interest rates sent to the House of Commons not long after the Revolution of 1688. England's prosperity, he argued, required abandoning conventional economic wisdom: "In a Country not furnish'd by Nature with mines of Gold and Silver . . . there are but two ways of growing Rich . . . either Conquest, or Commerce." By conquest "the Romans made themselves masters of the Riches of the world," but, since England was relatively deprived of precious metals and "no Body is vain enough to entertain a Thought of our reaping the Profits of the World with our Swords," commerce was, he reasoned, "the only way left to us, either for Riches or Subsistence."[68] The common view that Locke was rejecting was that wealth instead derives from value intrinsic to natural resources, a key part of what Adam Smith would later characterize as *mercantilist* assumptions, according to which the way to sustain and expand economic power was to hoard treasures (made of metals derived from mining), to expand territory (more land meant more sources of value), and to use the muscular power of the state to acquire and hold on to that territory.[69] The view Locke favored held, instead, that value was ultimately generated by labor. Locke and other Whigs were acutely aware of the fact that, despite a small population and a small landmass, Dutch industriousness and commerce had helped create a remarkably wealthy and autonomous society. There was no reason, they thought, that England could not follow the same path.[70]

But the salient point again operates in two ways. On the one hand, there was something anti-Augustinian in the reconsideration of labor. This is yet another way in which political economy and original sin were incompatible *morally*: work was coming to be characterized not as punishment but as the key to national prosperity. On the other hand (and as with selfishness, watching, and debt), labor possessed social value in its rootedness in long-standing skepticism about self-control. Once again, that is, political economy benefited from habits cultivated in the regime of original sin. Milton, Locke, and others who shared their outlook may not have been coming toward a Puritan work ethic in the way that Weber suspected. Milton and Locke, for example, both wanted little to do with what Weber thought was the all-important doctrine of predestination. But they both point to the phenomenon Weber did set out to explain: the conflation of life with *work*.

Admittedly, there are lots of opinion makers who had long recommended work as a countervailing habit. Biblical scripture clearly offers it as an antidote to disorder. "Let him that stole, steal no more, but rather let him labour," runs Ephesians 4: 28, which is quoted more than once in the Westminster Assembly, the Calvinist confession of faith—and quoted there in relation to the economically tinged Eighth Commandment ("thou shalt not steal"). And certainly these kinds of prescriptions were not unique to English or Puritan writers. "Chi fatica è tentato da un demonio, chi stà in otio da molti" (those who work hard are tempted by one devil, those who are idle are tempted by a hundred), runs an Italian expression noted in an eighteenth-century English collection of popular moral proverbs.[71] But there is nevertheless something even more economically tinged in the Janus-faced English writers who were situated between Puritanism and Enlightenment. For Richard Baxter, writing in the *Saints Everlasting Rest* (1650), the devil is kept away "by keeping the heart imployed." If *imployed* is not already loaded, Baxter explains in the rest of the text that, while keeping the heart busy matters, the saintly also needed to attend to mundane employment: "[A]s it is an encouragement to a Thief, to see your Doors open . . . so it will encourage Satan, to find your hearts idle; but when the heart is taken up with God, it cannot have while to hearken to Temptation. . . . If you were but busied in your lawful Callings, you would not be so ready to hearken to temptation."[72]

And once again there may be no author who so clearly reflected—and lastingly shaped—these broader changes as John Locke did. What gave Locke's thought "its integrity and human depth was," as John Dunn once wrote, "that of a deeply Puritan self," which is appreciable in Locke's most sustained blueprint for self-formation, *Some Thoughts concerning Education*.[73] Locke makes clear his aversion to *doctrinal* original sin when he asserts that, "of all the men we meet with, nine parts of ten are what they are, good or evil, useful or not, by their education" (the remaining 10 percent were, he thought, not unfixable but rather naturally smart enough to be spared the education others needed).[74] The pedagogy Locke assailed was, no less clearly, that of Reformed orthodoxy, with its unflinching advice to subdue the will of children, whose assumed depravity made them the long-suffering subjects of physical punishment and the inculcation of guilt.[75] Not least, what Locke promised for his theory verges on the transformation of human nature through controlled experience.

But all that said, Locke's alternative approach to education was not to leave children to their own agency. It was to shape their wills from the inside out. Alongside his comment about nine-tenths of humanity lies a more anthro-pessimistic assertion that, not far under the surface, we all possess a "natural propensity to indulge corporal and present pleasure," which was no less than "the root of all vicious and wrong actions." It may have been reasonable to believe that "every man must some time or other be trusted to himself, and his own conduct," but only after the cultivation of powerful habits that could countervail the corporeal urges.[76] The requisite skill of educators was therefore to find the right balance between discipline and restraint: to encourage self-control by betting against full-throated Augustinianism and granting a measure of individual freedom but to do so only after inculcating enough self-discipline to avoid Pierre Nicole's nightmare scenario of a self-absorbed free-for-all, a hypothetical scenario that Locke knew well from, among other things, having undertaken an English translation of Nicole's essays on morality.[77]

The grandson of a clothier, and perfectly aware of the importance of wool in the English economy at the time, Locke put forward the telling metaphor that, by education, good habits would be "woven into the very principle of [a student's] nature," a gradual, subtle, and thorough process that depended on a system of "esteem" and "disgrace." Like virtually everything in his education theory, the qualities—those both aimed for and unwanted—resonated economically. Apply "too strict a hand," and children "lose all their vigour and *industry*"; education should teach us to avoid "*luxury*" alongside pride and "*covetousness*"; worst is when bad educators break the mind, as Locke puts it, resulting in "a low spirited, moap'd [moped] creature . . . [who] will be, all his life, an *useless* thing to himself and others." By the same token, "esteem and disgrace" came down to something akin to solvency: "If you can once get into children a love of *credit*, and an apprehension of shame and disgrace, you have put into them the true principle, which will *constantly work*, and incline them to the right."[78] A proponent of the labor theory of value, Locke naturally looked toward the creation of valuable laborers. And key was a mode of self-discipline that too was born in residually Puritan watchfulness, although here retooled to prevent the excesses of commercial society from threatening otherwise useful habits, as happened when accumulation bled into luxury, or inutility and irregularity resulted from squandered autonomy, or insolvency arose from mishandled debt, and so on. In other words, Locke's pedagogy and the liberal society his model education was meant to sustain staked everything on the acquisition of self-control. And to fulfill that promise Locke drew from an Augustinian tradition that again possessed a dual legacy: it may have assumed self-control was profoundly elusive, but it nevertheless forged an array of methods to get as close to it as possible.

Even the otherwise anthro-optimistic Rousseau can be connected to this Augustinian habitus, if from a different angle and with a different aim. A recovering Augustinian with an abiding interest in the economy (he wrote the massive entry on the economy for Diderot and d'Alembert's *Encyclopédie*, which later became his *Discourse on Political Economy*), Rousseau was attuned to the political and social dangers of amour propre if not properly sublimated. In his own work on education, *Émile*, he also offered a theory built, more than Locke's, for an egalitarian economic and political purpose and even more ingenious in concealing the process of discipline. Also more bracingly than Locke, Rousseau denied original sin—the fact that the human heart possesses no "original perversity" he asserted as an "incontestable maxim" in *Émile*. But he recognized that there was no going back to a state of nature prior to amour propre, the mode of self-perception that he was at pains to identify as a social creation. Working with the tools at hand was unavoidable. Rousseau's optimistic solution was therefore "to extend *amour propre* to other people" in order to "transform it into a virtue," which would, he hoped, lead to an understanding of justice and "the moral relations of beings."[79] In a political sense, this meant that amour propre would need to be sublimated to align individual interests with the general will. But the emotionally tinged economic sense of his formulations was no less crucial. To return to a pivotal line from his *Discourse on Political Economy* that we noted earlier, Rousseau hoped that people could come to love the "greater whole . . . with that exquisite feeling that every isolated man has only for himself."

The trick to achieving that hopeful outcome—"to transform into a sublime virtue the dangerous disposition that gives birth to all our vices"—was understandably cast as a paradox.[80] Amour propre had an unrivaled capacity to act as an agent of material growth, sustaining all the advantages of commercial society. But daring to use it made self-control all the more crucial. Education—the most systematic component of self-formation—therefore had to ensure that self-love would not take expression in such an unbalanced way that it threatened civic virtue, eroded political stability, or aggravated economic inequality. By de-moralizing amour propre, enlighteners were not, after all, making selfishness less potent. Just the opposite. They were giving it a gain of function over the Augustinian tradition, which made the antidote all the more crucial, especially where it had to solve the paradox underlying Rousseau's all-important notion of the general will: the paradox of freedom *as* obedience.[81] Insofar as *general* implies structure and *will* implies agency, Rousseau's notion is infamously confounding—how can structure and agency not exist in tension? No less vexing is the problem to which *The Social Contract* proposed the general will as the solution: how to obey only ourselves and remain as free as we were in the state of nature. But this was exactly where sublimated love would align agency with the greater whole. A system of public education would create citizens whose self-cultivation had been carefully designed to give them a taste of their truest freedom in the very scenarios in which their actions fell in line with the actions of others. If their fellow citizens had gone through the same education and learned to crave that same freedom, individual wills would line up with one another, and obedience to the generality would overlap with obedience to the self. Pentecost Barker never read *The Social Contract*, although, as we will see, he read Rousseau's novel *Julie*. But he hoped for something remarkably similar when he envisioned reason and love bringing particles closer to *Nous* as they also brought them into alignment. For both Barker and Rousseau, enlightenment to an enormous degree *was* alignment.

To be sure, there is something profoundly optimistic in all this. Imagining a society in which individual actions are so guided by common principles that they seem to harmonize autonomously is the definition of dreaming big. But for that reason the wariness and cunning—the residual Augustinianism at its most insidious in the normally Pelagian Rousseau—is no less remarkable. In *Émile*, pupils are given the illusion that they are the ones in charge even as every situation that requires choices is carefully curated by the educator. All this is in one sense to say that, even among otherwise anthro-optimistic authors, amour propre seems to be there to some degree in writings on political economy, waiting in the wings to complicate the optimism.

If there is an exception, an enlightened anthro-optimist who was thorough in rejecting the Augustinian tradition even while focused on the economy, it is Etienne-Gabriel Morelly, author of the book that so impressed Barker and Merivale, *Code de la nature*. Morelly wholly rejects amour propre, the origins and artifice of which he ties, more radically than does Rousseau, to private property. He also repudiated amour propre as the necessary starting point for a social theory. If Rousseau wanted to get beyond egoism, Rousseau still assumed the same egoism was the key to the escape route. But Morelly, an obscure French tax official about whom virtually nothing is known, was different. With his protosocialist ambition to abolish property ownership, he was interested not just in social equality but in trying to interrupt inequality's recurrence by imagining how to abolish the vestiges of anthro-pessimism. Morelly was radical Enlightenment at its most radical, anthro-optimism taken to the furthest degree, and spread across discursive realms, transforming theology as much as the economy. (Recall that it was Morelly's passing comment about impostors—"Shout as much as you like, impostors or fanatics, who have an interest in persuading us of chimeras"—that Barker committed to memory.)

Yet, whoever exactly he was, Morelly was also not just an eighteenth-century outlier. He was an Enlightenment outlier.

Amour propre, acquisitiveness, spectating, labor, debt, credit, remission—these were key terms and concepts of Enlightened economic thought. And their cultural legitimation ran up against moral barriers that rested on a long-standing view of human nature according to which overvalued self-worth was exhibit A in the case for human depravity, acquisitiveness was a vice, labor was a form of punishment, debt was another way of saying sin, remission and credit were tropes for a power over which Christ was supposed to have a spiritual monopoly, and commercial society as a whole could be seen as a predicament of fallen humankind in making amour propre, arduous labor, acquisitiveness, and so on such recurring woes.[82] In all these ways, original sin, if understood theologically, hindered the Enlightenment's general economic aims. But when enlighteners argued that self-love would not run amok if culturally reframed as amoral, or that labor was the key to creating value, or that debt could be profitably managed, they drew on the promise of disciplinary techniques that had been forged in the same Augustinian tradition that they sought to de-moralize. Doctrinal original sin may have impeded the emergence of modern capitalism. But the habits Augustinians had developed in order to control themselves could also be put to work for the same purpose.

None of this necessarily means that the Enlightenment's political economists would have welcomed the more woeful developments that can be traced to their vision. It is true enough that there is a version of eighteenth-century political economy that sounds crass in direct proportion to its concision. Bernard Mandeville made his case by way of a doggerel poem whose argument hardly needed to extend beyond its four-word subtitle: "Private Vices, Public Benefits." François Quesnay's case could be encapsulated in the term *laissez-faire*, which has become only more totemistic by retaining its original French form after the death of French as a lingua franca. Plenty of other authors, however, can easily be seen wringing their hands.

The widely read and multiauthored *Histoire des deux Indes* (1770), which sold eight times as many copies as *The Wealth of Nations* in the eighteenth century, is often taken as an elaboration of the notion that the gentle mores that attend the spread of commerce can, as Montesquieu put it, "cure destructive prejudices."[83] But, in fact, ambivalence pervades the *Histoire*, particularly in its concern that among the natural consequences of commercial development are monopolies, piracy, and slavery. The authors of the *Histoire* (Guillaume-Thomas Raynal was behind less of this work than was once assumed) had already condemned slavery in the first edition, but by the third edition, heavily rewritten by Diderot and published in 1780, the condemnation of slavery was highly emotional, and the proposal for what to do about it is, as the historian Anoush Terjanian has shown in detail, revealing of double-mindedness about the benefits and mollifying effects of commerce. Had the *Histoire* simply been dogmatic about *doux commerce*, then commerce should have been consistently theorized as the antidote to the problems that commerce creates. Yet the proposals the *Histoire* makes for ending the slave trade deviate from letting the system take care of itself and include a joint effort to eradicate slavery undertaken by the "sovereigns of the earth."[84] That is hardly laissez-faire.

Or again there is Adam Smith. While in Glasgow, first as a student and then as a professor, Smith was made aware of the hazards of emerging capitalism by the port city's imperial ties. He could later point to a "disparity of benefits," writes one of his biographers, in the way in which Glasgow's trade in tobacco with Chesapeake stunted urban growth, limited opportunities for colonial merchants, and disproportionately rewarded Scottish factors. That he argued for the disutility of slavery may, in the same vein, owe something to his having been discomfited by Glaswegian merchants who profited from being shareholders in slave ships even after the city had given up the slave trade in the 1760s.[85] And while Mandeville laid out his economic theory in rhymed couplets, *The Wealth of Nations* tops out at nearly 400,000 words, with its caveats, qualifications, and concerns—about empire, slavery, monopolies, even the thought that the division of labor, so celebrated in the opening pages, might limit the occasions for a worker "to exert his understanding or to exercise his invention," leading him to a place where, without a system of public education, he would be "as stupid and ignorant as it is possible for a human creature to become."[86] Marx knew these words well and quipped that Smith nevertheless thought to offer a countervailing education in "homeopathic doses."[87] But Smith does not have to meet Marx's standards for his ambivalence to be taken seriously.

Again, we come to the fact that original sin was renounced by the Enlightenment but renounced *differently*. In relation to political economy, the renunciation was on one level dramatic: it amounted to a moral inversion, which aimed to turn unsavory tendencies into normative cultural habits. But on another level that very moral renunciation was assisted by a presumption of psychological continuity. This raises the question whether it is here in the retention of elements of the Augustinian tradition that the Enlightenment has been most unfinished, at least when imagined from the perspective of its anthro-optimists. If "St Augustine took the worst of St Paul, and Calvin the worst of St Augustine," as the Cambridge theologian Harry Williams once put it, then political economists may have found a way to one-up Calvin by taking something still worse—the eternal selfishness with none of the moral condemnation.[88]

Even Adam Smith weighed the costs and benefits of his new system. Even Smith, one could say, encourages its continual reappraisal. If modern capitalism settled into place as economic habits traded places with original sin, then any such reappraisal ought to begin with a basic question. What is it worth to remain in Augustine's debt?

CHAPTER NINE

"This is my Man"

I have no notion of a positive man, who will quarrel with me, or call me a Fool . . . for not pinning my faith on his sleeve. I love the diffident, such as conceive or say, these are my present thoughts. This is my Man.

PENTECOST BARKER
to Samuel Merivale, March 12, 1761

In 1760, the *London Magazine,* one of the longest-running periodicals in Britain and for Barker and Merivale a regular source of reviews of new books, reprinted a pamphlet with the lengthy, unsubtle, but revealing title "A Speech Delivered by an Indian Chief in Reply to a Sermon Preach'd by a Swedish Missionary, in Order to Convert the Indians to the Christian Religion." The prefatory paragraph offered the context:

> In 1710, a Swedish missionary preached a sermon at an Indian Treaty, held at [Conestoga in Pennsylvania], in which sermon he set forth original sin, and the necessity of a mediator; and endeavored by certain arguments to induce the Indians to embrace the Christian religion. After he had ended his discourse, one of the Indian chiefs made a speech, in reply to the sermons; the discourses on both sides were made known by interpreters. The missionary, on his return to Sweden, published his sermon, and the Indian's answer. Having wrote them in Latin, he dedicated them to the university at [Upsala], and desired them to furnish him with arguments to confute such strong reasoning of the Indian.[1]

What makes the pamphlet notable is not what it says about original sin being used to secure the need for Christ. We have seen this enough to recognize it as standard procedure. What was striking was that, after patiently listening to the Swedish missionary's sermon, one of the Susquehannock men in attendance countered with the deistic argument that he and his forebears had already lived moral lives, implying that religious truth comes not from a text like the Bible but from someplace more broadly accessible. Even more, this "Indian," with his "strong reasoning," turns the tables around, arguing that, despite the presumption of European missionaries to know more about morality than everyone else, their sordid deeds in America demonstrated that Christianity is as depraved as its invidious doctrines.

On the face of it, this looks too obviously like the enlightened conceit of using a counterfeited cultural outsider to comment on a European debate. Much as the fictional characters Uzbek and Reza operate as critics of eighteenth-century France in Montesquieu's *Persian Letters* (1721), this ingenious indigenous orator, pushing back against a Swedish evangelical, makes the case for rational religion too perfectly. But the "Indian's Speech," as it was later called, was not made up. A decade before 1710, a missionary named John Auren had preached on original sin and the necessity of Christianity to a group of people at Conestoga who found the sermon lacking.[2] Auren was struck enough by one man's counterargument to write it down and send it to a friend in Sweden, Eric Biörck, who several years later gave it to his son Tobias. In 1731, Tobias graduated from the University of Upsala and included the speech in his dissertation on the churches in America.[3] At some point shortly after, the speech was extracted from the dissertation—probably by a sympathetic deist—before it made its way into print as a stand-alone pamphlet and eventually as a reprint in the *London Magazine*.

Historians have noticed the "Indian's Speech" if only because it formed the basis of *Remarks concerning the Savages of North America* (1784), a late-life writing of Benjamin Franklin's that tried to upend the notion of savage. ("Savages we call them," the ironic first line of the *Remarks* reads, "because their manners differ from ours, which we think the Perfection of Civility; they think the same of theirs.")[4] Franklin found in the speech an encapsulation of deism, and he used it in his *Remarks* to illustrate the connection between religious orthodoxy and settler exploitation.[5] Having, like Barker, swerved from orthodoxy earlier in life, Franklin was also in the unusual position of being able to broadcast his ideas from a very public platform. And in the last and arguably most arresting of his "Thirteen Virtues," which he laid out to capture the ethos of his memoirs and to promote a model self for the young American republic, Franklin told his readers to "Imitate Jesus and Socrates."[6]

In so many words, that advice got at the heart of what, after finishing his sermon on original sin, the Swedish evangelical was so startled to hear from someone in his audience: Jesus does not necessarily matter. Franklin might have made the same point by telling his readers to imitate the Susquehannock philosopher whose oratory effectively expressed the same idea: Christianity does not necessarily matter.[7]

Much of what we have seen in this book can be drawn from the image of a Swedish missionary trying to impress on a non-Christian that, without original sin, there is no Christianity and that, without Christianity, there is no entrance into heaven. On the eve of the Age of Enlightenment, and on the frontier of the British Empire, it is not a European at all who articulates the universalist response that was later so important to Pentecost Barker, not to mention to Benjamin Franklin. Like the Bengalis in Devonshire, the figure who gets to this core idea is an *outsider*, a word used with some irony given that it signifies someone who says as much about connections as about spatial or cultural boundaries.

But there is more to the story. When the "Indian's Speech" found its way into print, it not surprisingly provoked an orthodox response. A year after printing it, the *London Magazine* published a rebuttal written by someone under the pen name Christianus Damnoniensis, Latin for "Devonshire Christian." "Christianus" had come across the "Indian's speech" in the *London Magazine* and wholly rejected its universalist case. Revelation and scripture are exactly what matter to salvation, Christianus replied. What Christianity therefore requires are precisely doctrinal guarantees—like original sin—of its exclusivity. At the end of the day, the "Indian Chief," Christianus concluded, was no more or less than an insensible "infidel."[8]

But the "Indian's Speech" also found defenders among figures less prominent than Franklin. In early 1762, six months after publishing Christianus's rebuttal, the *London Magazine* published one more piece on the pamphlet, a letter to the magazine written as a rejoinder to Christianus's rebuttal. "I have observed," it begins, "that disputants, instead of advertising to what is most likely to bring a controversy to an instructive, satisfactory conclusion, too frequently use methods productive of a contrary effect." In words that recall Barker and the "Methodistical gang," the letter implores an author—any author—never to use against an antagonist "the artillery of hell and damnation, personal reflection, malicious or futile expressions": "[N]or should he take anything for granted, that remains to be proved." The tone then turns polite but still pointed: "Your correspondent [Christianus] who favored us with remarks on the famous Indian speech, is one of the most moderate that I have read on his side of the question. But yet even him I think faulty in this, that he says, 'the infidel is worthy of the most dreadful condemnation.' For Sir, of what service can such expressions be to any cause? Till my judgment is convinced I can never truly, or acceptably believe. And if temporal or eternal punishments are threatened, to frighten me into a compliance, have I not great reason to suspect the truth of those opinions that need such a bugbear help? They may serve to intimidate children, but cannot in the least tend to convert men of common sense."[9]

The universalist defense of non-Christians, the aversion to threats of fire and brimstone, the repudiation of fear as a motive force, the invocation of sentiments held in common—all resonate with Barker's (or Franklin's) rationalist milieu. So, more curiously, does what comes next: the letter writer's list of his own thirteen virtues, although it would be better to call these thirteen *epistemological* virtues, characterized, as they were, as axioms in the service of religious knowledge: "I should be pleased if [Christianus] would first agree with me, concerning some axiomata, from which we might deduce and prove what may be advanced in the course of the controversy. If he does not object to the subsequent (what I think) self-evident truths, I shall have a right, with him, to take them for granted."[10]

The first three axioms, all enumerated in the original, are variations on the same theme:

1. A universal revelation should be such, as might be most easily, as well as universally understood.
2. It should not contradict itself.
3. Nor should it contradict experience, and demonstrable philosophy.

Rational and empirical criteria should be applied to religion, in other words. And any religion should sink or swim depending on whether it is obvious, free from contradictions, experientially intuitive, and expressible in philosophical terms. If it swims, then it should not produce disagreement among reasonable people, or so asserted the next axiom:

4. If learned and honest men (of both which qualities they have given the strongest proofs, by their writings, in vindication of, and sufferings for, their opinions) have differed, concerning what they call fundamentals and essentials in religion, deduced from any writing whatever; then those differences must be the result of want of capacity, in part, or in all of the persons differing, or in the writing itself.

Just as empty as contradictory religious precepts was the notion that a religion was accessible only to people who were closest to the moment of revelation, like the prophets of the Old Testament:

> 5. If there was as much necessity for mankind to understand a revelation now, as when it was first wrote, the same universally-benevolent and unerring spirit, that dictated it at first, would assist a number of translators, writing for publick benefit, so faithfully to translate it, that a true knowledge thereof might now be as easily attained as ever.

The divinity already implied in these precepts is then spelled out in the next four axioms, which invoke God both to check the hubris of Christianus and to establish the happy characteristics that belong to the deity but also, if to a lesser a degree, to human beings:

> 6. God is wiser than man.
> 7. With him is no variableness, nor shadow of turning.
> 8. He is so completely, so infinitely happy, that all that the whole of animated beings have done, now do, or ever can do, cannot in the least add to, or diminish from, the felicity of Deity; which is therefore unalterable.
> 9. The amiable qualities in man are possessed by the Deity in the highest degree.

Given the assertions listed above, smearing believers of any faith as *infidels* would be unfair. Much as Locke and Limborch thought every sect contained both evangelicals and papists, the axioms offered in the *London Magazine* suggest that every sect—even among the "Antichristians"—contains people driven by conscience, which is itself aimed at "the human race in general":

> 10. There are, or have been, good men among every sect of Christians, and among some Antichristians, *i.e.*, such men as have been desirous of thinking, speaking, and acting a-right, *i.e.*, of producing the greatest possible good, to the human race in general, and to themselves, in particular.

It was then left to the eleventh and twelfth axioms not only to rescue but also to venerate heterodoxy. Conscience demands unfettered opportunity to dissent. Heterodoxy should therefore always represent the avant-garde in the effort to find religious truth, while that avant-garde will for its part represent the more "valuable" members of any religion as it unrelentingly searches for the truth:

> 11. Should such persons be heterodox, either by want of capacity, or opportunity of better information, or both; yet, they must be more valuable, in the eye of Deity, than the more orthodox; who have acquired their orthodoxy otherwise than by a rational disquisition, a free enquiry.
> 12. It is every man's natural right and duty to think for himself; and, after he has done his utmost to get information, to judge upon such evidence as he may have procured.

Finally, axiom thirteen turns to the subject of sin, which was the issue that the Swedish missionary first claimed required Christ's intervention. But far from looking like an inherited stain, sin is simply an action that all rational beings know is wrong:

> 13. Sin, universally defined, is a violation of reason; particularly defined, it is an agent's violating what he thinks a law of Deity.

The "axiomata" thus expressed, the author signs off with a pen name, as did Christianus and countless other writers in the eighteenth century who were looking to refashion and protect their identities. Only this pen name, spelled out in all caps, PHILALETHES, we have seen before.

Was this *our* Philalethes? Was it Pentecost Barker giving us our one chance to witness him systematically lay out his views for theoretically all the world to see, writing not in the fragmented, casual, rambling prose of his letters but in the perspicacious and careful language of philosophy and theology? Admittedly, more than one writer in the eighteenth century used the pen name Philalethes—even more than one who published in the *London Magazine*. But neither the timing of the letter's publication nor the ideas it contains fit with any other author I can identify.[11] Barker also never mentions this letter in his correspondence with Merivale. On the surface that is odd. But the issue of the *London Magazine* I am quoting from came out in February 1762. By then old and infirm, Barker was hardly writing any letters to Merivale—there is not a single letter between January 23 and March 31, 1762. He may have had no occasion to tell Merivale that something he had written had gotten published. Three years earlier in their correspondence, on the other hand, he asks Merivale to read a letter—a different letter—that he expressly says he would eventually send to the *London Magazine*.[12] Two years after that, he again asks Merivale to read a letter he wants to place in a magazine, although here he doesn't say which one. We know Barker wrote a lot of letters. We know he read the *London Magazine* and tried to get at least one letter published in it. We know from many of his other comments that he defended—and borrowed from—non-Christians and their beliefs.[13] And we can only imagine that Barker might have felt emboldened to confront an opponent whose very name, Christianus Damnoniensis, said: "*I* am the Devonshire Christian." Being from Plymouth, Barker was of course from Devonshire too. And being a self-identifying Christian who also believed that "no man can be a Christian without being a deist," he would have had much reason to challenge Christianus's implicit claim about whom Christianity should exclude.[14]

On top of all that, what Philalethes's letter in the *London Magazine* conveys is what Barker believed. Here it is worth recalling the purser's image of "sinless beings" coming to earth from one of the "numberless worlds" of the universe in a "Fleet of Ships." In the logic of that image, any sin that an intelligent being commits is a deviation from its own inherent reasonableness. Just as in the thirteenth axiom, sin is unreason, while sinlessness is like the deity itself: reasonableness at its most eminent. As an act of being unreasonable, sinning meant even further that one had lost sight of *Nous*, which, given the particle's chip-off-the-old-block relationship to the divine, effectively meant that one had lost sight of oneself. The Susquehannock orator was told—by a different kind of alien who too had come in a fleet of ships—that he was contaminated by original sin. But Philalethes, his defender in the *London Magazine*, was implicitly saying that the whole notion of original sin—like the orthodox notion of sin itself—was wrong. People are not *contaminated* by sin. No one lives under its *dominion*. *Sin* is simply a word for what everyone has the sense to know is wrong.

Can we be sure that this was Pentecost Barker writing in the *London Magazine*? Not absolutely. But if this was not the purser from Plymouth, then there was another person in the English-speaking world sending off letters at the same moment that Barker was enlivened with ideas in his correspondence with Charistes, reading and writing to the same magazine, using the same pen name to express, in detail, the same beliefs. It seems unlikely that this was not our man. But if it is also not impossible, then a different Philalethes would be all the more suggestive. A remarkable archive exists for getting at the life of Pentecost Barker, understanding his motives, thinking about the ideas he reflected and, for his own purposes, reshaped. For those who left no archival trace, the stories are like sentient beings spread across the numberless worlds of the universe:

the details may have to be left to the imagination, but it is still easier to believe than to deny that such people existed.

When taken in their own way to the limits of the imagination, anthro-optimism and anthro-pessimism are paradoxical. Belief in the perfectibility of human beings looks toward a state in which cruelty and selfishness are effaced by benevolence. But how does this humane path to perfection not eventually carry us to the point where humanness, as it has long been understood, ends? When pushed to its extreme, anthro-optimism offers salvation by way of extinction, sparing us from ourselves if we cease *being* ourselves. Anthro-pessimism, for its part, entails a selfish indifference to other people, nowhere more obviously than in its reduction of humane feeling to a social illusion, a knock-on effect of selfishness enmeshed in a web of social interdependence. But it is that same hopeless assumption that our selfish ways will never change that guarantees that we remain recognizably human, for whatever that ends up being worth in the eternal recurrence of bad behavior.

Implied in these extremes may be part of the reason that Alexander Pope's anthro-irenic *Essay on Man* resonated with such opposed figures as Rousseau and Voltaire. For Pope, as we saw, extreme consequences in thinking about human nature could be avoided if "man" occupies "a middle state . . . with too much knowledge for the sceptic side . . . and too much weakness for the stoic's pride."[15] Barker's view of human nature—and for that matter his self-perception—was in a basic sense no different. He too thought that by being inexact Pope had gotten it exactly right. Yet just as with Voltaire and Rousseau, whose views varied dramatically despite their admiration of a moderate view of human nature, Barker too was located more toward one end of the anthropological continuum than the other.

One of the purser's last letters was in this respect one of his most intriguing. Written in January 1762, nine months before his death and six months before his final transmission to Merivale, Barker began by admitting that his taste for possessing physical books was beginning "to flag." He still believed that books were "mental food and exceedingly good diet," as Merivale had once described them. But he remembered too that as Sophron's estate was being settled, affairs got messy when the executors had to decide who should get which books from the minister's large library. Barker had lost out on some titles that Sophron had promised were coming his way, and now that he was cleaning his own house in preparation for the end, he seemed to believe that his heirs would be better off if he had fewer things for them to fight over.[16]

Possessing books was not the same as reading them, however. The latter activity Barker still enjoyed. And he assured Merivale in the same letter that he was especially enjoying reading an author never mentioned in the correspondence until late 1761, Jean-Jacques Rousseau. Merivale and Barker almost seem not to know who Rousseau is when his name first appears in their letters. "In the last Gentleman's Magazine," wrote Merivale in October 1761, "there is a very lively satire on Eloisa [*Julie; or, The New Heloise*] by Voltaire, who I suppose bears an enmity to the very name of Rousseau; for I know not that this author is related to his old poetical antagonist of that name."[17] The "old poetical antagonist" Merivale was thinking of was Jean-Baptiste Rousseau. Once again, Merivale indicated his savvy by knowing that Voltaire and Jean-Baptiste had a feud of their own. It is striking, all the same, that Merivale writes about Jean-Jacques as if the name was new to him. Rousseau had not yet published *The Social Contract* or *Émile*. But he had certainly established an international reputation with his *Second Discourse on Inequality* (1755), a book Barker and Merivale surprisingly never mention or even allude to.

Merivale, in any case, was more put off than entertained by Voltaire's disparaging comments about *Julie*, Rousseau's runaway bestseller and one of the century's most widely read books. He could admit that "there seems room given for many of [Voltaire's] reflections severe as they are." But he qualified: "[A]nd yet I should entertain no better an opinion than the author himself of the man or woman who can't read to the end of the work without being much more pleased than offended with it." Merivale was also, for his part, drawn to what Rousseau had to say about sexual attraction and unrequited love—*Julie* was in part a retelling of the story of Peter Abelard and Héloïse d'Argenteuil, whose tragic love affair in the twelfth century had ended with Abelard's castration. Merivale used the occasion to regale Barker with a story of his own frustrated early love.[18]

Barker was always interested, however, in what authors had to say about the divine intelligence. Rousseau was no exception. The purser could admit (without specifying) that in *Julie* there were "some things that I could wish had not been there," but he was "highly taken" with many things that were in the book, and "this particularly, with which I am charmed," he wrote before quoting a line from the earliest English translation of the novel: "'I could sooner be induced to believe the Bible corrupted and unintelligible than that God can be made violent or unjust.'"[19] One thing that resonated with Barker, that is, was Rousseau's Christian deism. But he rambled through digressions in his letter to get to something even more important to him: the subject of sin, to which he turned right after quoting from the novel. Merivale had brought up lust for sex. Barker was thinking about lust too, with the operative object of lust being, as ever, alcohol. But with Rousseau now fresh in his mind, he was also thinking about lust in and of itself. Rousseau found a way in almost everything he wrote to say that moral transgression could be discounted when defined by unthinking convention rather than authentic feeling. Barker latched onto that idea in relation to lust and sin. "I think I observed to you," he wrote Merivale, "that there are many who sin, not from Malice or repugnancy to the divine being, but are swayed by the impetuosity of their lusts." Then he moved even closer to the Rousseauian view—his own implied view too—that behavior is in some measure socially conditioned: "Some from bad example are led into sin without considering what [sins] are about. Boys at school are taught to sin before they know what sin is." He was careful, however, to separate these sinners whose actions derive from circumstances beyond their control from those who seem to exercise more agency: "[T]here are also calm, considerate sinners, who live on years in what to others appear great crimes. Now unless these have made themselves believe their practices are not sinful, the will must accompany such, and they are willful and presumptuous sinners."[20]

Before he has a chance to clarify, particularly what he means by people who believe "their practices are not sinful" (was he thinking of Antinomians, who in the assurance of their spiritual election often try to experience sin as if it is not sin?), Barker leaves Rousseau behind, temporarily. He takes a break from writing to Merivale and goes off to read a review of Robert Boulton's *Letters and Tracts on the Choice of Company* (1761), a recently published book that, among other things, warned against intemperance in drinking.[21] He did not say much about the review, but it seemed to push him further into reflection on his own past behavior, which in turn led him to wonder how responsible he, as opposed to the "wicked apprentices" who tempted him in his youth, had been for his alcoholism. Almost incredibly, this is the one moment in his letters when he intently raises the question of personal responsibility in relation to his drinking: "Myself having experienced the truths there [in Boulton] delivered, viz, that the very strict education, precepts, and example of my truly pious mother were defaced by the force and power of my father's (hell hounds I may call them) apprentices. It was beginning before her death but when that dreadful judgment came on the family no one now alive but poor I knows the lamentable consequences of it, to my dear father and his three unhappy children. I cannot proceed—the remembrance is so afflictively striking."[22]

Barker again seems to stop writing. Or, in any case, this is where the paragraph in his letter ends, and it is easy enough to imagine him pausing, given his painful memories of his mother's death, his father's anguish, and the bad things he had done both to his long-deceased parents and to himself. When he does eventually start a new paragraph, he returns to the topic of sin, but, almost as if led by his memories back to the mode of his diary, he merges the broader language of philosophy with the gospel and alludes to 1 John 3:9: "Whosoever is born of God doth not commit sin; for his seed remaineth in him: and he cannot sin, because he is born of God." It is a curious allusion. Barker almost always articulates his notion of the particle in the terms of abstract philosophy, while he quotes the Bible even more rarely in his letters than he references Jesus. In this late-life letter, however, he finds something analogous to the particle in the biblical metaphor of a seed. And as he returns to the subject of sin he now brings into the equation the question of how far one can go with perfection. One thing he says unambiguously is that full perfection—which we might translate into Barker's own terms as *sinlessness*—is impossible. Not for the first time can we see the limits of Barker's anthro-optimism. But his crucial point is that we can all still get out from underneath the *dominion* of sin. The meandering but coherent passage is worth quoting in full, not least to hear Barker's voice one last time:

> I've long thought that nothing can be meant by these words [1 John 3:9] but that a good man cannot sin with approbation or consent of will with a consciousness of what he is about, i.e., not to continue and carry on a course of sin, for as to perfection and living without some steps and falls it is out of the question. But such a one is not under the dominion of sin. He's not commanded or controlled by it. I entirely agree with you, that we all have a ruling passion, a sin that easily besets us. I know but too well. Truly. I never yet met with a truer account of man . . . than Pope's Essay. But what hath such a weak mortal as I am to do with such remarks? I look on myself of no more significance than a flea in the creation, but when the particle, which I cannot give up, comes into my mind, against this darling sin [the sin dictated by the ruling passion, i.e., drinking] a man should fight was he to live 100 years of age and die in the last dyke. Unless the mind or will accompany the act for the present there can be no act at all. Did not Peter know that he denied Christ? Did not [Thomas] Cranmer know that he put his name to a renunciation? Yet how soon did they both see their great sin? Yet I know not how to call even their sin a presumptuous one. A man in company resolves to come out sober yet, as it is too common, some favorite toast is proposed. He consents

> and is perhaps by one glass too much carried off from his resolution. This man is not a determined drunkard.[23]

It is worth saying again: not until this moment, and not after, does Barker so intently and extensively comment in his letters about his earlier drinking. Having thought about the nature of things through the perspective of countless figures, from the individualist Locke to the socialist Morelly, from mystical Islam to the anonymous author of the four lines handed to him by the French army captain, from Socrates to (very likely) the Susquehannock philosopher, he was also now thinking with Rousseau—and for that matter with Robert Boulton—and reaching the conclusion that drinking, his worst sin, never made him a "presumptuous sinner." Looking back at his past from the end of his life, and filtering virtually everything through his rejection of the determinisms of orthodoxy, he was here affirming that he was never a "determined drunkard."

In Barker's image of "sinless beings" from another world, there was no place for *original* sin, a doctrine that was already hard enough to sustain after the New World undermined the settlement story of Noah's son but that was provincialized, along with Eden, into total cosmic insignificance by the prospect of extraterrestrial life. Yet Barker was doing more with his otherworldly image than trying to drive a nail into Calvin's coffin. Beyond an innocent birth, a state of sinlessness meant a full life lived without moral error. Enlightenment *was* sinlessness. For that matter, sinlessness *was* enlightenment. And both conditions, or the same condition by two names, came into closer view in direct proportion to how fully someone could access the love of *Nous*. But if sinlessness was the maximum case scenario of anthro-optimism and perfectibility, it is telling that Barker had to go off world to imagine fully enlightened beings, as if no human example could make the point, not even Socrates or Jesus. It is tempting to wonder whether he had imagined perfection to the degree at which flawless moral conduct renders us unrecognizable to ourselves. It is not out of the question. The erasure of human form was exactly what he thought would occur in a future state in which erstwhile people dwell as particles. If he erased form from our essence as he contemplated eternity, he may have done the same as he imagined infinity, filled with the endless possibilities of "numberless worlds." All this suggests that, on the one hand, when it came to what could be accomplished on earth, he may have believed that true perfection was out of reach—as out of reach as Rousseau's state of nature. But on the other hand, in the same spirit in which Rousseau hoped that people would still improve the self and society by imagining how free we had once been, Barker's thought experiments made room for improvement. Even though he had a lifetime of heavy drinking to show for his flaws, the mark of his hope was that somewhere along the way he also began to believe—and by experience had proved to himself—that he was fixable.

~

As seems true for the Enlightenment as a whole, there is something both definite and indefinite about Pentecost Barker. Or should we call him Philalethes? Pamphilius Rekrab? Peter Bentcoskar? It is easy to imagine him nodding in agreement with the epigraph from T. S. Eliot that opened this book. What matters in determining someone's outlook is not communism, capitalism, or fascist military processions. What matters is whether one believes in original sin.[24] Barker did not believe in it. Eliot did. But they both thought the same doctrine was a cultural threshold that, if crossed, would permit the rest to follow. And to a significant degree they were both right in saying that, at the very least, Enlightenment modernity rested on the rejection of doctrinal original sin.

But I have also tried to stress that the way that enlighteners rejected original sin mattered. When they leaned toward anthro-optimism, fully rupturing the Augustinian inheritance, they opened up a path to more selfless personal and cultural aims. When they remained committed to anthro-pessimism, however much their secularity represented a break from Augustine's theology, they also remained committed to the individualist self as both the organizing principle and the desired end. Not only is this broader pattern already bifurcated into a "selfless Enlightenment" and a "selfish Enlightenment" that together entail something less unitary than "the Enlightenment" with a capital *E* and a definite article; there were also untold positions located and maintained in between these extremes of optimism and pessimism. As much, then, as the patterns of anthropological faith offer an organizing principle, the details of philosophical positions, where exactly one lands on the sliding scale, and what their reasons were for landing there, are harder things about which to generalize. Look no further than Barker. In one sense, his life has been worth examining at length because it is only in the details that his motives, emotions, and experiences are made intelligible. In another sense, it is sobering that, even in the weeds of his relatively well-documented case, it can be hard to pin down aspects of his outlook. Did he or did he not, to take only one example, believe that bad souls were annihilated after death? He never firmly answered that question. And the implications are not trivial when it comes to his views of divine nature, justice, the power of forgiveness, or whether forgiveness could take shape as mitigating good deeds or something more like contrition.

The indefinite lurking in the definite may, however, get at something definitive by another route: the end of Barker's story, whose fitting conclusion should involve a measure of inconclusiveness. If Barker was the Philalethes in the *London Magazine*, then there is something else I hope my liberal quotations from that letter convey: his prose at its stiffest. It may also be at its most perspicacious. His position is clear, and in its clarity it captures not only his argument but also his cultural milieu in published, polished form. Reading his letters to Merivale, in contrast, can be an interpretive chore. I hope my profuse quotations illustrate that too. But despite the rambling tone, in his letters to Merivale Barker was in motion intellectually. In his reasoning through possibilities, his candor about everything from the people he loved to the moral failures of his era, or his willingness to make mistakes and be wrong, he rescued himself from the overweening confidence more typical of the era's intellectuals. "I have no notion of a positive man who will quarrel with me, or call me a Fool . . . for not pinning my faith on his sleeve," he wrote to his confidant Charistes before professing his affection for the limits of confidence: "I love the diffident, such as conceive or say, these are my present thoughts. This is my Man."

Barker was in this sense his own man, his own iteration of human nature, a Dissenter reborn as a dissenter. Hope was the mood, love the emotion, experience the proof. But salvation—from the version of himself who was convinced he would never be saved—had come from the leap of faith he took away from faith, where he could see his image reflected like so much in his world: in a light that brilliantly revealed how much had gone wrong as it also made clear, to those not blinded by it, how much further there still was to go.

ACKNOWLEDGMENTS

Research and writing were supported by a yearlong Mellon Fellowship at the Huntington Library, the Willis F. Doney Membership at the Institute for Advanced Study in Princeton, a grant from the National Endowment for the Humanities, fellowships at the Institute for European Studies at Cornell University, and several Hobart and William Smith faculty research grants. I thank the library and research staff at the Devon Heritage Center in Exeter, the West Devon Record Office in Plymouth (now The Box), the British Library, the National Archives at Kew, the John Rylands Library in Manchester, the Museum of Freemasonry in London, the Huntington Library in San Marino, the Institute for Advanced Study and Firestone Library in Princeton, the Folger Shakespeare Library in Washington, DC, the Warren Hunting Smith Library at Hobart and William Smith Colleges, and the Olin Library at Cornell University. Three archivists in Exeter—Renée Jackaman, Stuart Tyler, and Jan Wood—deserve special thanks for helping me track down the Barker-Merivale correspondence. Parts of the argument here appeared in Matthew Kadane, "Original Sin and the Path to the Enlightenment," *Past and Present* 235, no. 1 (May 2017): 105–40, and for comments and suggestions I thank the journal's editor, Alexandra Walsham, and five anonymous reviewers. I am also grateful to people who offered commentary after reading draft chapters or hearing talks given over the past decade in the United States and Europe: Sebouh Aslanian, Lauren Benton, John Brewer, Guillaume Calafat, Jonathan Clark, David Cressy, Vincenzo Ferrone, Joseph Glatthaar, Frank Guridy, Deborah Harkness, Daniel Hershenzon, Steve Hindle, Lynn Hunt, Robert Ingram, Jonathan Israel, Chris Kyle, Kevin Lambert, Marc Lerner, Ann Little, Lindsay O'Neill, Julie Park, Hal Parker, Emma Planinc, John Pocock, Helena Rosenblatt, Jesse Sadler, Catherine Secretan, Stephen

Snobelen, Justin Stearns, Daniel Strum, Naomi Taback, Francesca Trivellato, James Vaughan, Rachel Weil, and Kathleen Wilson. Closer to home I thank my faculty colleagues for their input at our regular seminar and in other settings: Matt Crow, Jodi Dean, Laura Free, Janette Gayle, Leslie Hebb, Clif Hood, Eric Klaus, Derek Linton, David Ost, Colby Ristow, Nick Ruth, Dan Singal, Virgil Slade, Sarah Whitten, and Lisa Yoshikawa. I owe thanks to Matt Gallaway for publishing advice and to Darrin McMahon, Dylan Montanari, and Fabiola Enríquez Flores for seeing the book through to publication. I also owe an immense debt to friends whose expertise and time I have regularly asked for while writing this book: David Hall, Tim Harris, Sue Juster, Brent Sirota, Jake Soll, and Bill Taylor. Above all, I thank Peg Jacob for always finding time to read rough drafts and to try to see what I was after. It is no mystery to me that Pentecost Barker felt love and hope when talking about big ideas with thoughtful people. I am lucky to know so many of them, beginning with the three to whom I dedicate this book.

NOTES

Chapter One

1. Increase Mather, *Wo to Drunkards: Two Sermons Testifying against the Sin of Drunkenness: Wherein the Wofulness of That Evil, and the Misery of All That Are Addicted to It, Is Discovered from the Word of God* (Boston, 1673), 5.

2. "Journal of Pentecost Barker, 1729–31," West Devon Record Office, Plymouth (WDRO), MS 581/14. The manuscript was written inside Edward Leigh, *Critica Sacra in Two Parts: ... The Second [Part Containing] Philologicall and Theologicall Observations upon All the Greek Words of the New Testament in Order Alphabetical*, 3rd ed. (London, 1650).

3. H. J. Jackson, *Marginalia: Readers Writing in Books* (New Haven, CT: Yale University Press, 2001), 33–36.

4. For a rare example of Barker referencing *Critica Sacra*, see "Journal of Pentecost Barker," September 25, 1730.

5. "Journal of Pentecost Barker," August 16, 1730.

6. Devon Record Office (DRO), MS 3237M/F1.

7. Philip Gibbs, *A Letter to the Congregation of Protestant Dissenters at Hackney* (London, 1737), 31. "Demonist is their proper denomination," wrote Samuel Merivale to Pentecost Barker about the orthodox. DRO, MS 3237M/F1, April 30, 1760. Although Anthony Ashley Cooper, the Third Earl of Shaftesbury, never used these words, Merivale told Barker that he was here drawing on him. The likely source is where, in the broader context of an attack on enthusiastic Calvinism, Shaftesbury writes: "[W]e know very well that in some religions, there are those who expressly give no other idea of GOD, than of a Being arbitrary, violent, causing ill, and ordaining to Misery; which in effect is the same as to substitute a DAEMON, or *Devil*, in his room." *Characteristicks of Men, Manners, Opinions, Times* (London, 1711), 2:10.

8. Ryder describes a meeting he and his fellow congregants held after an incendiary sermon preached by Thomas Walker, his minister at Mill Hill Chapel: "[A]fter a little conversation we had a Long debate about two Opposite discourses, One denying Original Sin, Another asserting it, And if Ministers begin to deny the Scriptures, I know not what will become of our Religion." John Rylands University Library, Special Collections, University of Manchester (JRUL), Unitarian MSS, Q/6, "Diary of Joseph Ryder, in

41 Volumes," December 20–21, 1756. For more on Ryder, Thomas Walker, and Mill Hill, see Matthew Kadane, *The Watchful Clothier: The Diary of an Eighteenth-Century Protestant Capitalist* (New Haven, CT: Yale University Press, 2013), chap. 7.

9. For Wesley's sermon, which was delivered on Fletcher's death in 1785, see John Fletcher, *An Appeal to Matter of Fact and Common Sense; or, A Rational Demonstration of Man's Corrupt and Lost Estate . . . to Which Is Now Added, the Life of the Venerable Author, Compiled for This Work from the Most Authentic Source, by J. Kingston* (1772; expanded reprint, Baltimore, 1814), 12.

10. Fletcher, *An Appeal to Matter of Fact*, 13.

11. Aaron Crossley Hobart Seymour, *The Life and Times of Selina, Countess of Huntingdon* (London, 1839), 10–11.

12. Much of this paragraph is drawn from G. R. Evans, *Augustine on Evil* (Cambridge: Cambridge University Press, 1982); and St. Augustine, *Against Julian*, trans. Matthew Schumacher (Washington, DC: Catholic University of America Press, 2004). On the ideas behind the doctrine before Augustine, see Pier Franco Beatrice, *The Transmission of Sin: Augustine and the Pre-Augustine Sources*, trans. Adam Kamesar (Oxford: Oxford University Press, 2013). Also see Ian A. Mcfarland, *In Adam's Fall: A Meditation on the Christian Doctrine of Original Sin* (Malden, MA: Wiley Blackwell, 2010); and Isabella Image, *The Human Condition in Hilary of Poitiers: The Will and Original Sin between Origen and Augustine* (Oxford: Oxford University Press, 2017). For the view that Paul held these notions as much as Augustine, see William David Davies, *Paul and Rabbinic Judaism* (New York: Harper & Row, 1948), 31–57.

13. The sexually transmitted disease metaphor for original sin is not my invention. It was used in the seventeenth century, if not earlier. See Philip C. Almond, *Adam and Eve in Seventeenth-Century Thought* (Cambridge: Cambridge University Press, 1999), 197.

14. St. Augustine, *The Confessions*, trans. Henry Chadwick (Oxford: Oxford University Press, 1992), 29.

15. John Fletcher, *The Works of the Reverend John Fletcher* (New York, 1836), 4:51. On the Fall and epistemology, see Peter Harrison, *The Fall of Man and the Foundations of Science* (Oxford: Oxford University Press, 2008).

16. Joseph de Maistre, *St. Petersburg Dialogues*, trans. Richard Lebrun (Montreal: McGill-Queen's University Press, 1983), 33.

17. Maistre quoted in Richard Lebrun, "Joseph de Maistre and Edmund Burke: A Comparison," in *Joseph de Maistre's Life, Thought, and Influence: Selected Studies*, ed. Richard Lebrun (Montreal: McGill-Queen's University Press, 2001), 153–72, 165.

18. This argument is discussed at length in Isaiah Berlin, "Joseph de Maistre and the Origins of Fascism," in *The Crooked Timber of Humanity*, ed. Henry Hardy (Princeton, NJ: Princeton University Press, 1990); and Joseph Mali and Robert Wokler, eds., *Isaiah Berlin's Counter-Enlightenment*, Transactions of the American Philosophical Society, n.s., vol. 93, pt. 5 (Philadelphia: American Philosophical Society, 2003). For a broader range of views of Maistre's thought, see Carolina Armenteros and Richard Lebrun, eds., *Joseph de Maistre and His European Readers: From Friedrich von Gentz to Isaiah Berlin* (Leiden: Brill, 2011).

19. "Pour ne pas oublier la chose capitale, / Nous avons vu partout, et sans l'avoir cherché, / Du haut jusques en bas de l'échelle fatale, / Le spectacle ennuyeux de l'immortel péché." These lines, from the poem "Le voyage," first appeared in the expanded and more widely known second edition of *Les fleurs du mal*, which was published in 1861, four years after the first edition. Charles Baudelaire, *Les fleurs du mal* (Paris: Poulet-Malassis et de

Broise, 1861), 309. See Daniel Vouga, *Baudelaire et Joseph de Maistre* (Paris: José Corti, 1957); and Damian Catani, "Notions of Evil in Baudelaire," *Modern Language Review* 102, no. 4 (2007): 990–1007.

20. Georges Sorel, *Réflexions sur la violence* (Paris: Librairie de "Pages libres," 1908). On Sorel's Jansenist roots, see George Hunstson Williams, "Four Modalities of Violence, with Special Reference to the Writings of Georges Sorel: Parts Two and Three," *Journal of Church and State* 16, no. 2 (Spring 1974): 237–61. On Maurras and Bossuet, see Michael Sutton, *Nationalism, Positivism and Catholicism: The Politics of Charles Maurras and French Catholics, 1890–1914* (Cambridge: Cambridge University Press, 2002), 54–56, 295 n. 35. Also see Pierre Lasserre, *Le romantisme français: Essai sur la révolution dans les sentiments et dans les idées au XIXe siècle* (Paris: Société du Mercure de France, 1907); Michael H. Levenson, *A Genealogy of Modernism: A Study of English Literary Doctrine, 1908–1922* (Cambridge: Cambridge University Press, 1984), 82–86; and Martha Hanna, *The Mobilization of Intellect: French Scholars and Writers during the Great War* (Cambridge, MA: Harvard University Press, 1996), 43.

21. The insinuation that Pelagianism was Jewish goes back to Augustine. See Burton L. Visotzky, "Will and Grace: Aspects of Judaising in Pelagianism in Light of Rabbinic and Patristic Exegesis of Genesis," in *The Exegetical Encounter between Jews and Christians in Late Antiquity*, ed. Emmanouela Grypeou and Helen Spurling (Leiden: Brill, 2009), 43–62, 45.

22. Although Brunetière thought the classical spirit embodied a formalist approach to art (an orthodoxy in aesthetics that, like that in theology, could curtail the excesses of individualism), he still could not help but characterize Bossuet as a singular figure: "[Bossuet] était trop lyrique! Son eloquence avait quelque chose de trop personnel pour un siècle ou ce que l'on mettait au-dessus de tout, c'étaitt la raison, dans ce qu'elle a de plus raisonnable, et entendez par la de plus 'universel,' de plus 'general,' de plus 'commun.' Elle avait quelque chose de trop 'mouvemente,' de trop libre, et part consequent de trop irrégulier pour un siècle ou l'originalité meme ne consistait qu'a exprimer supérieurement les idées de tout le monde." Ferdinand Brunetière, *Bossuet* (Paris: Hachette, 1913), 60. This parallels the way in which enemies of the Enlightenment ascribed such cultural potency to the philosophes that they helped make "gods of men," as Darrin M. McMahon puts it in *Enemies of the Enlightenment: The French Counter-Enlightenment and the Making of Modernity* (Oxford: Oxford University Press, 2001), 202–3. On Bossuet, see Jacques Truchet, *La prédication de Bossuet: Étude des themes* (Paris: Éditions du Cerf, 1960); and Patrick Riley, introduction to *Politics Drawn from the Very Words of Holy Scripture* (1709), by Jacques-Bénigne Bossuet, ed. and trans. Patrick Riley (Cambridge: Cambridge University Press, 1999), xiii–lxviii. On Brunetière's religious conversion, see Ferdinand Brunetière, "Après un visite au Vatican," *Revue des deux mondes* 7, no. 127 (1895): 97–118.

23. On the context, see Charles Ferrall, *Modernist Writing and Reactionary Politics* (Cambridge: Cambridge University Press, 2001); and Christos Hadjiyiannis, *Conservative Modernists: Literature and Tory Politics in Britain, 1900–1920* (Cambridge: Cambridge University Press, 2018).

24. Eliot's syllabus and lecture notes have been reprinted in Ronald Schuchard, "T. S. Eliot as an Extension Lecturer, 1916–1919," *Review of English Studies*, n.s., 25, no. 98 (1974): 163–73. Given Eliot's association of the classicist view with the seventeenth century, the reference to Brunetière on the reading list very likely included *Bossuet*, which had just appeared in print in 1913.

25. For "a minor Brunetière," see E. K. Brown, "The National Idea in American Criticism," *Dalhousie Review* 14, no. 2 (1934): 133–47, 145. Brown himself does not describe Babbitt this way but writes: "It was a stroke of genius on someone's part to describe Babbitt as 'a minor Brunetière.'" Exactly who Brown is referencing is unclear, but Babbitt's association with Brunetière was well-known. See, e.g., Ferdinand Brunetière, "The French Mastery of Style," trans. Irving Babbitt, *Atlantic Monthly* 80 (October 1897): 442–51.

26. Eliot quoted in Schuchard, "T. S. Eliot as an Extension Lecturer," 165.

27. Ronald Schuchard, *Eliot's Dark Angel: Intersections of Life and Art* (Oxford: Oxford University Press, 1999), 67; Karen Csengeri, ed., *The Collected Writings of T. E. Hulme* (Oxford: Oxford University Press, 1994), 234. For Hulme's translation of and introduction to Sorel, see Georges Sorel, *Reflections on Violence*, trans. T. E. Hulme (New York: B. W. Huebsch, 1915).

28. In *Die Philosophie der Aufklärung* (Tübingen, 1932), Ernst Cassirer generally agreed with Eliot's description, writing that the odd humanist in "the seventeenth century tried in vain to contest [the] sentence" passed on the era by the Reformation. See Ernst Cassirer, *The Philosophy of the Enlightenment*, trans. Fritz C. A. Koelln and J. P. Pettegrove (Princeton, NJ: Princeton University Press, 1951), 140.

29. "The beginning of the twentieth century has witnessed a return to the ideals of classicism," Eliot announced in his second lecture, to which he added: "[T]he present-day movement is partly a return to the ideals of the seventeenth century." Schuchard, *Eliot's Dark Angel*, 61.

30. Valerie Eliot and John Haffensen, eds., *The Letters of T. S. Eliot* (New Haven, CT: Yale University Press, 2016), 6:290–91.

31. Eliot's reference to "the Church today" likely relates to Anglican debates in the early 1930s over revisions to the defining *Book of Common Prayer*. On formalist aesthetics and original sin, see Kenneth Asher, "T. S. Eliot and the New Criticism," *Essays in Literature* 20, no. 2 (1993): 292–309.

32. Carl Becker, "Brunetière und Bossuet," *Germanisch-Romanische Monatsschrift*, vol. 8 (Heidelberg: Carl Winter, 1920): 91–102, and *The Heavenly City of the Eighteenth-Century Philosophers* (New Haven, CT: Yale University Press, 1932), 102.

33. Cassirer, *The Philosophy of the Enlightenment*, 141.

34. The phrase is from Peter Gordon, *Continental Divide: Heidegger, Cassirer, Davos* (Cambridge, MA: Harvard University Press, 2010), 6. Another feature of the context was *Lebensphilosophie* (philosophy of life), on which see Edward Skidelsky, *Ernst Cassirer: The Last Philosopher of Culture* (Princeton, NJ: Princeton University Press, 2008), 160–94. Also worth noting is that Heidegger too read and deeply admired Brunetière. See Martin Heidegger, "Das Realitätsproblem in der modernen Philosophie," *Philosophisches Jahrbuch* 25 (1912): 353–63, 353, where Heidegger quotes from Ferdinand Brunetière, *Sur les chemins de la croyance: Première étape: L'utilisation du positivisme* (Paris: Perrin, 1905).

35. Martin Heidegger, *Being and Time* (1927), trans. John Macquarrie and Edward Robinson (Oxford: Blackwell, 1962), 492 n. iv, and "Das Problem der Sünde bei Luther" (1924), in *Sachgemäße Exegese: Die Protokolle aus Rudolf Bultmanns Neutestamentlichen Seminaren, 1921–51*, ed. Bernd Jaspert (Marburg: Elwert, 1996), 28–33.

36. Gordon, *Continental Divide*, 30–32.

37. Gordon, *Continental Divide*, 184–85.

38. Carl Schmitt, *Political Theology: Four Chapters in the Concept of Sovereignty* (1922), trans. George Schwab (Chicago: University of Chicago Press, 1985), "Der Begriff des Politischen," *Archiv für Sozialwissenschaft und Sozialpolitik* 58, no. 1 (1927): 1–33, and *Der*

Begriff des Politischen: Mit einer Rede über das Zeitalter der Neutralisierungen und Entpolitisierungen . . . (Munich: Duncker & Humblot, 1932).

39. Carl Schmitt, *Der Begriff des Politischen* (Hamburg: Hanseatische Verlagsanstalt, 1933).

40. It may be the brazen anti-Semitism that continues to make the third edition obscure. The more common 1963 reprint of the book is based verbatim on the less hostile second edition from 1932. See Heinrich Meier, *Carl Schmitt and Leo Strauss: The Hidden Dialogue*, trans. J. Harvey Lomax (Chicago: University of Chicago Press, 1994), 6–7 n. 5.

41. Meier, *Carl Schmitt and Leo Strauss*. Meier's reconstruction of the thick context makes for the most convincing argument. For a different angle, see Peter Schröder, "Carl Schmitt's Appropriation of the Early Modern European Tradition of Political Thought on the State and Interstate Relations," *History of Political Thought* 33, no. 2 (2012): 348–71.

42. For Strauss's assessment of Cassirer, see Leo Strauss, review of Ernst Cassirer, *The Myth of the State* (1946), *Social Research* 14 (1947): 125–28, 128. On the issue Strauss raises in the review, see Skidelsky, *Ernst Cassirer*, 232–33. Schmitt's operative term is *anthropologischen Glaubensbekenntnis*. Whether Schmitt knowingly borrowed this term is unclear, but it does appear earlier on at least one occasion in the widely read Hans Ferdinand Helmolt, *Weltgeschichte* (Leipzig, 1899), 10.

43. This is the major argument running through Meier, *Carl Schmitt and Leo Strauss*.

44. Schmitt, *Der Begriff des Politischen* (1933), 45 ("Die Leugnung der Erbsünde alle soziale Ordnung zerstört").

45. Meier, *Carl Schmitt and Leo Strauss*, 53–54.

46. The importance of original sin has often been recognized in passing, but without much elaboration. Max Weber noted: "[T]he contrast is striking between the pessimistic individualism [of people with 'a Puritan past'] and the entirely different way in which the 'Enlightenment' later viewed persons." Max Weber, *The Protestant Ethic and the Spirit of Capitalism with Other Writings on the Rise of the West*, ed. and trans. Stephen Kalberg, 4th ed. (Oxford: Oxford University Press, 2009), 107. He nevertheless did not mention the way in which the same people with "a Puritan past" also helped constitute a strain of Enlightenment pessimism. Writing largely about Maistre, Isaiah Berlin asserted that "what the entire Enlightenment has in common is denial of the central Christian doctrine of original sin," before offering the concise explanation that, contrary to the Augustinian tradition, enlighteners believed "that man is born either innocent and good, or morally neutral and malleable by education or environment, or, at worst, deeply defective but capable of radical and indefinite improvement by rational education in favourable circumstances, or by a revolutionary reorganization of society." Isaiah Berlin, "The Counter-Enlightenment" (1973), in *The Proper Study of Mankind: An Anthology of Essays* (London: Chatto & Windus, 1997), 243–68, 264. For context, see Mali and Wokler, eds., *Isaiah Berlin's Counter-Enlightenment*. When Hugh Trevor-Roper turned his attention to the Enlightenment's religious origins in an article from 1967, he located a proto-Enlightenment among religious philosophies for the express reason that they were Pelagian. See Hugh Trevor-Roper, "The Religious Origins of the Enlightenment," in *Religion, the Reformation and Social Change, and Other Essays* (London: Macmillan, 1967), 193–236; and John Robertson, "Hugh Trevor-Roper, Intellectual History and 'The Religious Origins of the Enlightenment,'" *English Historical Review* 124, no. 511 (2009): 1389–1421. Elsewhere in the historiography, the tensions between the Enlightenment and original sin have been implied if not always drawn out. In an influential interpretation of the seventeenth century, the more radical path to modernity, more befitting the powerless

than the bourgeoisie, came from what Christopher Hill too called *Pelagianism*. Christopher Hill, *The World Turned Upside Down: Radical Ideas during the English Revolution* (London: Temple Smith, 1972). Even the later revisionist critique of Hill's position implicitly accepted this premise. A subtext running through Hill's debate with J. C. Davis, e.g., is that it is disbelief in original sin that largely made one radical at the time. See Christopher Hill, *Winstanley: "The Law of Freedom" and Other Writings* (Cambridge: Cambridge University Press, 1973), 53. Compare J. C. Davis, *Utopia and the Ideal Society: A Study of English Utopian Writing, 1516–1700* (Cambridge: Cambridge University Press, 1981), 191 n. 104. Dale Van Kley has argued that, while Jansenists expressed interest in a handful of characteristic Enlightenment ideas, it was their attachment to original sin that made them "proto-Enlightenment" rather than full-throated defenders. See Dale Van Kley, "Pierre Nicole, Jansenism, and the Morality of Enlightened Self-Interest," in *Anticipations of the Enlightenment in England, France, and Germany*, ed. Alan Charles Kors and Paul J. Korshin (Philadelphia: University of Pennsylvania Press, 1987), 69–85. A point suggested by R. R. Palmer (Carl Becker's PhD student) and detectable in more recent work by Jeffrey D. Burson is that Jesuits belong in the Enlightenment precisely when they distanced themselves from a strenuous reading of original sin. See R. R. Palmer, *Catholics and Unbelievers in Eighteenth-Century France* (Princeton, NJ: Princeton University Press, 1939); and Jeffrey D. Burson, *Culture of Enlightening: Abbé Claude Yvon and the Entangled Emergence of the Enlightenment* (Notre Dame, IN: University of Notre Dame Press, 2019). J. G. A. Pocock identified an "Arminian Enlightenment" at the moment that Arminianism came to mean, above all, aversion to original sin. See J. G. A. Pocock, *Barbarism and Religion*, vol. 1, *The Enlightenments of Edward Gibbon, 1737–1764* (Cambridge: Cambridge University Press, 1999), 8–9, 50–71. The importance of original sin is not a feature of Jonathan Israel's work, but it is worth noting the number of times *original sin* appears in his books' indexes. See, e.g., Jonathan Israel, *Democratic Enlightenment: Philosophy, Revolution, and Human Rights, 1750–1790* (Oxford: Oxford University Press, 2011), 182, 203, 311, 312, 323, *A Revolution of the Mind: Radical Enlightenment and the Intellectual Origins of Modern Democracy* (Princeton, NJ: Princeton University Press, 2010), 23, 25, and *Enlightenment Contested: Philosophy, Modernity, and the Emancipation of Man, 1670–1752* (Oxford: Oxford University Press, 2006), 74–75, 121–26, 132–33, 213, 575, 583, 587, 599, etc. Most suggestively, Michael Heyd found a link between original sin's decline and the Enlightenment's origins among erstwhile Calvinists. See Michael Heyd, "Original Sin, the Struggle for Stability, and the Rise of Moral Individualism in Late Seventeenth-Century England," in *Early Modern Europe: From Crisis to Stability*, ed. Philip Benedict and Myron P. Gutmann (Newark, DE: University of Delaware Press, 2005), and "Changing Emotions? The Decline of Original Sin on the Eve of the Enlightenment," in *Representing Emotions: New Connections in the Histories of Art, Music and Medicine*, ed. Penelope Gouk and Helen Hills (Burlington, VT: Routledge, 2005), 123–38. For more on the historiography as it relates to political theology, see chap. 7 below.

47. The point was already apparent in Herbert Marcuse, *Studie über Autorität und Familie* (Paris: Félix Alcan, 1936).

48. See Max Horkheimer and Theodor W. Adorno, *Dialectic of Enlightenment: Philosophical Fragments* (1947), ed. Gunzelin Schmid Noerr, trans. Edmund Jephcott (Stanford, CA: Stanford University Press, 2002). See, too, Theodor W. Adorno, Else Frenkel-Brunswik, Daniel Levinson, and Nevitt Sanford, *The Authoritarian Personality* (New York: Harper, 1950).

49. On the critique of the Enlightenment from the left (and on Heidegger), see Jürgen Habermas, "The Entwinement of Myth and Enlightenment: Re-Reading *Dialectic of Enlightenment*," *New German Critique*, no. 26, Critical Theory and Modernity (Spring–Summer 1982): 13–30. On Marcuse and Benjamin, see, respectively, Michael Kohlhauer, "A Dialectal Reading of Joseph de Maistre by Herbert Marcuse," in Armenteros and Lebrun, eds., *Joseph de Maistre and His European Readers*, 171–88; and Ryohei Kageura, "Maistrian Themes in Walter Benjamin's Sociology," in ibid., 151–70. Horkheimer and Adorno cite Maistre more than once in *Dialectic of Enlightenment*. On Adorno's ambivalent relationship to existentialism, a movement of which Heidegger was a defining figure, see Peter Gordon, *Adorno and Existence* (Cambridge, MA: Harvard University Press, 2016).

50. Such comparisons were undertaken with the observer's boundless capacity to relate the other to itself, which Anthony Pagden memorably called the *principle of attachment*. See Anthony Pagden, *European Encounters with the New World: From Renaissance to Romanticism* (New Haven, CT: Yale University Press, 1993), passim. On the Enlightenment origins of comparative religion, see Lynn Hunt, Margaret C. Jacob, and Wijnand Mijnhardt, *The Book That Changed Europe: Picart and Bernard's Religious Ceremonies of the World* (Cambridge, MA: Harvard University Press, 2010).

51. For a fuller account of conjectural history, see Frank Palmeri, *State of Nature, Stages of Society: Enlightenment Conjectural History and Modern Social Discourse* (New York: Columbia University Press, 2016).

52. On the implication of historiography in this process, see Ranajit Guha, *Dominance without Hegemony: History and Power in Colonial India* (Cambridge, MA: Harvard University Press, 1997). Alongside *Dominance without Hegemony*, it is revealing to read Dipesh Chakrabarty, *Habitations of Modernity: Essays in the Wake of Subaltern Studies* (Chicago: University of Chicago Press, 2002), 3–19.

53. For an evangelical defense of the doctrine that is attuned to some of the ironies implicit in its relative decline, see Alan Jacobs, *A Cultural History of Original Sin* (New York: Harper One, 2008).

54. William Perkins, *Christian Oeconomie; or, A Short Survey of the Right Manner of Erecting and Ordering a Familie according to the Scriptures* (London, 1609), 162 (emphasis added). On Augustine and slavery, see David Wyatt, *Slaves and Warriors in Medieval Britain and Ireland, 800–1200* (Leiden: Brill, 2009), 247 n. 15.

55. David Brion Davis, *The Problem of Slavery in Western Culture* (Ithaca, NY: Cornell University Press, 1966), 91–92. For the argument that evangelicals were drawn to abolitionism because of their perceived sinfulness rather than their humanitarianism, see Christopher Brown, *Moral Capital: Foundations of British Abolitionism* (Chapel Hill: University of North Carolina Press, 2006). Original sin was not the only early modern way to justify slavery. The Spanish enslavement of the population of the New World rested on the assumption of "inferior intellect." See Anthony Pagden, *The Fall of Natural Man: The American Indian and the Origins of Comparative Ethnology* (Cambridge: Cambridge University Press, 1982), 27–56; and James H. Sweet, "The Iberian Roots of American Racist Thought," *William and Mary Quarterly* 54, no. 1 (1997): 143–66.

56. Davis, *The Problem of Slavery*, 392.

57. For the relevant numbers, see Alex Borucki, David Eltis, and David Wheat, "Atlantic History and the Slave Trade to Spanish America," *American Historical Review* 120, no. 2 (2015): 433–61, 440.

58. On the history of race and racism before 1700, see Benjamin Isaac, *The Invention of Racism in Classical Antiquity* (Princeton, NJ: Princeton University Press, 2004); Miriam Eliav-Feldon, Benjamin Isaac, and Joseph Ziegler, eds., *The Origins of Racism in the West* (Cambridge: Cambridge University Press, 2009); Robert Wald Sussman, *The Myth of Race: The Troubling Persistence of an Unscientific Idea* (Cambridge, MA: Harvard University Press, 2016); and Geraldine Heng, *The Invention of Race in the European Middle Ages* (Cambridge: Cambridge University Press, 2018). For a sustained case that even some of the ostensibly humanitarian enlighteners found new ways to justify slavery, see Louis Sala-Molins, *Dark Side of the Light: Slavery and the French Enlightenment*, trans. John Conteh-Morgan (Minneapolis: University of Minnesota Press, 2006).

59. Colin Kidd, *The Forging of Races: Race and Scripture in the Protestant Atlantic World, 1600–2000* (Cambridge: Cambridge University Press, 2006). On the broader story of race and human nature as part of Enlightenment taxonomy, see Justin E. H. Smith, *Nature, Human Nature, and Human Difference: Race in Early Modern Philosophy* (Princeton, NJ: Princeton University Press, 2015).

60. Kidd, *The Forging of Races*, 25.

61. On Hume and polygenesis, see John Immerwahr, "Hume's Revised Racism," *Journal of the History of Ideas* 53, no. 3 (1992): 481–86. Also see Kidd, *The Forging of Races*, 93.

62. Voltaire, "Relation touchant un Maure blanc amené d'Afrique à Paris en 1744," in *Oeuvres complètes de Voltaire*, ed. Louis Moland, 52 vols. (Paris: Garnier Frères, 1877–85), 23:190.

63. Andrew S. Curran, *The Anatomy of Blackness: Science and Slavery in an Age of Enlightenment* (Baltimore: Johns Hopkins University Press, 2011), 74–116.

64. Peter Harrison, "Linnaeus as a Second Adam? Taxonomy and the Religious Vocation," *Zygon: Journal of Religion and Science* 44, no. 4 (2009): 879–93.

65. Carl Linnaeus, *Systema naturae* (1735), 10th ed. (Stockholm: Laurentius Salvius, 1758), 20–22. For an overview, see Emmanuel Chukwudi Eze, introduction to *Race and the Enlightenment: A Reader*, ed. Emmanuel Chukwudi Eze (Cambridge, MA: Harvard University Press, 1997), 1–9.

66. Ter Ellingson, *The Myth of the Noble Savage* (Berkeley and Los Angeles: University of California Press, 2001). For a detailed account of how some Enlightenment authors in fact subverted the state-of-nature conceit, see Sankar Muthu, *Enlightenment against Empire* (Princeton, NJ: Princeton University Press, 2003).

67. David Hume, *Essays, Moral and Political* (Edinburgh, 1741), 161–62.

68. Other recent historians have noted the echo of theology but have not put it in terms of an opposition between Augustinians and Pelagians. On Augustinian-Epicureans, see John Robertson, *The Case for the Enlightenment: Scotland and Naples, 1680–1760* (Cambridge: Cambridge University Press, 2005). On Pelagians, see Eric Nelson, *The Theology of Liberalism: Political Philosophy and the Justice of God* (Cambridge, MA: Harvard University Press, 2019), 1.

69. For a summary of ancient Pelagianism, see Elizabeth A. Clark, *The Origenist Controversy: The Cultural Construction of an Early Christian Debate* (Princeton, NJ: Princeton University Press, 2016), 207–20.

70. The argument runs throughout Pierre Nicole, *Essais de morale* (1675), ed. Laurent Thirouin (Paris: Presses universitaires de France, 1999).

71. Van Kley, "Pierre Nicole, Jansenism, and the Morality of Enlightened Self-Interest," 72, 78.

72. Albert O. Hirschman, *The Passions and the Interests: Political Arguments for Capitalism Before Its Triumph* (Princeton, NJ: Princeton University Press, 1977); David Wootton, *Power, Pleasure, and Profit: Insatiable Appetites from Machiavelli to Madison* (Cambridge, MA: Harvard University Press, 2018). Still the classic account of the demoralization of the economy is E. P. Thompson, "The Moral Economy of the English Crowd in the Eighteenth Century," *Past and Present*, no. 50 (February 1971): 76–136.

73. For a definitive statement on Enlightenment secularity, see Margaret Jacob, *The Secular Enlightenment* (Princeton, NJ: Princeton University Press, 2019).

74. On the distinction between the historical and the philosophical Enlightenment, see Vincenzo Ferrone, *The Enlightenment: History of an Idea*, trans. Elisabette Tarantino (Princeton, NJ: Princeton University Press, 2015). For the most influential statements on Enlightenment incoherence, see Horkheimer and Adorno, *Dialectic of Enlightenment*; and Michel Foucault, *The Order of Things: An Archaeology of Human Sciences* (London: Vintage, 1970). A similar philosophical/historical distinction underpins Foucault's notion of what can usefully be saved from the Enlightenment. See Michel Foucault, "Qu'est-ce que les Lumières?," in *The Foucault Reader*, ed. Paul Rabinow (New York: Knopf Doubleday, 1984). In the same vein, see Jacques Derrida, "Une Europe de l'espoir," *Le monde diplomatique* 608 (November 2004): 3. On the philosophical incoherence as it relates to postcolonialism, see Chakrabarty, *Habitations of Modernity*, 20–47.

75. The overlap between theology and philosophical anthropology in early patristic sources is discussed in M. C. Steenberg, *Of God and Man: Theology as Anthropology from Irenaeus to Athanasius* (London: Bloomsbury, 2009).

76. I am using *belief* and *faith* relatively interchangeably and in the more pedestrian modern sense in which they mean something like the dogmatic opinion characteristic of much religious devotion. Ludwig Wittgenstein writes: "[Y]ou don't get in religious controversies, the form of the controversy where one person is *sure* of the thing, and the other says: 'well possibly.' You might be surprised that there hasn't been opposed to those who believe in Resurrection those who say 'well, possibly.'" Ludwig Wittgenstein, *Lectures and Conversations on Aesthetics, Psychology and Religious Belief: Compiled from Notes taken by Yorick Smythies, Rush Rhees and James Taylor*, ed. Cyril Barrett (Berkeley: University of California Press, 1966), 56. Anthropological faiths, as I understand them in their ideal typical forms, tend to operate the same way. The history and use of words like *belief* across time can admittedly be complicated. For one such history, see Ethan Shagan, *The Birth of Modern Belief: Faith and Judgment from the Middle Ages to the Enlightenment* (Princeton, NJ: Princeton University Press, 2018).

77. Alexander Pope, *Essay on Man* (1733–34), ed. Tom Jones (Princeton, NJ: Princeton University Press, 2016), xvi.

78. On Barker learning Pope's lines in 1739, see DRO, MS 3237M/F1, June 1, 1760, and January 15, 1762. Jenny Merivale, on whom more below, was encouraged by her father to do the same. See ibid., September 10, 1761.

79. These terms owed to the influence in Scotland of Cicero's *De finibus bonorum et malorum*. There is no reason to assume, however, that, simply because *Epicurean* and *Stoic* were actors' categories in the eighteenth century, they therefore accurately reflected what Epicureans and Stoics in the ancient world believed. Here see Istvan Hont, *Politics and Commercial Society: Jean-Jacques Rousseau and Adam Smith* (Cambridge, MA: Harvard University Press, 2015), 14–16.

80. The fullest account of Smith's tension and its resolution can be found in Nicholas

Phillipson, *Adam Smith: An Enlightened Life* (New Haven, CT: Yale University Press, 2010), passim.

81. See Keith Tribe, "'Das Adam Smith Problem' and the Origins of Modern Smith Scholarship," *History of European Ideas* 34, no. 4 (2008): 514–25. Also see Laurence Dickey, "Historicizing the 'Adam Smith Problem': Conceptual, Historiographical, and Textual Issues," *Journal of Modern History* 58, no. 3 (1986): 579–609. Smith was revising both his optimistic and his pessimistic books until the end of his life, and his revisions to the sixth edition of the *Theory of Moral Sentiments* relate to theology, self-control, and moral conduct, all issues that get at the heart of human nature and its limits. See D. D. Raphael, *The Impartial Spectator: Adam Smith's Moral Philosophy* (Oxford: Oxford University Press, 2007); and Daniel B. Klein, Erik W. Matson, and Colin Doran, "The Man within the Breast, the Supreme Impartial Spectator, and Other Impartial Spectators in Adam Smith's *The Theory of Moral Sentiments*," *History of European Ideas* 44, no. 8 (2018): 1153–68.

82. On the meaning of *Rational Dissent*, see Knud Haakonssen, ed., *Enlightenment and Religion: Rational Dissent in Eighteenth-Century Britain* (Cambridge: Cambridge University Press, 1996).

83. David Hume, *A Treatise of Human Nature* (1739), ed. Lewis Amherst Selby-Bigge and P. H. Nidditch (Oxford: Clarendon, 1978), 415. On Hume's much quoted line, see Nicholas L. Sturgeon, "Hume on Reason and Passion," in *The Cambridge Companion to Hume's Treatise*, ed. Donald C. Ainslie and Annemarie Butler (Cambridge: Cambridge University Press, 2015), 252–82. Experimental psychology has continued to support this view. For an overview of the relevant scholarship, see Jennifer S. Lerner, Ye Li, Piercarlo Valdesolo, and Karim S. Kassam, "Emotion and Decision Making," *Annual Review of Psychology* 66 (January 2015): 799–823. On emotion and belief in the early modern era, see Jessica Riskin, *Science in the Age of Sensibility: The Sentimental Empiricists of the French Enlightenment* (Chicago: University of Chicago Press, 2002); Jonas Liliequist, ed., *A History of Emotions, 1200–1800* (New York: Routledge, 2012), esp. chaps. 1 and 5; Alec Ryrie, *Unbelievers: An Emotional History of Doubt* (Cambridge, MA: Harvard University Press, 2019); Shagan, *The Birth of Modern Belief*; and Philip Nord, Katja Guenther, and Max Weiss, eds., *Formations of Belief: Historical Approaches to Religion and the Secular* (Princeton, NJ: Princeton University Press, 2019).

84. Toward the end of his life, when he could not access Hume's writings to quote straight from the source, Barker wrote: "Reason say some Gods noblest Gift to Man. I am one of those[.] Instinct says Hume is superior to Reason or something like it, for I can't go to the Page." DRO, MS 3237M/F1, January 15, 1762. Merivale understood Barker's reference and in his following letter wrote: "I can add nothing to your Remarks on the ruling Passion." Ibid., January 24, 1762.

85. Michel Foucault, "Une histoire restée muette," *La quinzaine littéraire*, no. 8 (July 1–15, 1966): 3–4. Also see James Schmidt, "On Foucault's Review of Cassirer's Philosophy of the Enlightenment" (2012), Persistent Enlightenment, https://persistentenlightenment.com/2013/07/02/foucaultcassirer.

86. For a comprehensive statement on the field, see Peter E. Gordon, "What Is Intellectual History? A Frankly Partisan Introduction to a Frequently Misunderstood Field" (paper presented to the Harvard Colloquium for Intellectual History, rev. Spring 2012), https://projects.iq.harvard.edu/files/history/files/what_is_intell_history_pgordon_mar2012.pdf.

87. On this issue, see Michel-Rolph Trouillot, *Silencing the Past: Power and the*

Production of History (Boston: Beacon, 1995); and Carlo Ginzburg, *Threads and Traces: True False Fictive*, trans. Anne C. Tedeschi and John Tedeschi (Berkeley and Los Angeles: University of California Press, 2012).

88. It is Hannah Arendt who calls *ideology* in a fundamental sense the *logic of an idea.* See Hannah Arendt, "Ideology and Terror: A Novel Form of Government," *Review of Politics* 15, no. 3 (1953): 303–27, 316.

Chapter Two

1. Peter Harrison, "Original Sin and the Problem of Knowledge in Early Modern Europe," *Journal of the History of Ideas* 63, no. 2 (2002): 239–59.

2. Owen Linzmayer, *Apple Confidential 2.0: The Definitive History of the World's Most Colorful Company* (San Francisco: No Starch, 2004); Rob Janoff, *Taking a Bite Out of the Apple: A Graphic Designer's Tale* (London: Balestier, 2018).

3. For just a few of the many recent works on religion and the Enlightenment, see Jonathan Sheehan, *The Enlightenment Bible: Translation, Scholarship, Culture* (Princeton, NJ: Princeton University Press, 2005); David Sorkin, *The Religious Enlightenment: Protestants, Jews, and Catholics from London to Vienna* (Princeton, NJ: Princeton University Press, 2008); Hunt, Jacob, and Mijnhardt, *The Book That Changed Europe*; and William J. Bulman and Robert G. Ingram, eds., *God in the Enlightenment* (Oxford: Oxford University Press, 2016).

4. For a clarifying distinction between residual culture and emergent culture, see Raymond Williams, *Marxism and Literature* (Oxford: Oxford University Press, 1977).

5. George Whitfield, *The Method of Grace: A Sermon, Preached on Sabbath Morning, September 13th, 1741: In the High-Church-Yard of Glasgow, upon Jer. vi. 14: By the Reverend Mr. George Whitfield: Taken from His Own Mouth, and Published at the Earnest Desire of Many of the Hearers* (Glasgow, 1741), 12.

6. Augustine's commentary on Jeremiah quoted in Benjamin Breckinridge Warfield, *The Plan of Salvation: Five Lectures Delivered at the Princeton Summer School of Theology* (Philadelphia: Presbyterian Board of Publication, 1914), 37–38.

7. On Augustine and Heb. 11:6, see William Mann, ed., *Augustine's Confessions: Philosophy in Autobiography* (Oxford: Oxford University Press, 2014), 81.

8. Diarmaid MacCulloch, *The Reformation: A History* (New York: Penguin, 2003), 106–15.

9. *Decrees of the Ecumenical Councils*, ed. Norman Tanner (Washington, DC, 1990), 2:657 (Council of Trent, session 5, June 17, 1546).

10. Puritans in New England, e.g., baptized their children within days of birth. David Hall, *Lived Religion in America: Toward a History of Practice* (Princeton, NJ: Princeton University Press, 1997), 53. This was one of the ways in which practice could deviate from theory. But even in theory some Calvinist could occasionally offer up baptism to deal with the problem of sin. The issue was still tricky, and one can detect in the qualifications both the pastoral need to offer assurance and the theological danger of doing so. William Perkins suggested that, in one sense, baptism was like clipping the hair of original sin. But the same trope gave him the chance to point to the limits of baptism, which was, he wrote, incapable of keeping sin from lingering in the root of the follicle. See William Perkins, *A Reformed Catholike; or, A Declaration Shewing How Neere We May Come to the Present Church of Rome in Sundrie Points of Religion* . . . (Cambridge, 1598), 37.

11. On the pre-Augustinian version of this argument, see Judith Lieu, *Marcion and the Making of a Heretic: God and Scripture in the Second Century* (Cambridge: Cambridge University Press, 2015), 352.

12. In the general and religion/philosophy categories searchable on the database *Eighteenth-Century Collections Online* (https://www.gale.com/primary-sources/eighteenth-century-collections-online), 3.18 percent of all texts written between 1701 and 1710 but only 0.92 percent of texts written between 1791 and 1800 contained the term *original sin*. In contrast, uses of *Trinity* (14.6 percent in 1701–10 and 13.4 percent in 1791–1800) and *predestination* (1.45 percent in 1701–10 and 1.56 percent in 1791–1800) stayed steady in the *general* category, while *doctrine of Trinity* increased (0.43 percent in 1701–10 and 0.89 percent in 1791–1800), and *baptism* declined only slightly (12.9 percent in 1701–10 and 8.02 percent in 1791–1800). That the doctrine of atonement was a softer replacement for that of original sin might be borne out by the increase in uses of *atonement* (4.4 percent in 1701–10 and 11.2 percent in 1791–1800). More dramatic is the increase in words that, in one sense or another, *original sin* opposes: *improvement* (15.4 percent in 1701–10 and 34.3 percent in 1791–1800), *happiness* (35.2 percent in 1701–10 and 52.2 percent in 1791–1800), *progress* (20 percent in 1701–10 and 42.8 percent in 1791–1800), and even to some degree *capital* (14 percent in 1701–10 and 33.8 percent in 1791–1800).

13. John Wesley, *The Doctrine of Original Sin: According to Scripture, Reason, and Experience* (Bristol, 1757).

14. G. K. Chesterton, *Orthodoxy* (New York: John Lane, 1908), 24.

15. Edwards's *Original Sin* constitutes vol. 3 of Clyde A. Holbrook, ed., *The Works of Jonathan Edwards* (New Haven, CT: Yale University Press, 1970). Alongside Edwards and Wesley, see David Jennings, *Vindication of the Scripture Doctrine of Original Sin, from Mr Taylor's Free and Candid Examination of It* (London, 1740); Samuel Niles, *The True Scripture-Doctrine of Original Sin Stated and Defended: In the Way of Remarks on a Late Piece . . . for Truth, and against Error* (Boston, 1757); and Isaac Watts, *The Ruin and Recovery of Mankind; or, An Attempt to Vindicate the Scriptural Account of These Great Events upon the Plain Principles of Reason: With an Answer to . . . Defilement of Sin* (London, 1740). On Taylor's reception, see Clyde A. Holbrook, introduction to Holbrook, ed., *The Works of Jonathan Edwards*, 3:1–101; and H. Shelton Smith, *Changing Conceptions of Original Sin: A Study of American Theology since 1750* (New York: Scribner's, 1955), chaps. 2–3. In these evangelical arguments, it is worth saying, reason was important only to understand doctrine, not to attain salvation. "Instead of going straight to Christ, I have wasted my time in fighting against sin with *the dim light of my reason*," wrote John Fletcher in his diary, alluding to the salvific futility of Enlightenment criteria before quoting Heb. 11:6. "I never had faith; and *without faith it is impossible to please God*. Therefore, all my thoughts, words, and works, however specious before men, are utterly sinful before God." Samuel Dunn, ed., *Selections from the Works of the Rev. John Fletcher* (London, 1837), 11 (diary entry, January 12, 1755).

16. Paola Bertucci, *Artisanal Enlightenment: Science and the Mechanical Arts in Old Regime France* (New Haven, CT: Yale University Press, 2017), 207–8. On d'Alembert, see Genevieve Lloyd, *Enlightenment Shadows* (Oxford: Oxford University Press, 2013).

17. Manuel Lima, *The Book of Trees: Visualizing Branches of Knowledge* (Princeton, NJ: Princeton University Press, 2014).

18. Bertucci, *Artisanal Enlightenment*, 47–53 and passim. Descartes too invoked conceptual trees, the traditional image of which helped soften his novelty. See Roger Ariew, *Descartes and the First Cartesians* (Oxford: Oxford University Press, 2014), 107.

19. Robert Darnton, *The Business of Enlightenment: A Publishing History of the Encyclopédie, 1775–1800* (Cambridge, MA: Harvard University Press, 1979), 7.

20. Francis Bacon, *The Works of Francis Bacon*, ed. James Spedding, Robert Leslie Ellis, and Douglas Denon Heath (Boston: Houghton, Mifflin and Co, 1900), 8:17.

21. Bacon, *The Works of Francis Bacon*, 8:77.

22. On Bacon's agenda as secular despite his use of religious imagery, see Mordechai Feingold, "'And Knowledge Shall Be Increased': Millenarianism and the Advancement of Learning Revisited," *Seventeenth Century* 28, no. 4 (2013): 363–93.

23. William H. Sewell Jr., "Visions of Labor: Illustrations of the Mechanical Arts Before, in, and After Diderot's *Encyclopédie*," in *Work in France: Representations, Meaning, Organization, and Practice*, ed. Steven Laurence Kaplan and Cynthia J. Koepp (Ithaca, NY: Cornell University Press, 1986), 277.

24. Harold J. Cook, *Matters of Exchange: Commerce, Medicine, and Science in the Dutch Golden Age* (New Haven, CT: Yale University Press, 2007), 166; Lucia Dacome, *Malleable Anatomies: Models, Makers, and Material Culture in Eighteenth-Century Italy* (Oxford: Oxford University Press, 2017), 85–86.

25. Diderot quoted in Michel Delon, ed., *Encyclopedia of the Enlightenment* (London: Routledge, 2001), 1:62.

26. Barbara B. Oberg, ed., *The Papers of Benjamin Franklin* (New Haven, CT: Yale University Press, 1995), 31:456.

27. Roy Porter, *The Creation of the Modern World: The Untold Story of the British Enlightenment* (New York: Norton, 2000), 364.

28. On the early iterations of Locke's anti-innatism, see Tim Stuart-Buttle, *From Moral Theology to Moral Philosophy: Cicero and Visions of Humanity from Locke to Hume* (Oxford: Oxford University Press, 2019), 45.

29. On the pre-Lockean and, for that matter, pre-Hobbesian uses of the state-of-nature conceit, see James J. Hamilton, "The Origins of Hobbes's State of Nature," *Hobbes Studies* 26, no. 2 (2013): 152–70.

30. John Marshall, *John Locke: Resistance, Religion and Responsibility* (Cambridge: Cambridge University Press, 1994), 145–48.

31. John Locke, *The Reasonableness of Christianity . . .* (London, 1695), 1–2. Locke does not deny the occurrence of the Fall, but the question he takes up in the opening pages of this work is what exactly humankind fell from. For a reader's response to this passage, see Philippus van Limborch to John Locke, Tuesday, October 8, 1697, in *Electronic Enlightenment Scholarly Edition of Correspondence*, ed. Robert McNamee et al., https://www.e-enlightenment.com/item/lockjoOU0060206a1c/?letters=decade&s=1690&r=1776.

32. Jean le Rond d'Alembert, *Preliminary Discourse to the Encyclopedia of Diderot*, trans. Richard N. Schwab with the collaboration of Walter E. Rex (Chicago: University of Chicago Press, 1995), 81.

33. On moral freedom, see Rob Iliffe, *Priest of Nature: The Religious Worlds of Isaac Newton* (Oxford: Oxford University Press, 2017), 8, 132. Also see Harrison, *The Fall of Man*, 235.

34. See William Stukeley, "Memoirs of Sr. Isaac Newton's Life. Wm. Stukeley 1752," Royal Society of London, MS 142, fols. 14r–15r, published in Rob Iliffe and Rebekah Higgitt, eds., *Early Biographies of Isaac Newton, 1660–1885* (London: Pickering & Chatto, 2006), 1:257–58. On the language of *downward fall*, see William Whiston, *Memoirs of the Life and Writings of Mr. William Whiston* (London, 1753), 32–34.

35. By the eighteenth century, the apple had become the operative fruit in Genesis. Its

displacement of other contenders—the fig, the pomegranate—was largely owing to John Milton. See Robert Appelbaum, *Aguecheek's Beef, Belch's Hiccup, and Other Gastronomic Interjections: Literature, Culture, and Food among the Early Moderns* (Chicago: University of Chicago Press, 2017).

36. In Greene's words: "Quae Sententia Celeberrima, Originem ducit, uti omnis, ut fertur, Cognitio nostra, a Pomo." See Robert Greene, *The Principles of the Philosophy of the Expansive and Contractive Forces* (Cambridge, 1727), 972.

37. Voltaire, *An Essay upon the Civil Wars of France . . . and Also upon the Epick Poetry of the European Nations from Homer down to Milton* (London, 1727), 103–4.

38. G. W. F. Hegel, "*Philosophical Dissertation on the Orbits of the Planets* (1801) Preceded by the 12 Theses Defended on August 27, 1801," trans. with a foreword and notes by Pierre Adler, *Graduate Faculty Philosophy Journal* 12, no. 2 (1987): 269–309, 293.

39. See Stephen I. Wagner, *Squaring the Circle in Descartes' Meditations: The Strong Validation of Reason* (Cambridge: Cambridge University Press, 2014), 29–32.

40. On sin and its absence in Hobbes, see Victoria Kahn, "What Original Sin? Political Theology, the Jewish Question, and the Work of Metaphor," *Telos* 178 (2017): 100–120, 106.

41. Spinoza writes that religious divines confuse rather than clarify the issue of human nature when they say our bad behavior derives "its origin from our first parents' fall": "For if it was even in the first man's power as much to stand as to fall, and he was in possession of his senses, and had his nature unimpaired, how could it be, that he fell in spite of his knowledge and foresight?" *The Chief Works of Benedict de Spinoza*, trans. R. H. M. Elwes (London: George Bell and Sons, 1891), 1:293.

42. Nicholas Jolley, "Is Leibniz's Theodicy a Variation on a Theme by Malebranche?," in *New Essays on Leibniz's Theodicy*, ed. Larry M. Jorgensen and Samuel Lewlands (Oxford: Oxford University Press, 2014), 63; Patrick Riley, "Leibniz's Political and Moral Philosophy in the *Novissima sinica*, 1699–1999," *Journal of the History of Ideas* 60, no. 2 (1999): 217–39, 238; Nelson, *The Theology of Liberalism*, 5, 8.

43. Edward Gibbon, *The History of the Decline and Fall of the Roman Empire* (Dublin, 1788), 4:166.

44. Joseph Priestley, *An Appeal to the Serious and Candid Professors of Christianity . . .* (London, 1771), 9.

45. Immanuel Kant, *Religion within the Boundaries of Mere Reason and Other Writings*, trans. and eds. Allen Wood and George di Giovanni (Cambridge: Cambridge University Press, 1998), 66. Here Kant also assumes that everyone has a natural tendency to do the wrong thing and at worst to be radically evil. But the point of the line quoted above is that, in theorizing ways to overcome such tendencies (whether the strategies are personal or take the form of civil religion), he also presupposes enough human agency to undermine original sin in its typical formulations.

46. "L'homme est comme Dieu ou la nature l'a fait; et Dieu et la nature ne font rien de mal." Denis Diderot, *L'addition aux pensées philosophiques; ou, Objections diverses contre les écrits de différents théologiens*, in *Oeuvres philosophiques*, ed. Paul Vernière (Paris, 1964), 58–72, 65.

47. Benjamin Franklin, *A Defence of the Rev. Mr. Hemphill's Observations; or, An Answer to the Vindication of the Reverend Commission* (Philadelphia, 1735), 6.

48. Voltaire, "Originel (péché)," in *Dictionnaire philosophique IV*, vol. 20 of *Oeuvres complètes de Voltaire* (Paris: Garnier, 1879), 151–56, 155–56. Also see Voltaire to René

Joseph Tournemine, ca. Thursday, June 16, 1735, in McNamee et al., eds., *Electronic Enlightenment Scholarly Edition of Correspondence*, http://www.e-enlightenment.com/item/voltfrVF0870155a1c/?letters=decade&s=1730&r=1975.

49. *Optimism* had just come into circulation in the 1730s from Leibniz's notion of the *optimum*.

50. DRO, MS 3237M/F1, May 28, 1759.

51. DRO, MS 3237M/F1, May 28, 1759.

52. The prize-winning essays are collected in Roger Tisserand, ed., *Les concurrents de J.-J. Rousseau à l'Académie de Dijon* (Vesoul: Imprimerie nouvelle, 1936). On the Académie de Dijon, see James E. McClellan, *Science Reorganized: Scientific Societies in the Eighteenth Century* (New York: Columbia University Press, 1985), 99.

53. On *perfectibilité*, see Florence Lotterie, *Progrès et perfectibilité: Un dilemma des Lumières françaises, 1755–1814* (Oxford: Oxford University Press, 2006), xviii.

54. On the appropriation of Augustinian religiosity to arrive at the general will, see Patrick Riley, *The General Will Before Rousseau: The Transformation of the Divine into the Civic* (Princeton, NJ: Princeton University Press, 1986). Insofar as amour propre is an Augustinian category, Istvan Hont has much to say in his *Politics in Commercial Society*. Many of the same core issues in Augustinian thought are raised in relation to Rousseau, Stoicism, and Epicureanism in Christopher Brooke, *Philosophic Pride: Stoicism and Political Thought from Lipsius to Rousseau* (Princeton, NJ: Princeton University Press, 2012), 181–202. For more on Rousseau, see chaps. 8–9.

55. "Posons pour maxime incontestable que les premiers mouvements de la nature sont toujours droits: il n'y a point de perversité originelle dans le coeur humain." Jean-Jacques Rousseau, *Émile; ou, De l'éducation* (Paris, 1762), 1:97.

56. On original sin and the decision of the authorities to condemn Rousseau's *Émile*, see Thomas Worcester, "Friends as Liabilities: Christophe de Beaumont's Defense of the Jesuits," in *The Jesuit Suppression in Global Context: Causes, Events, and Consequences*, ed. Jeffrey D. Burson and Jonathan Wright (Cambridge: Cambridge University Press, 2015), 65–79, 67–68. Also see Jeremiah L. Alberg, "Rousseau and the Original Sin," *Revista portuguesa de filosofia* 57, no. 4 (2001): 773–90.

57. Jean Starobinski, *Jean-Jacques Rousseau: Transparency and Obstruction* (1957), trans. Arthur Goldhammer (Chicago: University of Chicago Press, 1988), 115. On the other hand, W. H. Auden thought that "Augustine was the first real psychologist for he was the first to see the basic fact about human nature, namely that the Natural Man hates nature, and that the only act which can really satisfy him is the *acte gratuit*." Auden was here thinking of the gratuitous act of stealing pears that Augustine relates in the *Confessions* (see the previous chapter), which for Auden illustrated how much we all want to make choices only for the sake of making choices, a drive that fundamentally puts us at odds (hence "Man hates nature") with the more natural effort simply to meet our needs. W. H. Auden, "Squares and Oblongs" (1947), in *The Complete Works of W. H. Auden: Prose*, ed. Edward Mendelson (Princeton, NJ: Princeton University Press, 1996), 2:339–50, 341. It is worth noting that Auden was influenced by T. S. Eliot's views on original sin but also reflects an impression made by the Second World War. It is illuminating to compare one of Auden's college courses to the syllabus of Eliot's discussed in the previous chapter. Auden taught a class at Swarthmore College in Pennsylvania in 1943 called "Romanticism from Rousseau to Hitler" in which, according to Edward Mendelson, he argued that the view of human nature found in Rousseau had led straight to Nazism (see

Complete Works, 2:xxi n.). Auden may have never systematically examined original sin, but, particularly in some of what he writes about the triadic relationship among the anthropological faiths of Pascal, Rousseau, and Voltaire, he reflects, as does the Frankfurt school, if differently, the way in which the rise of Hitler complicated the story of the Enlightenment and original sin as *simply* antithetical. For Auden's ruminations on Voltaire, see, e.g., W. H. Auden, "The Great Democrat" (1939), in *Complete Works*, 2:8–11.

58. M. Mirabaud (Paul-Henri Thiry d'Holbach), *Système de la nature* (London, 1770), 1:214 n. 59.

59. Sorel quoted in Delon, ed., *Encyclopedia of the Enlightenment*, 1:xi. Also see Anton M. Matytsin, "Whose Light Is It Anyway? The Struggle for Light in the French Enlightenment," in *Let There Be Enlightenment: The Religious and Mystical Sources of Rationality*, ed. Anton M. Matytsin and Dan Edelstein (Baltimore: Johns Hopkins University Press, 2018), 62–85.

60. "Dès notre origine, nos sense sont rebelles: dès le ventre de nos mères, ou la raison est plongée et dominée par la chair, notre âme e nest l'esclave, et accablée de ce poids. Toutes les passions nous doominent tour à tour, et souvent toutes ensemble, et même les plus contraires. Dieu retire de nous les lumières, comme il avait fait à Adam, et encore plus. Ainsi nous comes frappes de la plaie de l'ignorance et de celle de la concupiscience; tout le bien, jusqu'au moindre, nous est difficile; tour le mal, quelque grand qu'il soit, a des attraits pour nous." Jacques-Bénigne Bossuet, *Élévations a Dieu sur tous les mystères de la religion Chrétienne* (1727), vol. 7 of *Oeuvres complètes de Bossuet*, ed. F. Lachat, 31 vols. (Paris: Vivès, 1862–75), 124–25.

61. Feingold, " 'And Knowledge Shall Be Increased.' " Compare Anton M. Matytsin and Dan Edelstein, introduction to Matytsin and Edelstein, eds., *Let There Be Enlightenment*, 1–20, 10–11.

62. I make this claim after searching for *enlightened age* on *Eighteenth-Century Collections Online*, still the most comprehensive database of works published in English in the century. On the narratological appeal of the Fall, see Stephen Greenblatt, *The Rise and Fall of Adam and Eve: The Story That Created Us* (New York: Norton, 2018).

63. John Laurence, *The Gentleman's Recreation; or, The Second Part of the Art of Gardening Improved . . .* (London, 1716), v.

64. Laurence, *The Gentleman's Recreation*, iv.

65. On gardening and legal and political analogies, see Rebecca Bushnell, *Green Desire: Imagining Early Modern English Gardens* (Ithaca, NY: Cornell University Press, 2003), 78.

66. Deborah Harkness, *The Jewel House: Elizabethan London and the Scientific Revolution* (New Haven, CT: Yale University Press, 2007), 248.

67. The practice is little understood in the early modern era, but for the nineteenth century see Philip Bowes, *Farm Book-Keeping by Double Entry* (London, 1853), 10–11.

68. George Berkeley, *Essay towards Preventing the Ruine of Great Britain* (London, 1721), 17.

69. "I cant forbear on this occasion telling you an Odd opinion," wrote Joseph Addison to a friend, "of a Holy Father, a Capuchin, who in a discourse on the Vanity of Mirth, told us that he did not question but laughter was the effect of Original Sin and that Adam was not Risible before the Fall." Joseph Addison to Henry Newton, February 1700, in McNamee et al., eds., *Electronic Enlightenment Scholarly Edition of Correspondence*, https://www.e-enlightenment.com/item/addijoOU0010019a1c/?letters=decade&s=1700&r=22.

70. DRO, MS 3237M/F1, September 17, 1759.

71. George Berkeley, *Alciphron; or, The Minute Philosopher: In Seven Dialogues: Containing an Apology for the Christian Religion, against Those Who Are Called Free-Thinkers* (Dublin, 1732), 109. The same opposition between being enlightened and being depraved subtly comes forward in Thomas Gordon's early use of the phrase *enlightened age* from around the same time. Gordon invoked it to emphasize keywords that were adjacent to the rejection of original sin: *liberty* and *anticlericalism*. In a 1732 defense of the power of the laity over the clergy, he writes: "I dread all great Changes, and all Approaches towards such. I would therefore have the Clergy provoke none. They must not, in an enlightened Age, and an Age of Liberty, think themselves a match for the Laity, were the Laity once attempted to exert themselves." Gordon's usage is additionally suggestive for invoking the power of ordinary people—or at least nonclerics—as representative of such a new age. See Thomas Gordon, *Supplement to the Sermon Preached at Lincoln's-Inn, on January 30. 1732 . . .* (1732), 15.

72. John Brine, *A Vindication of Some Truths of Natural and Revealed Religion: In Answer to the False Reasoning of Mr. James Foster, on Various Subjects . . . to Deism* (London, 1746), iii; and James Foster, *Sermons* (London, 1744), 1:91.

73. Alexander Pope nodded to him in the *Epilogue to the Satires*: "Let modest Foster, if he will, excel / Ten Metropolitans in preaching well." Alexander Pope, *The Works of Alexander Pope*, ed. Joseph Barton, 9 vols. (London, 1797), 4:314. Another contemporary compared Foster's preaching to Farinelli's singing, while yet another thought: "Here [when Foster sermonized] was a confluence of persons of every rank, station, and quality. Wits, freethinkers, and numbers of clergy; who, whilst they gratified their curiosity had their . . . prejudices loosened." J. Hawkins, *A General History of the Science and Practice of Music* (1776), 5:321. See also C. Fleming, *A Sermon Preached at Pinners-Hall, on Occasion of the Death of the Late Rev. James Foster, D.D. with Memoirs of His Life and Character* (1753); and C. Bulkley, *A Sermon Preached at the Evening-Lecture in the Old Jewry on Sunday November 18, 1753, on Occasion of the Death of the Late Rev. James Foster, D.D.* (London, 1753).

74. Antitrinitarianism was already apparent in James Foster, *Essay on Fundamentals* (1720).

75. DRO, MS 3237M/F1, February 9, 1759.

76. Brine, *Vindication*, iii.

77. James Foster, *Sermons on the Following Subjects* (London, 1735), 1:60, 62–63.

78. Brine, *Vindication*, v–vii (emphasis added).

79. DRO, MS 3237M/F1, May 30, 1760.

80. For the iteration of this argument during Baxter's time, see Mark Goldie, *Roger Morrice and the Puritan Whigs* (Woodbridge: Boydell, 2016), 268. Brunetière noted that Bossuet made the same argument, although the starting point was Protestantism itself: "Nul n'a mieux vu que lui [Bossuet], ni ne l'a dit plus clairement, que, du luthéranisme au calvinisme, du calvinisme a l'arminianisme, de l'arminianisme au socinianisme, l'evolution nécessaire du protestantisme tendait, avec une rapidité de jour en jour croissante, a l'indifférentisme." Brunetière, *Bossuet*, 198. It is unclear which passage from Bossuet Brunetière had in mind here. The likeliest possibility makes no mention of Arminianism, which seems to be Brunetière's addition. Bossuet himself writes: "Ainsi les calvinistes plus hardis que les luthériens, ont servi à établir les sociniens qui ont été plus loin qu'eux, et dont ils grossissent tous les jours le parti. Les sectes infinies des anabaptistes sont sorties de cette même source: et leurs opinions mêlées au calvinisme ont fait naître les indépendants, qui n'ont point eu de bornes; parmi lesquels on voit les trembleurs, gens fanatiques, qui croient que toutes leurs rêveries leur sont inspirées; et ceux

qu'on nomme Chercheurs, à cause que dix-sept cents ans après Jésus-Christ ils cherchent encore la religion et n'en ont point d'arrêtée." Jacques-Bénigne Bossuet, "Oraison funèbre de Henriette-Marie de France, reine de la Grande-Bretagne," in Lachat, ed., *Oeuvres complètes de Bossuet*, 12:440–66, 453. Among much later historians, one can still find the logic of the same argument used by, on one end of the spectrum, someone like C. F. Allison (*The Rise of Moralism* [Vancouver: Regent College Publishing, 1966]) and, on the other, someone like Christopher Hill (*The World Turned Upside Down*).

81. "A History of the Batter Street Congregational Church, 1704–1921," WDRO 2973/3.

82. DRO, MS 3237M/F1, January 1, 1759.

83. DRO, MS 3237M/F1, March 29, 1759.

84. In a rabbinic gloss, Adam is misled by Eve after she gets him drunk. Jordan D. Rosenblum, *Rabbinic Drinking: What Beverages Teach Us about Rabbinic Literature* (Oakland: University of California Press, 2020), 45–47. It is slightly suggestive in this context that Barker's physician was Jewish, but even if he or his physician knew this interpretation it is worth saying that Barker was making a different argument altogether. He was not trying to exonerate Adam by pinning the blame on Eve; he was trying to exonerate humanity by pinning the blame solely on Adam. On Barker's doctor, see DRO, MS 3237M/F1, April 19, 1759.

85. Mark A. Ellis, *Simon Episcopius's Doctrine of Original Sin* (New York: Peter Lang, 2006), 149–66.

86. "Journal of Pentecost Barker," August 30, 1730. Just as formulaic in the diary is his self-beratement for failing to be adequately self-denying. To take only one example: "[U]pon the whole I have not led a diligent, watchfull, self denying life this day." "Journal of Pentecost Barker," September 11, 1730.

87. Leigh, *Critica Sacra*, 509.

88. DRO, MS 3237M/F1, April 29, 1762.

89. See, e.g., "Journal of Pentecost Barker," March 19, 1731.

90. DRO, MS 3237M/F1, May 24, 1762.

91. DRO, MS 3237M/F1, August 6, 1761.

Chapter Three

1. R. D. Sheldon, "Barbon, Nicholas (1637/1640–1698/9), Builder and Economist," in *Oxford Dictionary of National Biography* (Oxford: Oxford University Press, 2004).

2. Charles Bardsley, *Curiosities of Puritan Nomenclature* (London: Chatto & Windus, 1880), 121–25.

3. Philip Benedict, *Christ's Churches Purely Reformed: A Social History of Calvinism* (New Haven, CT: Yale University Press, 2002), 505–7.

4. Barker's parents' marriage is recorded in 1688. For the reference to the number of Barker children, see "Journal of Pentecost Barker," June 1, 1730. Barker's grandfather had also apparently been named Pentecost. Here see "Will of Pentecost Barker, Gentleman of Plymouth, Devon," The National Archives (TNA), PROB 11/880/405.

5. "Batter Street Presbyterian Meeting Register," TNA, RG4/4091 fol. 18.

6. Barker was born on September 25, 1690, and baptized nearly three weeks later, on October 13. See "Journal of Pentecost Barker." For his will, see "Will of Pentecost Barker." Barker was buried at St. Andrews on September 8, 1762, as Samuel Merivale noted to his daughter Jenny. See DRO, MS 3237M/F4, September 19, 1762.

7. Mark Brayshay, Cynthia Gaskell Brown, and James Barber, "Plymouth," in *Historical*

Atlas of South-West England, ed. Roger Kain and William Ravenhill, cartographer Helen Jones (Exeter: University of Exeter Press, 1999), 514–40.

8. Gordon Jackson, “Ports, 1700 to 1840,” in *The Cambridge Urban History of Britain*, ed. Peter Clark (Cambridge: Cambridge University Press, 2000), 2:705–32.

9. John Ehrman, *The Navy in the War of William III, 1689–1697: Its State and Direction* (Cambridge: Cambridge University Press, 1953), 419. On Devonport’s size today, see https://www.royalnavy.mod.uk/our-organisation/bases-and-stations/naval-base/devonport.

10. In the form of beer, alcohol had long been tied to the war machine to provide nutrition to sailors, but by Barker’s lifetime it was coming to be meted out by pursers in more varied forms and for the express purpose of keeping sailors mildly drunk and, thus, under control. Karen McBride and Tony Hines, “What Shall We Do with the Drunken Sailor? Accounting and Controls for Alcohol in the Royal Navy in the Time of Nelson,” in *Accounting for Alcohol: An Accounting History of Brewing, Distilling and Viniculture*, ed. Martin Quinn and João Oliveira (London: Routledge, 2018), 85–101.

11. Barker had a brother too, but details about him are missing. See DRO, MS 3237M/F1, January 15, 1762.

12. “Journal of Pentecost Barker,” 1730.

13. “Journal of Pentecost Barker,” March 28, 1730. I am quoting here from the notes Barker took in his diary on the sermons he heard. One can only wonder whether his minister—in this case Peter Baron—really suggested that diligence could *earn* rather than simply suggest election. Or was this how Barker wanted to hear the argument?

14. “Journal of Pentecost Barker,” May 6, 1730.

15. Here I draw on my own work. See Kadane, *The Watchful Clothier*, esp. chaps. 3–4.

16. “Journal of Pentecost Barker,” February 23, 1730 (emphasis added). Barker came back to the subject of the household servants in a late-life letter, acknowledging that they “were made to learn the Assembly’s Catechism” but continuing: “I knew but one that ever had a sense of Religion. They corrupted each other and I could not have been worse placed onboard a Man of War, or Newgate, than I was at home, especially after my mother died.” DRO, MS 3237M/F1, April 19, 1759.

17. “Journal of Pentecost Barker,” January 29, 1730.

18. “Journal of Pentecost Barker,” January 29, 1730.

19. Whether Barker still had the same speech patterns in later life is a mystery. It may be suggestive that he does feel intimidated in the presence of what he calls *formidable opponents*. See the episodes related in chap. 5 below relating to “Pope Joan” and “R.” In both cases, Barker is proud of himself for getting his words out effectively, although he still says that Merivale could have said things better.

20. Barker also explained that he was “ruined when taken from school [by his] mother’s dying.” DRO, MS 3237M/F1, February 26, 1760.

21. DRO, MS 3237M/F1, January 1, 1759. Had he known “half the Latin” Merivale knew, Barker said, he could “turn every word” of Robert Barclay’s *Theologiae vere christianae apologia* (1676) into English. He also mentions that he could “understand a little Latin” in testimony during the court-martial of Admiral Thomas Mathews. “Copies of All the Minutes and Proceedings Taken at and upon the Several Tryals of Captain George Burrish, Captain Edmund Williams, Captain John Ambrose, Lieutenant Henry Page, Lieutenant Charles Davids, Lieutenant William Griffiths; and Lieutenant Cornelius Smelt, Respectively: Before the Court Martial Lately Held at Chatham: And All the Proceedings Relating Thereunto,” *House of Commons Sessional Papers of the Eighteenth Century: Naval Court Martial* (1746), 185.

22. Although Barker picked up French from his travels (during, e.g., his time in Provence), he still had to ask for Merivale's help with longer French passages. See chap. 4 below.

23. DRO, MS 3237M/F1, April 19, 1759. There were decades to go for Thomas Taylor's translation of Plato's complete works into English in 1804, but Barker missed Henry Spens's 1763 translation of the *Republic* by only a year. Much of what he and Merivale read was translated by Floyer Sydenham, knowledge of whose work Barker owed to his "Jew[ish] physician, who reads much, especially in new and curious books." Ibid.

24. "Journal of Pentecost Barker," September 20, 1730.

25. "Marriage Settlement, Pentecost Barker and Alice Beer of Plymouth," WDRO, MS 2929/4.

26. If Barker's father-in-law helped him become a purser, it was likely by way of an introduction to the most socially significant of the figures with whom Barker rubbed shoulders, Sir John Rogers (1676–1744), a Whig MP, occasional mayor of the town, and relative friend of Dissenters to whom Barker wrote in 1720 expressly to ask for help getting a job as a purser. See "Letters Addressed to Sir John Rogers," WDRO, MS 733/3358/17.

27. "Journal of Pentecost Barker," June 6, 1730.

28. "Journal of Pentecost Barker," June 8, 1730.

29. "Batter Street Presbyterian Meeting Register." On the early diary, see the last entry of the journal, in which Barker indicates that he wrote a diary before 1729. "Journal of Pentecost Barker," June 27, 1731. In his letters to Merivale, Barker also reveals that thirty years later he was still in regular conversation with Susan's husband, Peter Cock, who by then was his good friend. For the line about Baron's sermon, see DRO, MS 3237M/F1, June 25, 1759.

30. Here I am drawing on my own work on spiritual diaries. See Kadane, *The Watchful Clothier*, esp. chaps. 1–2. Also see Tom Webster, "Writing to Redundancy: Approaches to Spiritual Journals and Early Modern Spirituality," *Historical Journal* 39, no. 1 (1996): 33–56; Michael Mascuch, *Origins of the Individualist Self: Autobiography and Self-Identity in England, 1591–1791* (Stanford, CA: Stanford University Press, 1996); Paul S. Seaver, *Wallington's World: A Puritan Artisan in Seventeenth-Century London* (Stanford, CA: Stanford University Press, 1985), 42–43; Jürgen Schlaeger, "Self-Exploration in Early Modern English Diaries," in *Marginal Voices, Marginal Forms: Diaries in European Literature and History*, ed. Rachel Langford and Russell West (Amsterdam: Brill, 1999), 22–36; Philip Benedict, "Some Uses of Autobiographical Documents in the Reformed Tradition," in *Von der dargestellten Person zum erinnerten Ich, Europäische Selbstzeugnisse als historische Quellen (1500–1850)*, ed. Kaspar von Greyerz, Hans Medick, and Patrice Veit (Cologne: Böhlau, 2001), 357–58; D. Bruce Hindmarsh, *The Evangelical Conversion Narrative: Spiritual Autobiography in Early Modern England* (Oxford: Oxford University Press, 2005); John Stachniewski, *The Persecutory Imagination: English Puritanism and the Literature of Religious Despair* (Oxford: Oxford University Press, 1991); Alan Macfarlane, *The Family Life of Ralph Josselin: A Seventeenth Century Clergyman* (Cambridge: Cambridge University Press, 1977); and Andrew Cambers, "Reading, the Godly, and Self-Writing in England, circa 1580–1720," *Journal of British Studies* 46, no. 4 (2007): 796–825.

31. Among the most quoted authors are Richard Baxter, John Bunyan, George Trosse, Matthew Henry, and Philip Doddridge.

32. The diary also reflects Puritan practice, which was more or less traditional Dissenter practice too. Apart from writing in the diary and reading the literature of practical

divinity, both of which were devotional acts, Barker regularly attended two sermons on Sunday and one during the week.

33. "Journal of Pentecost Barker," February 1, 1730: "It is now seven years since I have kept a daily account of my conduct. . . . I have now as much reason to watch every day against earthly mindedness as I had at that time against drunkenness."

34. "Journal of Pentecost Barker," February 27, 1730.

35. "Journal of Pentecost Barker," October 31, 1729.

36. The argument I am referencing largely comes from Harry G. Levine, "The Discovery of Addiction: Changing Conceptions of Habitual Drunkenness in America," *Journal of Studies on Alcohol* 15 (1978): 493–506, although much of what Levine argues was suggested earlier in Joseph Hirch, "Enlightened Eighteenth Century Views of the Alcohol Problem," *Journal of the History of Medicine and Allied Sciences* 4, no. 2 (1949): 230–36. Levine has been challenged by Roy Porter and Jessica Warner. Here see Roy Porter, "The Drinking Man's Disease: The 'Pre-History' of Alcoholism in Georgian Britain," *British Journal of Addiction* 80, no. 4 (1985): 385–96; and Jessica Warner, "Before There Was 'Alcoholism': Lessons from the Medieval Experience with Alcohol," *Contemporary Drug Problems* 19 (1992): 409–28, and " 'Resolv'd to drink no more': Addiction as a Preindustrial Construct," *Alcohol* 55 (1994): 685–91. But more recently Warner has been challenged (and Levine mostly defended) by Peter Ferentzy, "From Sin to Disease: Differences and Similarities between Past and Current Conceptions of Chronic Drunkenness," *Contemporary Drug Problems* 28, no. 3 (2001): 363–90. A more synthetic view can be found in James Nicholls, "Vinum Britannicum: The 'Drink Question' in Early Modern England," *Social History of Alcohol and Drugs* 22, no. 2 (2008): 190–208. My point is not that Barker can solve the mystery of when excessive drinking came to be seen by opinion makers as a disease. Obviously no public was reading or influenced by his private diary. The point is that Barker himself at times entertained the idea that he had a disease. And that alone is culturally suggestive. For general insights about drinking and sociability in an earlier but still relevant era, see Phil Withington, "Intoxicants and Society in Early Modern England," *Historical Journal* 54, no. 3 (2011): 631–57.

37. For a definition of the *Puritan ethos*, see Christopher Durston and Jacqueline Eales, "Introduction: The Puritan Ethos, 1560–1700," in *The Culture of English Puritanism, 1560–1700*, ed. Christopher Durston and Jacqueline Eales (London: Macmillan, 1996), 1–31, 13.

38. In Shakespeare's *Twelfth Night*, Olivia is described in her endless mourning over her brother's death as "being addicted to a melancholy" (2.5.206–7). For a discussion of this and other literary uses of *addiction*, see Rebecca Lemon, *Addiction and Devotion in Early Modern England* (Philadelphia: University of Pennsylvania Press, 2018).

39. John Mason, *Self-Knowledge: A Treatise, Shewing the Nature and Benefit of That Important Science, and the Way to Attain It* (London, 1745), 55. Barker wrote Merivale: "Mason on Self Knowledge is a fine performance. To hear him preach as I did once at Cheshunt one should not think he was master of such learning and knowledge as he there displays." DRO, MS 3237M/F1, January 1, 1759.

40. Levine, "The Discovery of Addiction," 30.

41. Richard Baxter, *A Christian Directory; or, A Summ of Practical Theologie . . .* (London, 1673), 381.

42. Baxter's contemporaries saw no qualitative difference here either. Increase Mather presupposed wine could be an object of addiction. Witness Mather's *Wo to Drunkards*, which, as we have seen, uses the word *addicted* in its full title. Liquor was equally irrelevant to the fundamental problem for Benjamin Franklin, who in the 1720s patted himself

on the back for being able to perform his work in his London printshop so much more efficiently than his buzzed coworkers, whose inefficiency he thought came entirely from beer. Leonard W. Labaree, Ralph L. Ketcham, and Helen C. Boatfield, eds., *The Autobiography of Benjamin Franklin* (New Haven, CT: Yale University Press, 1964), 99–101.

43. Baxter, *Christian Directory*, 381–82.

44. George E. Valliant, *The Natural History of Alcoholism Revisited* (Cambridge, MA: Harvard University Press, 1995), 44–45.

45. Baxter, *Christian Directory*, 384–85.

46. See the many important correctives in David D. Hall, *The Puritans: A Transatlantic History* (Princeton, NJ: Princeton University Press, 2019).

47. Valliant, *The Natural History of Alcoholism*, 243.

48. "Journal of Pentecost Barker," January 17, 1731.

49. "Journal of Pentecost Barker," September 25, 1730.

50. C. E. Storey, "Apoplexy: Changing Concepts in the Eighteenth Century," in *Brain, Mind and Medicine: Essays in Eighteenth-Century Neuroscience*, ed. H. Whitaker, C. U. M. Smith, and S. Finger (Boston: Springer, 2007), 233–244.

51. Barker also seemed to make a distinction between *apoplectic* and *hysterical* fits. On one occasion, he remembered an "apoplectic fit" occurring in 1717. See "Journal of Pentecost Barker," May 2, 1731. But on another occasion he very specifically located his first "hysterical" fit on the first day of January 1724: "As on this day 6 years I was first seiz'd with those histerical fits, which have been such a Scourge to me." Ibid., January 1, 1730. It is of course also possible that he was using *apoplectic* and *hysterical* interchangeably and was just misremembering exactly when the first had occurred.

52. After a diary entry in which he describes "drink" and "flesh meats" his "very best friends," he writes: "I am undone forever. What is Man without his God. How painful is it to me to live now in this World, where friends pity me, medicines relieve me (Opium many times has lull'd me to sweet sleep) but in the other state, if I am not pardon'd punishments will act on the naked soul." "Journal of Pentecost Barker," November 7, 1729.

53. Francis Osborne, *Advice to His Son* (1658), 18.

54. On the ambiguities of the nineteenth-century intent behind *heroic* as a descriptor, see Robert B. Sullivan, "Sanguine Practices: A Historical and Historiographic Reconsideration of Heroic Therapy in the Age of Rush," *Bulletin of the History of Medicine* 68, no. 2 (1994): 211–34.

55. Thomas Edwards, *Gangraena; or, A Catalogue and Discovery of Many of the Errours, Heresies, Blasphemies and Pernicious Practices of the Sectaries of This Time* (London, 1646).

56. Thomas Tryon, *Wisdom's Dictates; or, Aphorisms and Rules, Physical, Moral, and Divine, for Preserving the Health of the Body, and the Peace of the Mind . . .* (London, 1691).

57. Barker read Richard Baxter avidly, and Baxter offered some of the same reasons for his own vegetarianism. But Baxter articulated his rationale only in his last treatise, which was not discovered and published until the twentieth century. See Richard Baxter, *The Poor Husbandman's Advocate to Rich Racking Landlords*, ed. F. J. Powicke (Manchester: Manchester University Press, 1926), 39.

58. DRO, MS 3237M/F1, August 1760.

59. On "managing populations," see Nicholas Rogers, *Mayhem: Post-War Crime and Violence in Britain, 1748–53* (New Haven, CT: Yale University Press, 2012), 153–57.

60. Proximity to the navy unavoidably meant proximity to drinking. N. A. M. Rodger, *The Wooden World: An Anatomy of the Georgian Navy* (New York: Norton, 1986), 72.

61. "Journal of Pentecost Barker," June 27, 1731.

62. "Journal of Pentecost Barker," February 1, 1731. If the math here does not add up, it is because Barker arrived at "eighth anniversary" counting by months instead of by days (he had started writing at the end of February 1723 rather than the beginning), and he also celebrated his eighth year at its commencement rather than conclusion.

63. "Journal of Pentecost Barker," February 15, 1730.

64. "Journal of Pentecost Barker," February 16, 1730.

65. "Journal of Pentecost Barker," February 15, 1730.

66. "Journal of Pentecost Barker," February 28, 1730. Sometimes it can admittedly be unclear what exactly Barker means by *drunk*: "I din'd in publick I may call it, with several of very good fashion, and broke away soon after Dinner to renew my Conduct since the last sacrament. My Management hath indeed bin very bad. I was soon drunk with Passion and Peevishness, Impatience and Discontent." Ibid., March 14, 1730.

67. "Journal of Pentecost Barker," September 22, 1730. As he continued in the same reflective entry, recognizing that the wheels had to be greased even as they ultimately drove everyone to the same place: "[W]hat will it signify a few years hence, who is Mayor of this Town, who hath the advantage of recommending men to Places? For this is what they chiefly mind. The Dust will cover us all, and Worms will feast upon us. What is Old King George the better for swaying the brittish sceptre from 1714 to 1727? He is now no more. I have seen the rise and fall of his Reign, and of his Predecessors. The Glories of Queen Ann's [*sic*], could not preserve her from the Dust." Ibid.

68. Barker notes in one of his diary entries that he was entrusted to resupply the lighthouse at Eddystone, a few miles off the coast from Plymouth. He conveys this detail in a state of panic after having forgotten to supply the lighthouse with candles. For the diary entry, see "Journal of Pentecost Barker," December 8, 1729. A nineteenth-century historian of lighthouses apparently took the time to look through Barker's diary and concluded—circumstantially—that the reason Barker forgot to supply candles was that he was too drunk to perform his job. See William John Hardy, *Lighthouses: Their History and Romance* (London: Religious Tract Society, 1895), 145–46.

69. Linda Colley, *The Ordeal of Elizabeth Marsh: A Woman in World History* (New York: Anchor, 2007), 142.

70. N. A. M. Rodger, *The Command of the Ocean: A Naval History of Britain, 1649–1815* (New York: Norton, 2005), 108 (quoting Pepys).

71. Karen McBride, Tony Hines, and Russell Craig, "A Rum Deal: The Purser's Measure and Accounting Control of Materials in the Royal Navy, 1665–1832," *Business History* 58, no. 6 (2016): 925–46, 931.

72. McBride, Hines, and Craig, "A Rum Deal," 931.

73. Edward Ward, *The Wooden World Dissected, in the Character of a Ship of War* (London, 1707), 55–59.

74. Rodger, *Wooden World*, 88. Rodger points out that in the eighteenth century pursers could still be responsible for the loss of victuals if they did not keep detailed accounting.

75. See Pentecost Barker to Philip Vanbrugh, April 18, 1740, TNA, ADM 106/947/58.

76. On John Rogers (1676–1744), see n. 26 above; and "Letters Addressed to Sir John Rogers." Also see John M. Triffitt, "Politics and the Urban Community: Parliamentary Boroughs in the South West of England, 1710–1730" (DPhil thesis, University of Oxford, 1985), 210–18, and "Believing and Belonging: Church Behaviour in Plymouth and Dartmouth, 1710–30," in *Parish, Church and People: Local Studies in Lay Religion, 1350–1750*, ed. S. Wright (London: Hutchinson, 1988), 179–80.

77. Barker also on one occasion records that on the previous night he had been up late dancing but was quick to qualify: "I have no Delight in these things, but to please my very good Friends I complyed with it, & hope I did not wilfully offend." "Journal of Pentecost Barker," December 29, 1729. On enthusiasm, see Michael Heyd, *"Be Sober and Reasonable": The Critique of Enthusiasm in the Seventeenth and Early Eighteenth Centuries* (Leiden: Brill, 1995).

78. "Journal of Pentecost Barker," September 18, 1730.

79. See, e.g., "Journal of Pentecost Barker," April 30, 1731.

80. "Journal of Pentecost Barker," February 25, 1731.

81. "Journal of Pentecost Barker," March 19, 1731.

82. "Journal of Pentecost Barker," April 24, 1731.

83. "Journal of Pentecost Barker," April 26, 1731.

84. "Journal of Pentecost Barker," April 28, 1731.

85. "Journal of Pentecost Barker," May 20, 1731.

86. "Journal of Pentecost Barker," June 16, 1731.

87. Labaree, Ketcham, and Boatfield, eds., *The Autobiography of Benjamin Franklin*.

88. Even earlier, Barker might have embraced the ideas he found in the writings of Origen. Sometime before the 1720s, his father, Gregory, had "bought at some auction Phoenix 1st Volume, wherein is the account of Origen and his opinions." "I dipt into it now and then," Barker recalled in late life to Merivale, "but rather look'd upon it as heresy." DRO, MS 3237M/F1, June 25, 1759. Barker knew well what heresy was in the 1720s, and if he dipped into a heretical work it was *as* a dangerous heretical work, not as a source of inspiration for a change in outlook, or at least not in any sense to which he was willing to admit. The book he is talking about here is, incidentally, John Dunton, *The Phoenix; or, A Revival of Scarce and Valuable Pieces . . . Being a Collection of Manuscripts and Printed Tracts, Nowhere to Be Found but in the Closets of the Curious* (London, 1707).

89. For an overview of some of these developments, see James Spalding, "The Demise of English Presbyterianism, 1660–1760," *Church History* 28, no. 1 (1959): 63–83.

90. See Benjamin Grosvenor, *An Authentick Account of Several Things Done and Agreed upon by the Dissenting Ministers Lately Assembled at Salters-Hall* (London, 1719). That the issue was subscription to the Thirty-Nine Articles rather than to the more strenuous Westminster Confession itself indicates Dissent's relative retreat from Calvinism.

91. The fuller story is told in C. Gordon Bolam, Jeremy Goring, H. L. Short, and Roger Thomas, *The English Presbyterians: From Elizabethan Puritanism to Modern Unitarianism* (London: Allen & Unwin, 1968), 175–232.

92. The same observation was made in the only piece of academic writing to dedicate attention—albeit just a few pages—to Barker's diary. See Triffitt, "Believing and Belonging."

93. See, e.g., "Journal of Pentecost Barker," April 11, 1731.

94. This point was made long ago in Paul Hazard, *La crise de la conscience européenne* (Paris: Boivin, 1935).

95. "Il a voulu encore que toutes les races humaines se réduisissent à la seule race d'Adam: en sorte que tous les hommes, et selon le corps et selon l'âme, dépendissent de la volonté et de la liberté de ce seul homme." Bossuet, *Élévations a Dieu sur tous les mystères*, 120.

96. The theme runs throughout Kidd, *The Forging of Races*.

97. "Journal of Pentecost Barker." Also see Osborne, *Advice to His Son*.

98. "Journal of Pentecost Barker," September 10, 1730.

99. "Journal of Pentecost Barker," September 10, 1730.

100. I mistakenly thought this was Morley in Yorkshire until coming across an earlier spelling of Moreleigh (then and now a tiny village of just a few dozen houses). Compare Matthew Kadane, "Original Sin and the Path to the Enlightenment," *Past and Present* 235, no. 1 (May 2017): 105–40, 118.

101. Michael Fisher, *Counterflow to Colonialism: Indian Travellers and Settlers in Britain, 1600–1857* (Delhi: Permanent Black, 2004).

102. On Britons' relative indifference to skin color in the early eighteenth century, see Dror Wahrman, *The Making of the Modern Self: Identity and Culture in Eighteenth-Century England* (New Haven, CT: Yale University Press, 2004), esp. chap. 3.

103. Barker indicates that Peter Baron, a.k.a. Sophron, had also swerved from orthodoxy in later life even if he kept his true belief under wraps. For more on Baron, see chap. 5.

104. "Journal of Pentecost Barker," November 30, 1729.

105. That Baron could have made this same point using the Trinity only makes it more interesting that he draws on original sin. About the Trinity, Joseph Priestley would later write in terms expressly sensitive to the other Abrahamic religions: "The doctrine of the trinity, having been one of the earliest, corruptions of Christianity, will probably be one of the last to be completely eradicated. But the time, I trust, is fast approaching, when, by means of the zeal of truly enlightened and good men in this great cause, this fundamental error, which gives such great and just cause of offence to Jews and Mahometans, will be removed, and all that has been built upon it will fall to the ground." Joseph Priestley, *An Appeal to the Serious and Candid Professors of Christianity . . .* (Birmingham, 1784), 29.

106. On early modern British perceptions of Islam, see Nabil Matar, *Islam in Britain, 1558–1685* (Cambridge: Cambridge University Press, 1998), 108–10; Humberto Garcia, *Islam and the English Enlightenment, 1670–1840* (Baltimore: Johns Hopkins University Press, 2011), 1–29; James R. Jacob, *Henry Stubbe, Radical Protestantism and the Early Enlightenment* (Cambridge: Cambridge University Press, 1983), 64–77; and J. A. I. Champion, *The Pillars of Priestcraft Shaken* (Cambridge: Cambridge University Press, 1992), 99–132. Compare the more negative perception of Islam associated with Lancelot Addison in William J. Bulman, *Anglican Enlightenment: Orientalism, Religion and Politics in England and Its Empire, 1648–1715* (Cambridge: Cambridge University Press, 2015), 121–28.

107. "Journal of Pentecost Barker," March 26, 1730.

108. See, e.g., DRO, MS 3237M/F1, February 9, June 16, and September 1, 1759.

109. DRO, MS 3237M/F1, May 21, 1759.

110. DRO, MS 3237M/F1, June 2, 1759. On Le Clerc's aversion to original sin, see Annie Barnes, *Jean Le Clerc (1657–1736) et la république des lettres* (Paris, 1938), 106. Barker invokes the same metaphor (Tokay, Champs, etc.) when, on a different occasion, he tells Merivale how much more pleasurable it was to have a conversation about books with a friend's housekeeper, an "intelligent woman," than to take part in "carnal pleasures." DRO, MS 3237M/F1, May 5, 1760.

Chapter Four

1. The details here are well covered in Dorinda Outram, *The Enlightenment* (1995), 4th ed. (Cambridge: Cambridge University Press, 2019), 1–9, 168–76.

2. "Diary of Joseph Ryder," October 31, 1749.

3. DRO, MS 3237M/F1, January 12, 1759.

4. Barker's letters ended up in the possession of the Merivale family, no doubt because their ancestor Samuel Merivale was the recipient. As for the survival of Merivale's letters, my guess is that one of Barker's survivors at some point returned Merivale's letters to the Merivale family, although this is nowhere detailed in Barker's will. On letter writing in this era, see Lindsay O'Neill, *The Opened Letter: Networking in the Early Modern British World* (Philadelphia: University of Pennsylvania Press, 2015).

5. William Stephens, *An Account of the Growth of Deism in England* (London, 1696).

6. See "An Elegy Made on the Rev. Mr. William Stephens, Late Vicar of St. Andrew's Church in Plymouth . . . ," West Sussex Record Office, Add. MS 8122.

7. On the mechanics of the process, see Sarah L. C. Clapp, "The Beginnings of Subscription Publication in the Seventeenth Century," *Modern Philology* 29, no. 2 (1931): 199–224.

8. "Will of Pentecost Barker." On St. Andrews's wealth, see Peter Virgin, "Mudge, Zachariah (1694–1769), Church of England Clergyman," in *Oxford Dictionary of National Biography*. Barker was buried at St. Andrews on September 8, 1762.

9. "Marriage Settlement, Pentecost Barker and Alice Beer of Plymouth."

10. "Journal of Pentecost Barker," September 20, 1730.

11. WDRO, MS 457/533.

12. "Will of Gregory Barker, Wine Cooper of Plymouth, Devon," TNA, PROB 11/703/279. A letter survives from 1740 in which Barker writes one of his late father Gregory's clients asking to fulfill an outstanding order. See Pentecost Barker to Philip Vanbrugh. Barker's father had died earlier that year, leaving his son £20 in addition to an unspecified amount of property. The inheritance no doubt helped. So too did the fact that Barker had the option to consolidate his capacity to provide the navy with goods, which in turn may have made him an even more attractive purser.

13. In his diary-keeping years, Barker viewed promotion to a third-rate ship as a great success. See "Journal of Pentecost Barker," December 24, 1729.

14. DRO, MS 3237M/F1, February 26, 1760.

15. On Barker and the *Barfleur*, see TNA, ADM 106/1004/188. On the *Sandwich*, see TNA, ADM 106/1079/277. On the *Ocean*, see TNA, ADM 354/161/325. On the *Dover*, see DRO, MS 3237M/F1, April 20, 1759.

16. DRO, MS 3237M/F1, August 6, 1761.

17. No notice of this appointment exists in the Admiralty Papers, but a newspaper account reports that in 1755 Barker was appointed purser of the *Norfolk* for "his faithful Service in the Mediterranean." See *Whitehall Evening Post; or, London Intelligencer*, no. 1370, February 18–20, 1755. One wonders whether Barker himself provided this press release to boost his reputation after the fallout with Marsh. See the discussion at the end of this chapter.

18. "Copies of All the Minutes and Proceedings," 185–86.

19. Another glimpse of Barker and Mathew's relationship appears in a letter to Merivale in which Barker reports that he had a conversation with Mathews as the admiral was awaiting his court-martial: "Till about that time I never thought that [Mathews] thought at all about religion." But here apparently Mathews did think about it. "Take away Gods Omniscience, and you un-God him," Barker recalled Mathews as saying. "Another time, [Mathews] surprised me more, talking about Faith & Works, & sent me to borrow a Volume of the Spectators, where was an admirable chapter upon the subject." DRO, MS 3237M/F1, June 10, 1760.

20. DRO, MS 3237M/F1, May 21, 1759.

21. Marsh was the uncle of the now better-known Elizabeth Marsh. See Colley, *The Ordeal of Elizabeth Marsh.*

22. "Diary of George Marsh," University of London, Wellcome Library, MSS 7628–29, March 19, 1750.

23. "Diary of George Marsh," March 19, 1750.

24. "Diary of George Marsh," May 8, 1755.

25. "Diary of George Marsh," March 19, 1750.

26. "Diary of George Marsh," April 7, 1750.

27. The National Archives, "Currency Converter: 1270–2017," https://www.nationalarchives.gov.uk/currency-converter, accessed Aug. 14, 2023.

28. By his death in 1800, Marsh was worth £34,575, an amount at the end of which one can add three zeros to get the rough equivalent in today's terms. Colley, *The Ordeal of Elizabeth Marsh*, 38.

29. On the *Renommée*, see Jean-Michel Roche, *Dictionnaire des bâtiments de la flotte de guerre française de Colbert à nos jours*, vol. 1, *1675–1870* (Toulon: Roche, 2005), 372–73. There is no indication that Barker was serving on the *Dover*. At the time he was still purser on the *Barfleur*.

30. TNA, HCA 30/244. Brent Sirota writes that the eighteenth-century sea "was acquiring a reputation as a moral hazard, a zone of irreligion and immorality." See Brent Sirota, "The Church: Anglicanism and the Nationalization of Maritime Space," in *Mercantilism Reimagined: Political Economy in Early Modern Britain and Its Empire*, ed. Philip J. Stern and Carl Wennerlind (Oxford: Oxford University Press, 2014), 196–217, 199.

31. DRO, MS 3237M/F1, April 20, 1759.

32. DRO, MS 3237M/F1, April 29, 1759.

33. DRO, MS 3237M/F1, May 3, 1759. See Sabina Pavone, "Between History and Myth: The Monita secreta Societatis Jesu," in *The Jesuits II: Cultures, Sciences, and the Arts, 1540–1773*, ed. John W. O'Malley, Gauvin Alexander Bailey, Steven J. Harris, and T. Frank Kennedy (Toronto: University of Toronto Press, 2019), 50–65.

34. The slight difference in wording and the absence of accent marks may mean that Barker was here working from memory. DRO, MS 3237M/F1, March 27, 1759.

35. Robert Darnton, *The Forbidden Best-Sellers of Pre-Revolutionary France* (New York: Norton, 1996), 115. Darnton discusses the book throughout chap. 4.

36. For more on Mercier's work, see Diane Berrett Brown, "The Pedagogical City of Louis-Sébastien Mercier's 'L'an 2440,'" *French Review* 78, no. 3 (2005): 470–80.

37. Mercier was not the first author to put the words into print. Described simply as *ces quatre beaux*, they also appear in Le Maître de Claville (Charles-François Nicolas), *Traité du vrai mérite de l'homme, considéré dans tous les âges et dans toutes les conditions* (Amsterdam, 1738), 167. But here too the author indicates that he heard them elsewhere.

38. Merivale wrote: "[T]hose French lines are beautiful & grand, There is I think a great justness as well as sublimity of thought in them, providing we take not, rien decider, in too rigorous a sense." DRO, MS 3237M/F1, March 30, 1759.

39. For a revision of the view of Britain and France as intractable enemies, see John Shovlin, *Trading with the Enemy: Britain, France, and the 18th-Century Quest for a Peaceful World Order* (New Haven, CT: Yale University Press, 2021).

40. Two other appearances in this historical record are not particularly revealing. In 1749, Barker hired a man named Thomas Bewes to be his attorney. See WDRO, 572/11/4 1749. The reasons are never clear, although the need for legal services may have had

something to do with the partnership with Marsh. In 1750, Barker's name also appears among the subscribers to Thomas Riley's *Naval Expositor* (1750).

41. This book confusingly shared the short title *Sermons* with the book to which, as we saw in chap. 2, John Brine had a negative reaction. But the *Sermons* from 1733 was a different work, which is to say a different collections of sermons. Also, if Barker had only one copy of Foster's writing, namely, the sermons from 1733, then the implication is that by then he had lost his subscription copy of *Discourses on All the Principal Branches of Natural Religion*.

42. "It is used as fuel for burning; some of it he takes and warms himself, he kindles a fire and bakes bread. But he also fashions a god and worships it; he makes an idol and bows down to it."

43. DRO, MS 3237M/F1, June 14, 1760.

44. *Whitehall Evening Post*, no. 1412, May 29–31, 1755. For a further suggestion that Barker maintained a residence in London after 1755, there is a reference (which can be inferred as having been made in 1757) to "Pentecost Barker" as a "London gentleman" in a survey of private British archives written in the 1880s and drawn from Historical Commissions material. See William B. Weeden, "Bits of English History from the Manuscripts," *Unitarian Review and Religious Magazine* 22, no. 5 (1884): 446–58, 456.

45. Two lodges met at the Rainbow Coffee House: the Britannic Lodge, no. 33 (from 1730 to 1739), and the Imperial George Lodge, no. 92 (from 1754 to 1757). Barker might have been part of the latter, but the available information from this lodge covers a later era. See Library and Museum of Freemasonry, London, GBR 1991 AR/290. I owe thanks to Martin Cherry and Susan Snell from the Museum of Freemasonry for their help. On Freemasonry and the Enlightenment, see Margaret C. Jacob, *The Origins of Freemasonry: Facts and Fictions* (Philadelphia: University of Pennsylvania Press, 2006).

46. An 1870 report on historical manuscripts that were then scattered throughout private estate archives in the United Kingdom records "several letters" sent between Harry Trelawny, a well-known army officer from Cornwall, and "Pentecost Barker." The manuscript cataloger was apparently struck enough by Barker's letters to describe a few of them. For example (and here we can unmistakably hear his voice): "In one [Barker] 'wonders that no one had translated the Moyen de Parvenir [by Béroalde de Verville],' which he had been reading: 'it would sell better than Whitfield's Sermons.'" Barker also apparently writes in a letter from 1750 that he heard that *Letters Writ by a Turkish Spy* (Amsterdam, 1684–94)—now attributed to Giovanni Paolo Marana—was written by Roger L'Estrange. Was Barker sardonically suggesting that the Tory L'Estrange was a closet deist? In yet another letter, Barker smeared the 1713 *The System of English Ecclesiastical Law* (i.e., the *Codex*) by Edmund Gibson, bishop of London, as being "as useless as a Church Bible." Not least, in a letter from May 16, 1760, Barker says that he had—to quote from the manuscript cataloger—"credible information that Mr. [Laurence] Sterne, one of the Prebendarys of York, was the author of Tristram Shandy." (Barker wrote much the same thing about Sterne in a letter to Merivale sent two weeks earlier. See DRO, MS 3237M/F1, May 1, 1760.) See *First Report of the Royal Commission on Historical Manuscripts* (London, 1870), 51. Access to these letters would no doubt flesh out Barker's image. But the letters did not turn up among some of the Trelawny papers that ended up in the British Library in the 1920s. Most likely they were lost in France during the Second World War. According to one local history, after the Trelawny (Trelawne) estate was sold, "many of the important manuscripts . . . were retained by Sir John Salisbury when he went to live in the south of France": "He and his wife both died there in Vaucluse in 1944 while

the country was under German occupation." The author further speculates that the family papers were therefore lost. See James Derriman, "The Trelawny Muniments," *Devon and Cornwall Notes and Queries* 35, no. 5 (1984): 225–28. My thanks to Angela Broome, library archivist at the Royal Cornwall Museum, for helping me try to find these letters.

Chapter Five

1. Pamphilus was also a pseudonym later used by David Hume in the *Dialogues concerning Natural Religion* (1779). Hume was persuaded to wait to publish the *Dialogues* until after his death in 1776. He had finished this work by 1761, however, and a shorter, preliminary version was in circulation among his friends by the early 1750s. But there is no indication at all in their correspondence that Barker or Merivale knew of the work or had access to Hume's illustrious inner circles. See Robert John Sheffler Manning, "David Hume's 'Dialogues concerning Natural Religion': Otherness in History and in Text," *Journal of Religion* 70, no. 4 (1990): 589–605.

2. DRO, MS 3237M/F1, June 27, 1759. Barker would also on occasion refer to his view as "the Pamphilian scheme." See, e.g., ibid., June 26, 1760.

3. DRO, MS 3237M/F1, July 10, 1760.

4. DRO, MS 3237M/F1, June 20, 1759. On Morgan, see Jan van den Berg, *A Forgotten Christian Deist: Thomas Morgan* (New York: Routledge, 2021). Barker also may have intended his pen name to be a subtle rebuke of John Brine. The evangelical author John Johnson's *Evangelical Truths Vindicated: In an Epistle to the Readers of Mr. John Brine's Two Pamphlets . . .* (London, 1758) invented a character named Philalethes to serve as a cautionary tale about deism. Barker of course wanted to throw that kind of caution to the wind and may have therefore ironically appropriated the character's name.

5. That Barker does occasionally reverse his last name suggests that Philalethes was a substitute not for his whole name but just for Pentecost. See, e.g., DRO, MS 3237M/F1, February 21, 1760.

6. Maurice Wiles, *Archetypal Heresy: Arianism through the Centuries* (Oxford: Oxford University Press, 2001), 153 n. 673. Some information on Merivale can be gleaned from J. M. Rigg, "Merivale, John Herman (1779–1844)," rev. Ralph Lloyd-Jones, in *Oxford Dictionary of National Biography*. The invaluable secondary source on Merivale is, however, a self-published family history: Anna E. Merivale, *Family Memorials* (Exeter, 1884). For the essays, both defenses of the recently deceased Arian minister Nathaniel Lardner (1684–1768), see Joseph Priestley, ed., *The Theological Repository: Consisting of Original Essays, Hints, Queries, etc. Calculated to Promote Religious Knowledge*, 6 vols. (London, 1769–88), 2:73–82, 3:58–70.

7. The *Old Whig* author Charistes is identified as George Benson in Herbert McLachlan, *The Unitarian Movement in the Religious Life of England* (London: George Allen & Unwin, 1934), 1:167. Also see Lady Tranquilla (Thomas Bradbury), *The Triumphs of Bigotry: A Poem, Sacred to the Peaceful Memory of Charistes* (London, 1749).

8. The Barker-Merivale correspondence also contains a fragment of a letter Barker sent in 1746. See DRO, MS 3237M/F1.

9. Charles E. Lart, "The Huguenot Settlements and Churches in the West of England," *Proceedings of the Huguenot Society of London* 7, no. 2 (1901–4): 286–98, 288. Lart makes a passing reference to a letter between Barker and Merivale but does not cite it in his very slim documentation or explain how he came to see it.

10. The one exception here is John Triffitt, who dedicated a few pages to Barker's

business connections as part of his larger attempt to understand the politics of religion in the southwest of England. Triffitt gives no indication that he knew anything about Barker's life after the end of his diary in 1731. See Triffitt, "Believing and Belonging," 179–84.

11. DRO, MS 3237M/F1, August 29, 1759.

12. DRO, MS 3237M/F1, September 3, 1759.

13. DRO, MS 3237M/F1. See the letter numbered 90 by an early archivist. Context indicates that it was written in August 1759. In the same vein, Barker writes Merivale: "Philalethes trusts you [Charistes], with all his secrets, and I do the same by you." Ibid., June 30, 1759.

14. Barker too indicates that he tried to keep his views somewhat secret. "A young man," he explained to Merivale, "put me to my Trumps by saying Calvin and Beza were esteem'd very good Preachers. (N. B., This is a way that some take—they affirm a thing and then ask your opinion.)" Barker was here using *Calvin* and *Beza* as coded nicknames for two local orthodox preachers whom he did not like. And Barker's point, in case it is not clear, is that the young man was trying to suss out his opinions ("putting someone to their trumps," i.e., getting him to show his hand, as in playing cards) by getting him to express an opinion about two orthodox ministers. DRO, MS 3237M/F1, July 16, 1759.

15. DRO, MS 3237M/F1, July 12, 1759. Barker also sent Jenny a rebus that Merivale suggests involved the word *Tullibardine*, a village in Scotland. What exactly the rebus was is unclear. But Merivale congratulated Barker for it being one of his best "conundrums."

16. Several of Merivale's letters indicate that he also knew how to write in James Weston's shorthand. See James Weston, *Stenography Compleated; or, The Art of Shorthand Brought to Perfection* (London, 1727).

17. DRO, MS 3237M/F1, December 11, 1759.

18. Both Sophron (Sophronius) and Logisto are names found in Isaac Watts, *The Strength and Weakness of Human Reason* (1737). Logisto is an interlocutor who represents the deist position, which Watts argued against by insisting that sinful postlapsarian human nature disallows the full potential of human reason. Barker, however, appropriates the name in a thoroughly positive sense.

19. On the "Methodistical gang," see DRO, MS 3237M/F1, September 25, 1759.

20. DRO, MS 3237M/F1, September 1, 1759.

21. Weber, *The Protestant Ethic and the Spirit of Capitalism*, 60.

22. DRO, MS 3237M/F1, August 29, 1759. For readability, I have fixed an obvious mistake here in the original, changing *lovely* to *loves* in "Philalethes loves Charistes."

23. The letters that Merivale wrote near the time of his wife Elizabeth's death do not survive.

24. Merivale's memorandum book (DRO, MS 3237M/F4) records Jenny's birth on April 12, 1749, and death on January 27, 1763.

25. DRO, MS 3237M/F4.

26. We know little about Barker's death, but in a letter dated September 19, 1762, Samuel explains to Jenny that it was "immediately owing to a strangury that racked him grievously for some few days before he died." DRO, MS 3237M/F4.

27. DRO, MS 3237M/F4.

28. DRO, MS 3237M/F4, November 9, 1759.

29. DRO, MS 3237M/F4, February 26, 1760.

30. *Rex v. Barker* (1762), 97 Eng. Rep. 823–26.

31. *Sophronize* eventually came into use in English to describe the process of imbuing

someone with self-control but, according to the *Oxford English Dictionary*, not until the 1820s.

32. Even to his close friend Barker, Peter Baron waited until he was on his deathbed to admit that he believed in "the inferior scheme," i.e., the antitrinitarian belief that Christ is inferior to God. DRO, MS 3237M/F1, April 27, 1760.

33. DRO, MS 3237M/F1, June 16, 1759.

34. DRO, MS 3237M/F1, June 16, 1759.

35. Merivale's frank language in his letters to Barker stands in contrast to the cautious tone he assumed when writing publicly, even under the protection of a pseudonym. See Merivale's two essays in Priestley's *The Theological Repository*, cited above in n. 6. Merivale was still more conventional in the one work to which his actual name was attached, albeit posthumously. See Samuel Merivale, *Daily Devotions for the Closet . . .*, 3rd ed. (London, 1796). Merivale drew many of his devotions from the traditional formula of Isaac Watts and Philip Doddridge and managed to avoid statements about doctrine altogether.

36. JRUL, MSS, 6, B114/4, Samuel Bourn to George Benson, December 29, 1744.

37. DRO, MS 3237M/F1, October 5, 1759.

38. DRO, MS 3237M/F1, September 15, 1759.

39. Later in their correspondence, Merivale notes that in Barnstable a similar preaching arrangement had been agreed to. See DRO, MS 3237M/F1, March 21, 1762.

40. DRO, MS 3237M/F1, September 25, 1759.

41. DRO, MS 3237M/F1, October 3, 1761.

42. DRO, MS 3237M/F1, January 28, 1760. Merivale asked Barker to "forgive this freedom" in speaking: "[Y]ou are the only person I have ever corresponded with on this subject." Merivale also had more to say. The dangers of orthodoxy were the reason there should be no "publick stipends" for ministers, unless one could "make those stipends common to all parties without Distinction, in some proportion to the numbers of which each society consisted." Ibid.

43. DRO, MS 3237M/F1, September 25, 1759.

44. DRO, MS 3237M/F1, September 25, 1759.

45. Phyllis Mack, *Heart Religion in the British Enlightenment: Gender and Emotion in Early Methodism* (Cambridge: Cambridge University Press, 2008). Also see Susan Juster, *Doomsayers: Anglo-American Prophecy in the Age of Revolution* (Philadelphia: University of Pennsylvania Press, 2006), esp. chaps. 3 and 6; and Catherine A. Brekus, *Strangers and Pilgrims: Female Preaching in America, 1740–1845* (Chapel Hill: University of North Carolina Press, 1998).

46. DRO, MS 3237M/F1, March 10, 1760.

47. DRO, MS 3237M/F1, March 26, 1760.

48. All the quotations in this paragraph are from DRO, MS 3237M/F1, April 15, 1760.

49. Barker complained about George Whitfield precisely because of Whitfield's emphasis on Jesus. A follower of Whitfield's, Barker wrote, "actually said . . . that had it not been for X, the whole Creation must have perished." DRO, MS 3237M/F1, April 19, 1759. The idea offended Barker not only because it made Christ necessary but also because it implied that, rather than God, it was a man, namely, Jesus, who had control over the future state.

50. See the exchange with a man named "R" discussed below.

51. DRO, MS 3237M/F1, March 25, 1761.

52. James Bagg's Case (1615), 77 Eng. Rep. 1271–81.

53. *Rex v. Barker* (1762).

54. DRO, MS 3237M/F1, March 26, 1760.

55. The argument that Mansfield was an ally of all Dissenters is not so obvious given that Dissent was itself changing. For that questionable argument, see Charles F. Mullett, "Lord Mansfield and English Dissenters," *Missouri Law Review* 2, no. 1 (1937): 46–62.

56. Kevin Butterfield, *The Making of Tocqueville's America: Law and Association in the Early United States* (Chicago: University of Chicago Press, 2015), 74. Also see Timothy Endicott, *Administrative Law* (2009), 3rd ed. (Oxford: Oxford University Press, 2015), 412.

57. DRO, MS 3237M/F1, March 3, 1760.

58. On Barker and Baron being neighbors, see "Plymouth, Passage between Houses in Great Hoe Lane, Agreement," WDRO, MS 2919/11.

59. DRO, MS 3237M/F1, July 6, 1762.

60. DRO, MS 3237M/F1, September 1, 1759.

61. Merivale, *Family Memorials*, 5.

62. Isabel Rivers, "Doddridge, Philip (1702–51), Independent Minister and Writer," in *Oxford Dictionary of National Biography*.

63. On Tavistock's population, see Jonathan Barry, "Towns and Processes of Urbanization in the Early Modern Period," in Kain and Ravenhill, eds., *Historical Atlas of South-West England*, 417.

64. Merivale, *Family Memorials*, 15.

65. In their correspondence during their courtship, Merivale called himself "Fidelio" and Elizabeth "Charissa" (which may be another clue about his later nickname "Charistes").

66. McLachlan, *The Unitarian Movement in the Religious Life of England*, 92.

67. When Barker determined that Sophron was an Arminian, he passed the information along to Merivale as if it was a great discovery. On Baron's admission to believing in the "inferior scheme," which is to say that Jesus was not part of a Trinity but inferior to God, see n. 32 above.

68. DRO, MS 3237M/F1, June 26, 1760.

69. DRO, MS 3237M/F1, April 29, 1759.

70. Several letters from Merivale to Barker were lost—it is easy to tell they were written in the first place because Barker references them, but it is hard to tell how many are missing. Regardless, even if these were accounted for (I estimate no more than two dozen are missing), Barker was still the far more prolific correspondent.

71. DRO, MS 3237M/F1, March 27, 1759.

72. DRO, MS 3237M/F1, June 14, 1759.

73. DRO, MS 3237M/F1, June 16, 1759.

74. On the obscure authorship of *Code de la nature*, see Nicholas Wagner, "Etat actuel de nos connaissances sur Morelly," *Revue: Dix-huitième siècle* 10 (1978): 259–68. For the sake of convenience, I consistently refer to Morelly as the author of the *Code*.

75. Michael Sonenscher, "Property, Community, and Citizenship," in *The Cambridge History of Eighteenth-Century Political Thought*, ed. Mark Goldie and Robert Wokler (Cambridge: Cambridge University Press, 2006), 465–94.

76. Michael Sonenscher, *Sans-Culottes: An Eighteenth-Century Emblem in the French Revolution* (Princeton, NJ: Princeton University Press, 2018), 229–30.

77. See Abbé Noël Antoine Pluche, *Spectacle de la nature*, 8 vols. (1732–51).

78. Karl Marx, *Capital: A Critique of Political Economy* (1867), trans. Ben Fowkes (London: Penguin, 2004), 1:873.

79. DRO, MS 3237M/F1, November 7, 1759.

80. Barker first quotes these lines on June 12, 1759. Merivale does not read the text until November 7, 1759. For the passage, see [Etienne-Gabriel Morelly], *Code de la nature; ou, Le véritable esprit de ses loix, de tout tems négligé ou méconnu* (1755), 154.

81. Barker too endorses Morelly's assessment that the sole vice in the universe is avarice. DRO, MS 3237M/F1, November 10, 1759.

82. The possibility came up after Barker and Merivale read Samuel Bourn's *A Letter to the Rev. Samuel Chandler, D.D., concerning the Christian Doctrine of Future Punishment* (London, 1759).

83. On these terms, see Margaret C. Jacob, *The Secular Enlightenment*, 163–66.

84. For the broader context, see Jan Fergus, *Provincial Readers in Eighteenth-Century England* (Oxford: Oxford University Press, 2007).

85. On the other hand, apart from commentary on a few well-known works like *Candide* or Rousseau's *Julie*, many of the texts Barker and Merivale discuss seem disproportionately important when they were probably just timely. See, e.g., the abundant space given John Edmunds, who had just published a book, but whom Barker and Merivale reference only on that brief occasion. DRO, MS 3237M/F1, October 31, 1761.

86. On Rousseau's *Julie*, see chap. 9 below.

87. The text Merivale is referencing is *Some Familiar Letters between Mr. Locke and Several of His Friends* (London, 1708).

88. Merivale leaves the lines of Locke's that he transcribes in Latin so he "won't spoil the beauty" by translation. He quotes the following from Locke: "Viros probos fovendos colendosque semper existimavi. Ignoscant alii meis erroribus; nemini propter opinionum diversitatem bellum indico, ignarus ego & fallibilis homuncio. Evangelicus sum ego christianus, non papista. Hucusque scripseram die supra notato, quo autem die epistolam hanc finiri permissum est, infra videbis. Quod velim cum me christianum Evangelicum, vel si mavis orthodoxum, non papistam dico, paucis accipe. Inter christiani nominis professores duos ego tantum agnosco classes, evangelicos & papistas. Hos, qui tanquam infallibiles dominium sibi arrogant id aliorum conscientias: i llos, qui quaerentes unice veritatem, illam & sibi & aliis, argumentis solum rationibusque persuasam volunt; aliorum erroribus faciles, suae imbecillitatis haud immemores: veniam fragilitati & ignorantiae humanae dantes petentesque vicissim." Merivale then quotes this from Limborch: "Quae de christianis evangelicis & papistis disseris, optima sunt & verissima. Ego utramque classem in omnibus christianorum sectis reperiri credo. Nullum enim coetum ita prorsus corruptum mihi persuadeo, ut nemo in tanto numero sit evangelicus; licet enim coetus ipse professionem edat papismi, nonnullos tamen in eo latere credo evangelicos, quibus dominatus ille in aliorum conscientias displicet, ac dissentientibus salutem abjudicare religio est. Rursus licet coetus evangelicam charitatem profiteatur, non adeo in omnibus & per omnia purgatum, sperare ausim, quin & degeneres aliquot in eo reperiantur, qui professionis suae obliti, tyrannidem animo fovent, libertatemque sentiendi, quam sibi cupiunt, aliis invident. Ita ubique zizania tritico permixta in hoc saeculo habebimus. Evangelicos ego, quocunque in coetu sunt, amo ac fraterna charitate complector. Papistas, licet ejusdem mecum coetus membra, tanquam spurios Christianos considero, nec genuina esse corporis Christi membra agnosco, utpote charitate, ex qua discipulos suos agnosci vult Christus, destitutos."

89. DRO, MS 3237M/F1, November 6, 1761. Merivale ends his letter to Barker "Vale vir amicissime, cum tua, & me ama." It is doubtful that Barker knew—Merivale in any case did not explain—that Locke ends his letter to Limborch (access to the original of

which Barker did not have) virtually the same way: "Vale, vir amicissime, & me ama." As further testament to the layers and layers of intimacy in these letters, Merivale simply seems to have been making an allusion for his own pleasure.

90. DRO, MS 3237M/F1, May 1, 1762.

91. DRO, MS 3237M/F1, March 31, 1762.

92. DRO, MS 3237M/F1, August 1760. This letter was at some point numbered 308 by an archivist, but it fits chronologically between letters 217 and 218.

93. DRO, MS 3237M/F1, April 27, 1760.

94. DRO, MS 3237M/F1, June 10, 1760.

95. The argument that Taylor's book was of critical importance in contemporary debates about original sin runs throughout Smith, *Changing Conceptions of Original Sin.*

96. DRO, MS 3237M/F1, February 11, 1760.

97. DRO, MS 3237M/F1, April 27, 1760. Barker was here no doubt thinking of the opening pages of *The Reasonableness of Christianity,* where Locke discusses death as the outcome of the Fall.

98. DRO, MS 3237M/F1, March 28, 1760.

99. See the letters from August through October 1759 in DRO, MS 3237M/F1.

100. This is the thesis of Alan Charles Kors, *Atheism in France, 1650–1729* (Princeton, NJ: Princeton University Press, 1990), vol. 1.

101. Barker also may have read Samuel Colliber, whose *Free Thoughts concerning Souls* (1734) compares the soul to a particle. Colliber was also connected to the Royal Navy. But there is no mention of Colliber in Barker's letters.

102. DRO, MS 3237M/F1, November 13, 1759.

103. Annemarie Schimmel, *My Soul Is a Woman: The Feminine in Islam,* trans. Susan H. Ray (New York: Continuum, 1997), 34–35.

104. DRO, MS 3237M/F1, September 12, 1760.

105. The ceremonial minimalism, or reductionism, of rationalized, Protestant-inflected Enlightenment religiosity is a theme throughout Hunt, Jacob, and Mijnhardt, *The Book That Changed Europe.*

106. Barker and Merivale rejected predestination. Here by *necessity* Barker refers to the view that God's existence was necessary.

107. DRO, MS 3237M/F1, May 30, 1759.

108. DRO, MS 3237M/F1, May 5, 1760.

109. DRO, MS 3237M/F1, April 27, 1760.

110. Phillipson, *Adam Smith,* 42.

111. See DRO, MS 3237M/F1, May 9, 1762, where Merivale writes: "I can't help thinking with [Henry] Grove, [John] Balguy, [Richard] Price and many others, that by the mere force of our understanding we are capable of discerning a moral difference in things; of perceiving what is right and wrong, good and evil in actions, as well as what is true and false in matters of speculation; and consequently of judging what ought, or ought not to be done. And here methinks the foundation of morality should be laid; or otherwise virtue . . . will appear to be a very unstable and precarious thing as the perceptions of mere sense [i.e., Hutcheson's 'moral sense'] are often deceitful. Nevertheless I am thoroughly persuaded that to supply the defects of our reason, and aid the cause of virtue as well as promote the general good, our kind and bountiful creator has implanted generous instincts and affections in our nature, and given us a strong sense of what is amiable or hopeful in actions and characters as well as judgment [*sic*] more calmly two approve of the one, and condemn the other; and I suppose what we call the principle of conscience

within us, may generally be understood as comprehending that moral sense as well as this moral judgement. And what I think defective in some of our great reasoners, particularly Locke, [Samuel] Clarke, [William] Wollaston, [Arthur] Syke[s], [Richard] Price and others, is their attributing so much to the right apprehensions and judgments of the mind, as in a manner to overlook the good affections and dispositions of the heart, and declaring that there can be no virtue in acting from the best affections, any further than those affections are the proper offspring of reason."

112. David Brion Davis, "New Sidelights on Early Antislavery Radicalism," *William and Mary Quarterly* 28, no. 4 (1971): 585–94. For the claim that the pamphlet was not widely circulated, see ibid., 592.

113. J. Philmore, *Two Dialogues on the Man-Trade* (London, 1760), 54.

114. "We [English] might justly be considered as the aggressors; for in truth we are now at war (we Englishmen, we Christians, to our shame be it spoken) and have been for above a hundred years past, without any cessation at all, at war and enmity with mankind in general, and in this war we have destroyed every year, at least for some years past, near as many of the human race, who never did us any injury, as have been destroyed in the same time by the war now carried on in Europe." Philmore, *Two Dialogues*, 55.

115. *Monthly Review; or, Literary Journal*, 24 (February 1761): 160.

116. DRO, MS 3237M/F1, May 1, 1761.

117. *Monthly Review; or, Literary Journal*, 24 (February 1761): 160.

118. DRO, MS 3237M/F1, May 1, 1761.

119. DRO, MS 3237M/F1, May 1, 1761. This last sentence is oblique, but it can be deciphered. Barker consistently says that anything brought into being—any being that, in other words, has "been made"—was never made for the sake of being wicked. His logic ran like this: something has to have been *made* for it to be wicked, but, if it was made in the first place, it was ultimately made by God, and, in being made by God, it cannot be resolutely wicked. Barker spells out his reasoning in another letter, in which he cautiously presents his view of God's omniscience to Merivale. It is worth reading in full: "By one means or another I have for some years past been quite satisfied, that [things] cannot be, as our fiery divines, or merciless doctors [of theology] represent [them]. I have had one argument for my own satisfaction frequently working in my mind (whether standard or no, I know not). It is the omniscience or prescience of God. But with the profoundest humility would I dare to say it. Did God know, that his own creature would so behave as to be irredeemably and eternally miserable surely he would not bring him into being. You [Merivale] can better express what I would say than I can myself. It appears to me, that it is utterly inconsistent with the goodness of God to sustain one that owes his very being to him, to endure never ending misery—Cui Bono? The opinion, or belief, that he will [i.e., that God would do such a thing] fights as much against his justice as his mercy. It cannot be. For this reason (as above). If such a creature could not have been, but to be always miserable, infinite goodness would not have brought him out of nothing into being, to suffer Eternally. It is possible that Louis 15, who they call Bien Aimé and his Leonical [*sic*], Tygeratical [*sic*] ministers would have kept [Robert-François] Damien [the attempted regicide] alive to this day between 4 Horses [i.e., perpetually drawn and quartered]. I can't think it of them, nor of the diabolical inquisitors, nay even that the tormentors themselves in the hell on earth would so behave. Then say I, shall these wretches more cruel than Libyan lion or Hyrcanian tiger, be more merciful than God? Nothing humane can thus spin out misery much less what is Divine. Shall the mercy of God be outdone by the mercy of men? No, it cannot." DRO, MS 3237M/F1, June 25, 1759.

It is interesting to think about what Barker is saying here alongside his gloss on 1 John 3:9 discussed in chap. 9.

120. DRO, MS 3237M/F1, May 23, 1761.

121. Tamara Elisabeth Lewis, "'To Wash a Blackamoor White': The Rise of Black Ethnic Religious Rhetoric in Early Modern England" (PhD diss., Vanderbilt University, 2014), 271–89.

122. Lewis, "'To Wash a Blackamoor White,'" 274.

123. Merivale's letters from these months do not survive, so we miss a real opportunity to hear his thoughts on slavery and race.

124. DRO, MS 3237M/F1, June 27, 1759. Barker would also on occasion call his view "the Pamphilian scheme." See DRO, MS 3237M/F1, June 26, 1760.

125. DRO, MS 3237M/F1, June 26, 1760.

126. DRO, MS 3237M/F1, March 31, 1762.

Chapter Six

1. The Dutch boy Otto Van Eck is a rare exception. See Arianne Baggerman and Rudolf Dekker, *Child of the Enlightenment: Revolutionary Europe Reflected in a Boyhood Diary*, trans. Diane Webb (Leiden: Brill, 2009). Van Eck is interesting to compare to Jenny. But the differences are significant. He and his parents bear the influence of Rousseau. He was from an elite Dutch family, born in the aftermath of the French Revolution and raised, as a man, to take over the estate. Otto also lived to be eighteen, while Jenny made it only past her thirteenth birthday.

2. Quoted in Porter, *The Creation of the Modern World*, 157.

3. DRO, MS 3237M/F1, July 12, 1760.

4. DRO, MS 3237M/F1, July 16, 1759.

5. DRO, MS 3237M/F1, June 12, 1759.

6. DRO, MS 3237M/F1, November 25, 1759.

7. See DRO, MS 3237M/F1, February 21, 1760, where Barker writes: "I remember when a Fryar, a good natured man, had hope that I might see my error and become a Catholic before death, and was talking with one Mr Reynaud, a friend to the English, about purgatory, that it should restrain men from sin. Reynaud rallied, la Purgatoire, n'est pas pour tout jamais [i.e., Purgatory is not forever], slighting it upon that account for you know as well as I do that they scarce think any man so wicked, as to be sent to Hell, and Purgatory has but little effect upon them, especially as the pains may be bought off. The opulent are in no danger. . . . This tenet of theirs and confession are the grand pillars by which the church is upheld and the people kept steady to it." A few days later, Merivale agreed and piled on the criticism, although curiously rolling the notion of purgatory into his and Barker's general doubts about hell too: "[T]he popish purgatory is a wretched contrivance; Of no use, that I know of but to bring grist to the priest's mill. As scarce any are thought so bad to be in danger of Hell amongst them (which is designed rather for heretics and infidels) so very few indeed are so good as to go directly to Heaven. Purgatory therefore is what they must expect, behave how they will; and from this they may be delivered if the priests are well paid, even without repentance and amendment, for anything in their creed that I know to the contrary: and if so what motives are there left, likely to reclaim a Sinner, or preserve a Saint? That the profligate would be apt to comfort themselves, with the hope of their Punishments ceasing at last, is very natural to suppose;

but whether this thought would harden them in their vices more than the contrary I know not; but this we see plain enough, that very few who have been long accustomed to sin, are reclaimed by the fears of endless torments, any more than by the hopes of mercy." DRO, MS 3237M/F1, February 26, 1760. Here, as elsewhere, one can sense that Merivale was less anthro-optimistic than was Barker.

8. DRO, MS 3237M/F4, July 13, 1759.

9. DRO, MS 3237M/F4, June 30, 1761.

10. DRO, MS 3237M/F4, January 27, 1760. Around the same time, Merivale mentions to Barker that he was reading Virgil with Jenny. DRO, MS 3237M/F1, January 11, 1760.

11. DRO, MS 3237M/F4, September 10, 1761.

12. DRO, MS 3237M/F1, October 5, 1759.

13. Barbara Pitkin, "'The Heritage of the Lord': Children in the Theology of John Calvin," in *The Child in Christian Thought*, ed. Marcia J. Bunge (Grand Rapids, MI: Eerdmans, 2001), 161–69. Augustine thought that all non-Christian children would go to hell, but he imagined their punishment, even if eternal, would be relatively mild. See J. N. D. Kelly, *Early Christian Doctrine* (New York: Harper Collins, 1978), 366.

14. Their practice also suggests lingering belief in baptism as a ritual capable of washing away original sin. See chap. 2, n. 10.

15. Peter Gregg Slater, *Children in the New England Mind in Death and in Life* (Hamden, CT: Archon, 1977), esp. chap. 2.

16. Richard Baxter, *Two Disputations of Original Sin . . .* (London, 1675), 12.

17. DRO, MS 3237M/F1, April 9, 1759.

18. DRO, MS 3237M/F4, September 16, 1762. Barker refers to her as his "dear wife Jane Barker" in his will, but he also acknowledges that "by some [she is] called Jane Mills, during her life." "Will of Pentecost Barker." I have found no record of their marriage in any marriage register. This is a mystery I have not been able to solve.

19. DRO, MS 3237M/F1, March 14, 1760.

20. DRO, MS 3237M/F4, December 4, 1761.

21. DRO, MS 3237M/F1, January 17, 1762.

22. DRO, MS 3237M/F1, September 15, 1759.

23. DRO, MS 3237M/F1, August 1760.

24. DRO, MS 3237M/F1, January 17, 1762.

25. DRO, MS 3237M/F4.

26. DRO, MS 3237M/F1, August 1760.

27. Phyllis Mack, *Visionary Women: Ecstatic Prophecy in Seventeenth-Century England* (Berkeley and Los Angeles: University of California Press, 1995). Barker indicates that one of his grandfathers was a Quaker. See DRO, MS 3237M/F1, April 4, 1759. The connection is suggestive but hard to follow given the available evidence.

28. DRO, MS 3237M/F1, October 31, 1761.

29. Lebrun, "Joseph de Maistre and Edmund Burke," 165; Maistre, *St. Petersburg Dialogues*, xx. On the nuance in Maistre's thought, see Armenteros and Lebrun, eds., *Joseph de Maistre and His European Readers*.

30. Thomas Paine, *Common Sense* (Philadelphia: R. Bell, 1776), 14.

31. Edmund Burke, *Reflections on the Revolution in France* (London, 1790), 89.

32. Mary Wollstonecraft, *A Vindication of the Rights of Woman* (Boston, 1792), 199.

33. Mary Wollstonecraft, *An Historical and Moral View of the Origin and Progress of the French Revolution and the Effect It Has Produced in Europe* (London, 1794), 17. On

this text as a response to Burke, see Daniel I. O'Neill, *The Burke-Wollstonecraft Debate: Savagery, Civilization, and Democracy* (University Park: Pennsylvania State University Press, 2007), 227.

Chapter Seven

1. Martin Luther quoted in Volker Leppin, "Luther's Transformation of Medieval Thought: Continuity and Discontinuity," in *The Oxford Handbook of Martin's Luther's Theology*, ed. Robert Kolb, Irene Dingel, and L'Ubomír Batka (Oxford: Oxford University Press, 2014), 115–25, 119. On Luther's distinction between universal priesthood and ministry, see David P. Daniel, "Luther on the Church," in ibid., 333–52. Quentin Skinner notes that Luther did not explicitly rest his political views on the Fall. See Quentin Skinner, *The Foundations of Modern Political Thought*, 2 vols. (Cambridge: Cambridge University Press, 1978), 2:18.

2. In the context of his discussion in the *Institutes* of democracy and civil government, Calvin writes: "Pourquoy le vice, au défaut des hommes, est cause que l'espèce de supériorité la plus passable et la plus seule, est que plusieurs gouvernement, aidant les uns aux autres, et s'avertissants de leur office: et si queleun s'esleve trop haut, que les autres luy soyent comme censeurs et maistres." See *Institution de la religion chrétienne par Jean Calvin*, ed. Frank Baumbartner (Geneva, 1888), 683 (4.20.8).

3. Theodore Beza, *Right of Magistrates* (1574); *Vindiciae contra tyrannos* (1579). On the varied origins of resistance theory, see Robert M. Kingdon, "Calvinism and Resistance Theory, 1550–1580," in *The Cambridge History of Political Thought, 1450–1700*, ed. J. H. Burns and Mark Goldie (Cambridge: Cambridge University Press, 1991), 193–218. Also see Martin van Gelderen, "'So meerly humane': Theories of Resistance in Early-Modern Europe," in *Rethinking the Foundations of Modern Political Thought*, ed. Annabel Brett and James Tully (Cambridge: Cambridge University Press, 2006), 149–70.

4. The radical potential of the Jansenists is taken up in Dale K. Van Kley, *The Religious Origins of the French Revolution: From Calvin to the Civil Constitution, 1560–1791* (New Haven, CT: Yale University Press, 1999).

5. On original sin as the crucial organizing principle of the "Puritan ethos," see Durston and Eales, "Introduction: The Puritan Ethos." On the alleged Pelagianism of early Arminians in England, see Nicholas Tyacke, *Anti-Calvinists: The Rise of English Arminianism, c. 1590–1640* (Oxford: Oxford University Press, 1987), 52.

6. Simon Critchley, *The Faith of the Faithless: Experiments in Political Theology* (London, 2012), 108 (emphasis added). Also see Jerry Z. Muller, "Conservatism," in *The Cambridge History of Modern European Thought*, ed. Warren Breckman and Peter E. Gordon (Cambridge: Cambridge University Press, 2019), 1:232–54, 234; John Dunn, *The Cunning of Unreason: Making Sense of Politics* (New York: Basic, 2000), passim; Michael Oakeshott, *The Politics of Faith and the Politics of Scepticism* (New Haven, CT: Yale University Press, 1996); J. Roland Pennock and John W. Chapman, eds., *Human Nature in Politics* (New York: New York University Press, 1977), 6; and Erich Auerbach, "On the Political Theory of Pascal," in *Scenes from the Drama of European Literature* (New York: Meridian, 1959). For the importance of original sin as asserted by conservatives themselves, see, among others, James Burnham, *Suicide of the West: An Essay on the Meaning and Destiny of Liberalism* (New York: John Day, 1964); and Ernest Van den Haag and Ralph Gilbert Ross, *Passion and Social Constraint* (New York: Stein & Day, 1963). Outside academic writing, see, among others, Robert Leonard, "Why Rural America Voted for Trump,"

New York Times, January 5, 2017; and Jason Crowley, "Theresa May: Quickfire Questions on Jane Austen, Late Nights and Original Sin," *New Statesman*, February 8, 2017. For an older but insightful article, see Andrew Hacker, "On Original Sin and Conservatives," *New York Times*, February 25, 1973.

7. Nelson, *The Theology of Liberalism*, 1 (emphasis added).

8. "For he is freely in bondage who does with pleasure the will of his master. Accordingly, he who is the servant of sin is free to sin. And hence he will not be free to do right, until, being freed from sin, he shall begin to be the servant of righteousness. And this is true liberty, for he has pleasure in the righteous deed; and it is at the same time a holy bondage, for he is obedient to the will of God." St. Augustine, *The Enchiridion on Faith, Hope and Love*, ed. Henry Paolucci, trans. J. F. Shaw (Chicago: Henry Regnery, 1961), 37.

9. Peter Riedemann, *Rechenschafft unserer Religion, Leer und Glaubens, von den Bruedern so man die Hutterischen nennt* (1540); Gary K. Waite, "'Man is a devil to himself': David Joris and the Rise of a Sceptical Tradition towards the Devil in the Early Modern Netherlands, 1540–1600," *Nederlands Archief voor Kerkgeschiedenis / Dutch Review of Church History* 75, no. 1 (1995): 8–9, 23.

10. Schmitt, *Political Theology*, 5.

11. Jacques Derrida, *Rogues: Two Essays on Reason* (Stanford, CA: Stanford University Press, 2005), 154.

12. Schmitt, *Der Begriff des Politischen* (1933), 45.

13. DRO, MS 3237M/F1, January 1, 1759.

14. "The Augsburg Confession" (1530), in *Documents from the History of Lutheranism, 1517–1750*, ed. Eric Lund (Minneapolis, MN: Augsburg Fortress, 2002), 60 ("Item docent, quod post lapsum Adae omnes homines, secundum naturam propagati, nascantur cum peccato, hoc est, sine metu Dei").

15. DRO, MS 3237M/F1, January 1, 1759.

16. Barker's argument with his captain can also be set against a transition in the navy. "The eighteenth-century Navy lacked even a single world for 'discipline' . . . in its modern English sense," writes the historian N. A. M. Rodger. Where something that looks like discipline did exist on ships, Rodger argues, it was instead a function of everyone on board naturally coming together to survive whatever threats the ocean posed. Rodger, *Wooden World*, 202. Around the time of Barker's death, top-down discipline was therefore starting to become more common, which might help explain why Barker and his captain were having this conversation in the first place. Or, looked at another way, at the time Barker's aversion to the sort of discipline of which the tyrannical captain wanted more still had the force of naval custom to back it up.

17. Christopher Hill, "Antonio Gramsci," *New Reasoner* 4 (1958): 107–13, 111.

18. A point made in Corey Robin, *Fear: The History of a Political Idea* (Oxford: Oxford University Press, 2004), 1.

19. Compare Jonathan Scott, *Algernon Sidney and the Restoration Crisis, 1677–1683* (Cambridge: Cambridge University Press, 1991), 214–20.

20. Robert Filmer, *Patriarcha and Other Political Works*, ed. Peter Laslett (New York: Routledge, 1984), 53.

21. John Milton, *Paradise Lost*, ed. Alastair Fowler, 2nd ed. (New York: Routledge, 2007), 614–15 (emphasis added). On Milton and Filmer, see Roger Lejosne, "Milton, Satan, Salmasius and Abdiel," in *Milton and Republicanism*, ed. David Armitage, Arman Himy, and Quentin Skinner (Cambridge: Cambridge University Press, 1998), 115. In the same vein, the republican Algernon Sidney argued that liberty in Genesis is not the

same as liberty in late Stuart politics. What Filmer needed to prove but did not, Sidney wrote, was "that the law which [Adam] transgressed was imposed upon him by man, and consequently that there was a man to impose it." Adam breaking *God's* law was hardly relevant, in other words, in the face of unjust human laws. There may have nevertheless been enough residual religion in Sidney for him to admit that since "the sin of our first parents the earth hath brought forth briars and brambles, and the nature of man hath been fruitful only in vice and wickedness." But Sidney's counter to his own point was an encapsulation of early Enlightenment anthro-optimism. Just as heart implanted in our nature, he added, are "common sense, virtue, and humanity." Algernon Sydney, *Discourses concerning Government* (London, 1698), 3, 6.

22. John Locke, *Two Treatises of Government*, ed. Peter Laslett (Cambridge: Cambridge University Press, 1988), 172.

23. W. M. Spellman, *John Locke and the Problem of Depravity* (Oxford: Oxford University Press, 1988).

24. Marshall, *John Locke*, 145–48. For a nuanced view of Locke's attitudes, see Aderemi Artis, "Locke and Original Sin," *Locke Studies* 12 (2012): 201–19. On "inconveniences," see A. John Simmons, *On the Edge of Anarchy: Locke, Consent, and the Limits of Society* (Princeton, NJ: Princeton University Press, 1993), 27–30. What Locke was getting at, from another angle, is the problem that arises when people in a state of nature are judges in their own case and virtually certain, to the detriment of others, to overvalue their position.

25. "La monarchie ébranlée jusqu'aux fondements, la guerre civile, la guerre étrangère, le feu au dedans et au dehors; les remèdes de tous côtés plus dangereux que les maux. . . ." Jacques-Bénigne Bossuet, "Oraison funèbre d'Anne de Gonzague," in Lachat, ed., *Oeuvres complètes de Bossuet*, 12:539–67, 546.

26. This is the running theme in Hill, *The World Turned Upside Down*.

27. See Hill, *Winstanley*, 53.

28. Stephen Ward Angell and Pink Dandelion, eds., *The Oxford Handbook of Quaker Studies* (Oxford: Oxford University Press, 2013), 172.

29. On this subtle point, see Rachel Foxley, "The Levellers: John Lilburne, Richard Overton, and William Walwyn," in *The Oxford Handbook of Literature and the English Revolution*, ed. Laura Knoppers (Oxford: Oxford University Press, 2012), 272–85, 280.

30. Bossuet quoted in Paul Kléber Monod, *The Power of Kings: Monarchy and Religion in Europe, 1589–1715* (New Haven, CT: Yale University Press, 2001), 213.

31. On the links between England and France at midcentury, see Philip A. Knachel, *England and the Fronde: The Impact of the English Civil War and Revolution on France* (Ithaca, NY: Cornell University Press, 1967).

32. On Sexby, see Laurent Curelly, "'The French, those Monkies of Mankind': The Fronde as Seen by the Newsbook *Mercurius Politicus*," *XVII–XVIII: Revue de la Société d'études anglo-américaines des XVIIe et XVIIIe siècles* 69 (2012): 29–50.

33. Most Mazarinades were admittedly pious and royalist in tone. But not all. See, e.g., *Que la voix du people est la voix de Dieu* (1649); or *De la puissance qu'ont les roys sur les peoples, et du pouvoir des peoples sur les roys* (1650). More generally, see Hubert Carrier, *La presse de la Fronde (1648–1653): Les Mazarinades, la conquête de l'opinion* (Geneva: Droz, 1989).

34. See Bossuet, "Oraison funèbre de Henriette-Marie de France." Worth noting is that Bossuet also does not hesitate here to place the ultimate blame on Henry VIII and the Reformation: "Donc la source de tout le mal est que ceux qui n'ont pas craint de

tenter au siècle passé la réformation par le schisme, ne trouvant point de plus fort rempart contre toutes leurs nouveautés que la sainte autorité de l'Eglise, ils ont été obligés de la renverser." Ibid., 452.

35. According to H. M. Bourseaud, Bossuet began his "universal history" in either 1677 or 1678. See H. M. Bourseaud, *Histoire et descriptions des manuscrits et des éditions originales des ouvrages de Bossuet* (Paris: A. Picard & fils, 1898), 37. Bossuet first started writing *Politics Drawn from the Very Words of Holy Scripture* in 1679. Themes that emerge in both books were, however, apparent in sermons from the 1660s.

36. Jean Bodin, *Les six livres de la république* (1576).

37. Skinner, *The Foundations of Modern Political Thought*, 2:292.

38. On Bodin's Pelagian belief that human corruption has its source in custom as much as in nature, see Maryanne Cline Horowitz, *Seeds of Virtue and Knowledge* (Princeton, NJ: Princeton University Press, 1998), 187–88, 203–4.

39. "Les hommes meme les plus savans, les plus éloquents, n'ont servi quelquefois qu'a embellir le trône de l'erreur au lieu de le renverser. Bossuet en est un grand example dans sa prétendue Histoire universelle, qui n'est que celle de quatre à cinq peuples, et surtout de la petite nation juive, ou ignorée, ou justement méprisée du reste de la terre, à laquelle pourtant il rapporte tous les èvènements, et pour laquelle il dit que tout à été fait, comme si un écrivain de Cornouaille disait que rien n'est arrivé dans l'empire romain qu'en vue de la province de Galles." Voltaire, "Le Pyrrhonisme de l'histoire," in Moland, ed., *Oeuvres complètes de Voltaire*, 27:236.

40. Sanjay Subrahmanyam, "On World Historians in the Sixteenth Century," *Representations* 91, no. 1 (2005): 26–57, 28.

41. Jean Bodin, *Methodus ad facilem historiarum cognitionem* (1566).

42. Jacques-Bénigne Bossuet, *Discours sur l'histoire universelle* (1681; Paris, 1839), 349. Ernst Cassirer called Bossuet's book "the last great attempt at a purely theological presentation of history." Cassirer, *The Philosophy of the Enlightenment*, 207.

43. Skinner obliquely credited J. N. Figgis for noting the Lutheran overlap in Bossuet's thought: "[H]ad there been no Luther there could never have been a Louis XIV." Skinner, *The Foundations of Modern Political Thought*, 2:113.

44. Dale K. Van Kley, "Piety and Politics in the Century of Lights," in Goldie and Wokler, eds., *The Cambridge History of Eighteenth-Century Political Thought*, 110–43, 112.

45. Bossuet, *Élévations a Dieu sur tous les mystères*, 125.

46. On the importance of Malebranche, see Truchet, *La prédication de Bossuet*, 154. However, for a penetrating account of Malebranche's relation to Bossuet's crucial political concept of particular grace, see Riley, introduction to *Politics Drawn from the Very Words of Holy Scripture*. Brunetière grasped the same point and drew a direct connection to original sin. Nevertheless, he found Bayle rather than Malebranche to be the culprit. See Brunetière, *Bossuet*, 199.

47. Riley, *The General Will Before Rousseau*.

48. Riley, introduction to *Politics Drawn from the Very Words of Holy Scripture*, xxv.

49. J. H. Burns, "Conclusion," in Burns and Goldie, eds., *The Cambridge History of Political Thought*, 653–56, 653.

50. For the argument that Locke's perception of absolutism was partly rooted in the reality rather than simply the abstract idea of slavery, see Holly Brewer, "Slavery, Sovereignty, and 'Inheritable Blood': Reconsidering John Locke and the Origins of American Slavery," *American Historical Review* 122, no. 4 (2017): 1038–78.

51. The early rejection of innatism can be found in Locke's manuscript "Lectures on the Law of Nature" from 1663–64. For more here, see Stuart-Buttle, *From Moral Theology to Moral Philosophy*, 45.

52. John Locke, *Essay concerning Human Understanding* (1689); Marshall, *John Locke*, 346.

53. John Locke, *Some Thoughts concerning Education* (London, 1693).

54. Locke, *The Reasonableness of Christianity*, 6.

55. Bossuet was widely read, and Locke read widely. No one with Locke's interests would have been a stranger to Bossuet's arguments. See Justin Champion, *Republican Learning: John Toland and the Crisis of Christian Culture, 1696–1722* (Manchester: Manchester University Press, 2003), 38.

56. Tyacke, *Anti-Calvinists*, 52. On the subtle theological shifts away from Arminius, also see Ellis, *Simon Episcopius's Doctrine of Original Sin*.

57. It was because of this rising moralism that Mark Goldie has said the Puritan Whigs "stood poised between Puritanism and the Enlightenment." Goldie, *Roger Morrice and the Puritan Whigs*, 268.

58. Roger L'Estrange, *The Dissenter's Sayings* (London, 1681), 7.

59. L'Estrange also tried to curry favor with Huguenot exiles to keep the Whigs from using the revocation of the Edict of Nantes to draw a connection between Louis XIV and the Stuarts. Anne Dunan-Page, "Roger L'Estrange and the Huguenots: Continental Protestantism and the Church of England," in *Roger L'Estrange and the Making of Restoration Culture*, ed. Anne Dunan-Page and Beth Lynch (Burlington: Ashgate, 2008), 109–30, 129–30.

60. Baxter, *Two Disputations of Original Sin*.

61. John Dryden, *Absalom and Achitophel* (1681), 3rd ed. (London, 1682), 21. Both Whigs and Tories had, as it were, social chaos theories: each argued that victory for the other would lead to "arbitrariness," whether, as the Whigs saw it, in the form of a bad king's arbitrary rule or, as the Tories saw it, via the arbitrariness of social disorder. Tim Harris, *Restoration: Charles II and His Kingdoms* (London, 2005), 258.

62. Jacques Truchet, *Politique de Bossuet* (Paris: Armand Colin, 1966).

63. For a comparison of these texts, see Anne Barbeau Gardner, "Spinoza vs. Bossuet: The European Debate behind Dryden's *Religio Laici*," *Restoration* 28, no. 1 (2004): 1–14. In *Dryden and Enthusiasm: Literature, Religion, and Politics in Restoration England* (Oxford: Oxford University Press, 2018), John West suggests Dryden's interest in the irrational in his treatment of "enthusiasm." Dryden was also admired by the Tory modernists. Here see *The Complete Prose of T. S. Eliot: The Critical Edition*, vol. 2, *The Perfect Critic, 1919–1926*, ed. Anthony Cuda and Ronald Schuchard (Baltimore: Johns Hopkins University Press, 2014), 350–61.

64. Mark Goldie, "The Damning of King Monmouth: Pulpit Toryism in the Reign of James II," in *The Final Crisis of the Stuart Monarchy: The Revolutions of 1688–91 in Their British, Atlantic and European Contexts*, ed. Tim Harris and Stephen Taylor (Woodbridge: Boydell, 2013), 33–56, 35 (emphasis added). It is suggestive that Goldie implicates the Fall in the difference he recognizes between prerevolutionary and implicitly postrevolutionary (1688–) absolutist thought.

65. Goldie, "The Damning of King Monmouth," 46–47.

66. Goldie, "The Damning of King Monmouth," 47–51; Tony Claydon, *Europe and the Making of England, 1660–1760* (Cambridge: Cambridge University Press, 2007), 302.

67. Smith, *Changing Conceptions of Original Sin*, 10–13. Also see the commentary on

Romans 13 in Daniel Whitby, *Paraphrase and Commentary on the New Testament* (London, 1700).

68. DRO, MS 3237M/F1, June 25, 1759.

69. Edward Gibbon, *Miscellaneous Works* (London, 1837), 29.

70. Brunetière, *Bossuet*, 216. "C'est le guide et c'est le maitre, c'est le conducteur d'ames, c'est le directeur d'esprit, je dirais volontiers le directeur d'etudes, c'est le penseur dont les leçons n'ont pas cesse ni jamais ne cesseront d'être actuelles, d'etre vivantes."

71. Voltaire, *Oeuvres complètes* (Stuttgart, 1829), 14:147.

72. Cassirer, *The Philosophy of the Enlightenment*, 207.

73. Becker, "Brunetière und Bossuet," 94.

74. Riley, introduction to *Politics Drawn from the Very Words of Holy Scripture*, lxviii.

75. *Oeuvres de Messire Jacques-Benigne Bossuet, évêque de Meaux* (1772), 2:89.

76. "Pesez ces paroles: Toutes les pensées, et celles-ci: En tout temps. Nous ne faisons pas tout le mal, mais nous y penchons; il ne manque que les occasions, et les objets déterminent: l'homme laissé à lui-même n'éviterait aucun mal. Ajoutez ces paroles qui précèdent: 'La malice des hommes était grande sur la terre;' et celles-ci: 'Mon esprit ne demeurera pas en l'homme, parce qu'il est chair.'" *Oeuvres de Messire Jacques-Benigne Bossuet*, 2:104–5.

77. "Regardons-nous tout en cette source: regardons-y notre être et notre bien-etre, notre bonheur et notre Malheur. Dieu ne nous voit qu'en Adam, dans lequel il nous a tous faits." *Oeuvres de Messire Jacques-Benigne Bossuet*, 2:100.

78. I am taking liberty with pronouns for readability. "Quoi qu'Adam fasse, nous le faisons avec lui, parce qu'il nous tient renfermés, et que nous ne sommes en lui moralement qu'une seule et même personne: s'il obéit, j'obéis en lui; s'il pèche, je pèche en lui: Dieu traitera tout le genre humain comme ce seul homme, où il a voulu le mettre tout entier, l'aura mérité." *Oeuvres de Messire Jacques-Benigne Bossuet*, 2:100. On the notion that all human souls were contained in Adam, see Kelly, *Early Christian Doctrine*, 175–78.

79. Milton, *Paradise Lost*, ed. Fowler, 585.

80. On habeas corpus as a seventeenth-century creation, see Paul D. Halliday, *Habeas Corpus: From England to Empire* (Cambridge, MA: Harvard University Press, 2012).

81. Brunetière, *Bossuet*, 86–87.

82. The novelist Marilynne Robinson finds much to praise in Edwards but not particularly the prose. See Marilynne Robinson, "Jonathan Edwards in a New Light: Remembered for Preaching," *Humanities*, vol. 35, no. 6 (2014), https://www.neh.gov/humanities/2014/novemberdecember/feature/jonathan-edwards-in-new-light-remembered-preaching-fire-and.

83. Here see Jacob Soll, *Free Market: The History of an Idea* (New York: Basic, 2022), chap. 7.

84. Jacob Soll has stressed the importance of the 1670s. See Jacob Soll, *The Information Master: Jean-Baptiste Colbert's Secret State Intelligence System* (Ann Arbor: University of Michigan Press, 2009), and *Free Market*.

85. As Patrick Riley noted, the revocation of the Edict of Nantes was a rare occasion when the atavistic Bossuet recognized the success of modernity over antiquity. Riley, introduction to *Politics Drawn from the Very Words of Holy Scripture*, liii. To add another layer to the story, the exiled Huguenots often saw their plight in terms of the Fall, hoping their new surroundings foretold a new Eden. Owen Stanwood, "Between Eden and Empire: Huguenot Refugees and the Promise of New Worlds," *American Historical Review* 118, no. 5 (2013): 1319–44.

86. "Voilà, MESSIEURS, ce que nos pères ont admiré dans les premiers siècles de l'Église. Mais nos pères n'avaient pas vu, comme nous, une hérésie invétérée tomber tout à coup; les troupeaux égarés revenir en foule, et nos églises trop étroites pour les recevoir; leurs faux pasteurs les abandonner, sans même en attendre l'ordre, et heureux d'avoir à leur alléguer leur bannissement pour excuse; tout calme dans un si grand mouvement; l'univers étonné de voir dans un événement si nouveau la marque la plus assurée, comme le plus bel usage, de l'autorité, et le mérite du prince plus reconnu et plus révéré que son autorité même." Jacques-Bénigne Bossuet, "Oraison funèbre de Michel Le Tellier," in Lachat, ed., *Oeuvres complètes de Bossuet*, 12:573–602, 595 (emphasis added).

87. It is not that earlier royalists in France had never made the case that kings are divinely ordained to govern the depraved. Here see Anne-Marie Lecoq, "La symbolique de l'état: Les images de la monarchie des premiers Valois à Louis XIV," in *Les lieux de mémoire*, ed. Pierre Nora (Paris, 1986), 2:145–92, 173, 190 n. 71. Or see a pamphlet from earlier in the century that can even be read as invoking something like the concept of particular grace. H. Du Boys, *De l'origine et autorité des roys* (1604), 35. John McManners is not incorrect to say that "Bossuet's reactionary certainties were dated even as he proclaimed them." John McManners, *Church and Society in Eighteenth-Century France: The Religion of the People and the Politics of Religion* (Oxford: Oxford University Press, 1998), 301. But selling an outdated argument for sovereignty in a culture transformed by political crisis and new secular claims of legitimacy by itself represented a kind of novelty. Brunetière recognized this when he ironically titled one of his essays "La modernité de Bossuet" (1913). Equally to the point, Bossuet, speaking from a massive platform, made the case with unprecedented clarity and far more attuned than were earlier writers to the objections of rationalists and democratic-leaning Augustinians.

88. For the early biographer's comparison to Bossuet, see John Morley, *Burke* (London: Macmillan, 1879), 59; and Edmund Burke, *Reflections on the Revolution in France and the First Letter on a Regicide*, ed. Iain Hampsher-Monk (Cambridge: Cambridge University Press, 2014), 79.

89. Bossuet, *Politics Drawn from the Very Words of Holy Scripture*, 87.

Chapter Eight

1. A point made with respect to France but applicable more broadly in William H. Sewell Jr., *Capitalism and the Emergence of Civic Equality in Eighteenth-Century France* (Chicago: University of Chicago Press, 2021), 44.

2. Hirschman, *The Passions and the Interests*, 13. The effort proved successful when critical voices came to lament, as Hirschman writes, capitalism's obstruction of "the development of the 'full human personality.'" Ibid., 132. Herbert Marcuse had in the previous decade published his *One-Dimensional Man: Studies in the Ideology of Advanced Industrial Society* (Boston: Beacon, 1964).

3. Joyce Appleby, *Economic Thought and Ideology in Seventeenth-Century England* (Princeton, NJ: Princeton University Press, 1978), 26, 242, 247.

4. Michel Foucault, *The Birth of Biopolitics: Lectures at the Collège de France, 1978–1979*, trans. Graham Burchell (New York: Picador, 2008), 15–16. On Foucault's ruminations on the Fall, see Michel Foucault, *Les aveux de la chair* (Paris: Gallimard, 2018), esp. app. 4.

5. Three disparate writers in three dispersed locations reaching the same conclusion in the 1970s curiously echoes the marginal revolution a century earlier, when a narrative

resting on the same circumstances (three writers in three different locations independently reaching the same conclusion) lent weight to the naturalness of *homo economicus* through the "discovery" of marginal utility. A century after Jevons, Walras, and Menger, one could say, if with some exaggeration, that Hirschman, Foucault, and Appleby helped *undiscover* economic man. (The phrase *homo economicus* is not used until the nineteenth century, but the concept emerges in the eighteenth. See Joseph Persky, "The Ethology of Homo Economicus," *Journal of Economic Perspectives* 9, no. 2 [1995]: 221–31.)

6. Pierre Bourdieu, *The Logic of Practice*, trans. Richard Nice (Stanford, CA: Stanford University Press, 1990), 56.

7. Marcuse again comes to mind. He writes: "[S]o-called consumer society and the politics of corporate capitalism created *a second nature of man*." Herbert Marcuse, *Essays on Liberation* (Boston: Beacon, 1971), 11 (emphasis added).

8. The fuller story behind Weber's image is in Peter Baehr, "The 'Iron Cage' and the 'Shell as Hard as Steel': Parsons, Weber, and the Stahlhartes Gehäuse Metaphor in the Protestant Ethic and the Spirit of Capitalism," *History and Theory* 40, no. 2 (2001): 153–69.

9. Rousseau is admittedly here talking about the state as the "greater whole," but the point I am making is simply about the relationship between the self and a broader group. ("Si, par exemple, on les exerce assez-tôt à ne jamais regarder leur individu que par ses relations avec le Corps de l'Etat, et à n'appercevoir, pour ainsi dire, leur propre existence que comme une partie de la sienne, ils pourront parvenir enfin à s'identifier en quelque sorte avec ce plus grand tout, à se sentir membres de la patrie, à l'aimer de ce sentiment exquis que tout homme isolé n'a que pour soi-même, à élever perpétuellement leur ame à ce grand objet, & à transformer ainsi en une vertu sublime, cette disposition dangereuse d'où naissent tous nos vice.") Jean-Jacques Rousseau, *Discours sur l'economie politique* (4th ed.), in *Collection complète des oeuvres* (Geneva, 1780–89), 1:388.

10. DRO, MS 3237M/F1, November 11, 1759.

11. Barker nevertheless reserved praise for Bernard Mandeville's *An Enquiry into an Origin of Honour; and the Usefulness of Christianity in War* (London, 1725). See DRO, MS 3237M/F1, March 17, 1759.

12. Martin Luther, *The Ninety-Five Theses and Other Writings*, trans. and ed. William Russell (New York: Penguin, 2017), 3.

13. Jean Calvin, *Institutio christianae religionis*, ed. A. Tholuck (London, 1833), 163.

14. Josselin quoted in Durston and Eales, "Introduction: The Puritan Ethos," 13.

15. Michael Wigglesworth, *The Diary of Michael Wigglesworth, 1653–1657: The Conscience of a Puritan*, ed. Edmund Morgan (New York: Harper & Row, 1965), 5.

16. See Michel Foucault, *Technologies of the Self: A Seminar with Michel Foucault*, ed. Luther H. Martin, Huck Gutman, and Patrick H. Hutton (Amherst: University of Massachusetts Press, 1988). The phrase *technologies of the self* is discussed in relation to spiritual diaries in Webster, "Writing to Redundancy."

17. Blaise Pascal, *Pensées*, trans. A. J. Krailsheimer (London: Penguin, 1966), 84, 194, 109.

18. Seaver, *Wallington's World*.

19. "Journal of Pentecost Barker," November 30, 1729.

20. Pascal, *Pensées*, 70.

21. Weber, *The Protestant Ethic and the Spirit of Capitalism*, 88. There is a vast literature on the relationship between capitalism and the major Christian denominations, not to mention capitalism and religion more broadly. For a recent overview of the former, see Benjamin M. Friedman, *Religion and the Rise of Capitalism* (New York: Knopf Doubleday, 2022).

22. As Weber writes at the end of his essay: "[I]t cannot be the intention here to set a one-sided spiritualistic analysis of the causes of culture and history in place of an equally one-sided 'materialistic' analysis. *Both* are *equally possible*." Weber, *The Protestant Ethic and the Spirit of Capitalism*, 159.

23. For an elaboration of this argument, see Kadane, *The Watchful Clothier*, esp. chap. 7.

24. Hirschman, *The Passions and the Interests*, 9 (emphasis added).

25. Schama, *Embarrassment*, 215; Freya Sierhuis, *The Literature of the Arminian Controversy: Religion, Politics and the Stage* (Oxford: Oxford University Press, 2016).

26. For an analogous development later in the century, see Willem J. van Asselt, "Expromissio or Fideiussio? A Seventeenth-Century Theological Debate between Voetians and Cocceians about the Nature of Christ's Suretyship in Salvation History," in *Mid-American Journal of Theology* 14 (2003): 37–57.

27. Karen Hollewand, *The Banishment of Beverland: Sex, Sin, and Scholarship in the Seventeenth-Century Dutch Republic* (Leiden: Brill, 2019).

28. Michael R. Watts, *The Dissenters*, 3 vols. (Oxford: Oxford University Press, 1978–2015), 2:333–39.

29. For a recent work that assumes such elective affinities, see Anton van der Lem, *De Opstand in de Nederlanden, 1568–1648* (Nijmegen: Vantilt, 2014).

30. Daniel Walker Howe, *The Unitarian Conscience: Harvard Moral Philosophy, 1805–1861* (Cambridge, MA: Harvard University Press, 1970); Philip Goff, Detlef Junker, and Jan Stievermann, eds., *Religion and the Marketplace in the United States* (Oxford: Oxford University Press, 2015).

31. Philip Gorski, *The Disciplinary Revolution: Calvinism and the Rise of the State in Early Modern Europe* (Chicago: University of Chicago Press, 2003).

32. On the consistory, see Patrick Collinson, *Godly People: Essays in English Protestantism and Puritanism* (London: Hambledon, 1983); and Benedict, *Christ's Churches Purely Reformed*, 317–29.

33. A point made in Margo Todd, "Puritan Self-Fashioning: The Diary of Samuel Ward," *Journal of British Studies* 31, no. 3 (1992): 236–64.

34. I have made these arguments in more detail elsewhere. See Kadane, *The Watchful Clothier*, chap. 3.

35. Heyd, "Original Sin," and "Changing Emotions?"

36. The earliest use of *calvinophobia* I have found is in the evangelical *The Christian's Magazine* 4 (1811): 267. The same rejection of Calvin could also occur in Baptist and Independent congregations. See Watts, *The Dissenters*, 3:42–47.

37. Philip Gorski argues that the conspicuous absence of external secular policing in the early modern Dutch Republic and in Bradenburg Prussia owes to the Calvinist influence. See Gorski, *The Disciplinary Revolution*, passim.

38. The image of the panopticon runs throughout Michel Foucault, *Discipline and Punish: The Birth of the Prison*, trans. Alan Sheridan (New York: Vintage, 1977).

39. Jeremy Bentham, *Panopticon; or, The Inspection-House . . .* (Dublin, 1791), 2.

40. For an overview of various positions on Smith with respect to Augustinianism, see Eric Gregory, "Sympathy and Domination: Adam Smith and the Virtues of Augustinianism," in *Adam Smith as Theologian*, ed. Paul Oslington (New York: Routledge, 2011), 33–45.

41. Gary Anderson, *Sin: A History* (New Haven, CT: Yale University Press, 2009), 13.

42. Anderson, *Sin*, chap. 3.

43. Anderson, *Sin*, ix.

44. These are formalist terms first laid out systematically in I. A. Richards, *The Philosophy of Rhetoric* (New York: Oxford University Press, 1936). Depending on who is using the metaphor, of course, the tenor and the vehicle can switch roles. Sin (the tenor) is like debt (the vehicle) to the theologian. Debt (the tenor) is like sin (the vehicle) to the economist. When I call debt the *vehicle* in this chapter, I am assuming, in this sense, the theological perspective.

45. Bartolomé Yun-Casalilla and Patrick K. O'Brien, eds., *The Rise of Fiscal States: A Global History, 1500–1914* (Cambridge: Cambridge University Press, 2012).

46. Quoted in Julian Hoppit, "Attitudes to Credit in Britain, 1680–1790," *Historical Journal* 33, no. 2 (1990): 305–22, 318.

47. Karl Marx, *Grundrisse: Foundations of the Critique of Political Economy (Rough Draft)*, trans. Martin Nicolaus (London: Penguin, 1973), 842.

48. Richard Price, *Observations on Reversionary Payments; on Schemes for Providing Annuities for Widows, and for Persons in Old Age; on the Method of Calculating the Values of Assurances on Lives; and on the National Debt* (London, 1771), xxxi n. a.

49. Carl B. Cone, "Richard Price and Pitt's Sinking Fund of 1786," *Economic History Review* 4, no. 2 (1951): 243–51, 251.

50. Peter Buck, "People Who Counted: Political Arithmetic in the Eighteenth Century," *Isis* 73, no. 1 (1982): 28–45, 38.

51. On Richard Price and rational calculation, see William Deringer, *Calculated Values: Finance, Politics, and the Quantitative Age* (Cambridge, MA: Harvard University Press, 2018), 266–69.

52. Tawny Paul, *The Poverty of Disaster: Debt and Insecurity in Eighteenth-Century Britain* (Cambridge: Cambridge University Press, 2019), 2, 222.

53. DRO, MS 3237M/F1, October 20, 1761.

54. "Journal of Pentecost Barker," December 29, 1730.

55. Simon Critchley, "The Null Basis-Being of a Nullity, or between Two Nothings: Heidegger's Uncanniness," in *Interpreting Heidegger: Critical Essays*, ed. Daniel O. Dahlstrom (Cambridge: Cambridge University Press, 2011), 69–78, 73.

56. The line also appears in Luke 11:4: "[V]ergib uns unsre Sünden, denn auch wir vergeben allen, die uns schuldig sind."

57. For more on Heidegger's complicated relationship to original sin, see Stephen Mulhall, *Philosophical Myths of the Fall* (Princeton, NJ: Princeton University Press, 2005), 1–15, 46–84.

58. DRO, MS 3237M/F1, April 4, 1759. Barker is here quoting the sonnet of Milton's that begins "Cyriack, whose grandsire." See John Milton, *The Complete Poems*, ed. John Leonard (London: Penguin, 1999), 85. He often quotes lines to Merivale with the implied understanding that Merivale will know the fuller passage, and, thus, the operative part of the quotation often remains unsaid. Here, e.g., it is what Milton's sonnet says next that captures Barker's concept of liberty of conscience: "What supports me, dost thou ask? / The conscience, friend, to have lost them overplied / In liberty's defence, my noble task, / Of which all Europe talks from side to side." Ibid.

59. Milton's Arianism became clear when *De doctrina christiana* was finally published in 1823. Barker and Merivale obviously did not know that text. But there were many in the eighteenth century who, even without *De doctrina christiana*, thought Milton was heretical. See Stephen M. Fallon, "Milton, Newton, and the Implications of Arianism," in *Milton in the Long Restoration*, ed. Blair Hoxby and Ann Baynes Coiro (Oxford: Oxford University Press, 2016), 324.

60. Merivale's comments are worth seeing in full: "I have long esteemed Milton as a Unitarian, and so indeed some have represented him. The passage you quote is so strong to the purpose that I see not how it can be reconciled with that opinion which makes the son in any respect distinct from, and coequal with the father. He everywhere plainly represents them as two different persons, holding communion with each other; and if they were up on a footing of equality, there could be no room for adding what immediately follows, 'how have I then with whom to hold converse safe with the creatures which I made,' though as Adam is made to reply (perhaps on purpose to account for these strong expressions of scripture which speak of the son as one with the father) 'so pleas'd, Canst raise thy Creature to what height thou wilt, of Union or Communion, deified.' In short Milton everywhere contents himself with adhering to scripture representations . . . and seems cautiously to avoid the unwarranted language of Athanasius and tritheists. A subordination is always most religiously kept up; and in the highest things that are spoken of the son, he appears but as the image of the father, receiving and reflecting his glories, and appointed to be the grand medium of the divine manifestations and operations. Let anyone compare what is attributed to the father and to the son in the Angels song B[ook] 3 v[erse] 372 etc they must need to be sensible of the difference. Tis pretty plain I think that Satan considered the Messiah but as on par with himself originally; and this very consideration seems to give rise to that envy which he feels on the superior dignity to which he was by merit advanced. And it is in consequence of the sons being armed with his father's might that he gains that effectual conquest over his potent adversaries. Yet there are perhaps some few expressions to be met with that may look the other way; particularly b[ook] 3 v[erse] 305 etc those throned in highest bliss, equal to God, and equally enjoying God like fruition, which Dr [Thomas] Newton says deserves notice as an instance of Milton's orthodoxy, with relation to the divinity of God the son. I suppose the word equal is here used in a laxer sense, as denoting rather a high degree of similitude than strict equality; And the poet might think himself warranted to make use of this language for once by Saint Paul Phil[ippians] 2:6. I will only add that I don't find he anywhere speaks of the spirit as a 3rd person distinct from the father and the son but rather uses the word when it occurs merely to express a divine influence or energy; and herein too if I mistake not he makes these scripture his guide. Upon the whole I've sometimes wondered that Milton should not have been put down on the blacklist; But a poet is entitled to greater license then a preacher." DRO, MS 3237M/F1, March 21, 1762.

61. DRO, MS 3237M/F1, March 31, 1762. Barker's letter that prompted Merivale's long explication does not survive.

62. Barbara K. Lewalski, *The Life of John Milton: A Critical Biography* (2000), rev. ed (Malden, MA: Blackwell, 2008), 482.

63. Greenblatt, *The Rise and Fall of Adam and Eve*, 6, 59.

64. For an overview of the Christian-inflected meaning of labor, see Raffaella Sarti, Anna Bellavitis, and Manuela Martini, introduction to *What Is Work? Gender at the Crossroads of Home, Family, and Business from the Early Modern Era to the Present*, ed. Raffaella Sarti, Anna Bellavitis, and Manuela Martini (New York: Berghahn, 2018), 1–84.

65. Jacques Le Goff, *Un long moyen âge* (Paris: Tallandier, 2004).

66. Matthew Henry, *An Exposition of All the Books of the Old and New Testament* (London, 1721–25), 1:18.

67. Adam Smith, *An Inquiry into the Nature and Causes of the Wealth of Nations* (London, 1776), 1:99.

68. John Locke, *Some Considerations of the Consequences of the Lowering of Interest and Raising the Value of Money* (London, 1691), 15.

69. For a recent overview, see Stern and Wennerlind, eds., *Mercantilism Reimagined.*

70. On the development of the labor theory of value, see Steve Pincus, *1688: The First Modern Revolution* (New Haven, CT: Yale University Press, 2009), 366–72; Appleby, *Economic Thought and Ideology*, 129–57; and D. C. Coleman, "Labour in the English Economy of the Seventeenth Century," *Economic History Review* 2, no. 8 (1955–56): 280–95. For the internalist history, see Ronald Meek, *Studies in the Labor Theory of Value* (New York: Monthly Review Press, 1956).

71. John Mapletoft, *Select Proverbs, Italian, Spanish, French, English, Scotish, British, &c. Chiefly Moral: The Foreign Languages Done into English* (London, 1707), 17.

72. Richard Baxter, *Practical Works* (London, 1707), 247.

73. This theme runs throughout John Dunn's work on Locke. I am quoting here from John Dunn, *Locke: A Very Short Introduction* (Oxford: Oxford University Press, 2003), 2. On Locke and self-control, also see James Tully, "Governing Conduct: Locke on the Reform of Thought and Behavior," in *Approach to Political Philosophy: Locke in Contexts* (Cambridge: Cambridge University Press, 1993).

74. Locke, *Some Thoughts concerning Education*, 2.

75. See Philip Greven, *Spare the Child: The Religious Roots of Punishment and the Psychological Impact of Physical Abuse* (New York: Knopf, 1991), and *The Protestant Temperament: Patterns of Child-Rearing, Religious Experience, and the Self in Early America* (New York: Knopf, 1977), 192–220.

76. Locke, *Some Thoughts concerning Education*, 48, 43–44.

77. For Augustine, self-control while awake was one thing, but nocturnal emissions indicated that the same degree of control was not possible while sleeping. See William E. Mann, "The Life of the Mind in Dramas and Dreams," in Mann, ed., *Augustine's Confessions*, 108–34, 120. Locke's translation can be found in Pierre Nicole, *Discourses: Translated from Nicole's Essays by John Locke with Important Variations from the Original French* (London, 1828).

78. Locke, *Some Thoughts concerning Education*, 44, 47, 52, 50, 55.

79. Rousseau, *Émile*, 97, 155.

80. Rousseau, *Discours sur l'economie politique*, 388.

81. The theme here has been covered by others, as made particularly clear by many of the essays in *The Cambridge Companion to Rousseau*, ed. Patrick Riley (Cambridge: Cambridge University Press, 2001). Also see Patrick Riley, *Will and Political Legitimacy: A Critical Exposition of Social Contract Theory in Hobbes, Locke, Rousseau, Kant, and Hegel* (Cambridge, MA: Harvard University Press, 1982), and *The General Will Before Rousseau.*

82. The point about commercial society as a whole is made in Hont, *Politics in Commercial Society*, 47.

83. Montesquieu quoted in Anoush Terjanian, *Commerce and Its Discontents in Eighteenth-Century French Political Thought* (Cambridge: Cambridge University Press, 2013), 18.

84. Terjanian, *Commerce and Its Discontents*, 89, 73–92.

85. Both points are made in Ian Simpson Ross, *The Life of Adam Smith*, 2nd ed. (Oxford: Oxford University Press, 2008), 32–34.

86. Smith, *An Inquiry into the Nature and Causes of the Wealth of Nations*, 1:178.

87. Marx, *Capital*, 1:484.

88. Quoted in Brinley Roderick Rees, *Pelagius: Life and Letters* (Woodbridge: Boydell, 1998), 53.

Chapter Nine

1. "A Speech Delivered by an Indian Chief in Reply to a Sermon Preach'd by a Swedish Missionary, in Order to Convert the Indians to the Christian Religion." London Magazine; or, Gentleman's Monthly Intelligence 29 (Appendix 1761): 695–96, 695.

2. For the authenticity of the speech, see Alfred Owen Aldridge, "Franklin's Deistical Indians," *Proceedings of the American Philosophical Society* 94, no. 4 (1950): 398–410.

3. Tobias E. Biörck, *Dissertatio gradualis, de plantatione eclesiae svecanae in America, quam . . . in Regio Upsal. athenaeo, praeside . . . Andrea Bronwall . . . in audit* (Upsala, 1731). As Aldridge writes: "[W]e must of course have faith in the reliability of the Swedish minister's record and of Biörck's transcript, but since neither obviously would have any interest in inserting deistical arguments—in fact their natural tendency would be the opposite—there is no reason to suspect the authenticity of the account published at Uppsala." Aldridge, "Franklin's Deistical Indians," 402.

4. Benjamin Franklin, *Remarks concerning the Savages of North America* (1784), in *The Papers of Benjamin Franklin*, vol. 41, *September 16, 1783, through February 29, 1784*, ed. Ellen R. Cohn (New Haven, CT: Yale University Press, 2014), 412–23, 412.

5. See Aldridge, "Franklin's Deistical Indians," 398.

6. Labaree, Ketcham, and Boatfield, eds., *The Autobiography of Benjamin Franklin*, 150.

7. Here it is worth noting that the philosopher Charles Taylor considered the reduction of Christianity to guidelines for moral conduct to lie at the heart of secularity. In his words, secularity is the move from a society "where belief in God is unchallenged and indeed, unproblematic, to [a society] in which it is understood to be one option among others, and frequently not the easiest to embrace." Charles Taylor, *A Secular Age* (Cambridge, MA: Harvard University Press, 2007), 3. With his ostensibly simple advice, Franklin was not just asking for room to be made for Socrates alongside Jesus. He was, by Taylor's terms, pushing for secularity. So were all Rational Dissenters who, like Barker, thought similarly.

8. *London Magazine; or, Gentleman's Monthly Intelligence* 30 (August 1761): 407–9, 409.

9. *London Magazine; or, Gentleman's Monthly Intelligence* 31 (February 1762): 73–74.

10. London Magazine; or, Gentleman's Monthly Intelligence 31 (February 1762): 73.

11. The name was also popular among early modern alchemical writers. George Starkey (1628–65) writes as Eirenaeus Philalethes, and Thomas Vaughan (1621–66) wrote as Eugenius Philalethes, as did a later translator, Robert Samber (1682–1745). A closer contemporary of Barker's was the physician James Jurin (1684–1750), who wrote (in among other places the *London Magazine*) as Philalethes Cantabrigiensis. As the dates of all these figures indicate, however, none were alive in the 1760s.

12. DRO, MS 3237M/F1, June 16, 1759.

13. See the discussion of Francis Osborne in chap. 3.

14. DRO, MS 3237M/F1, April 29, 1762.

15. Pope, *Essay on Man*, 29.

16. DRO, MS 3237M/F1, January 15, 1762.

17. DRO, MS 3237M/F1, October 20, 1761.

18. DRO, MS 3237M/F1, October 20, 1761.

19. The edition Barker was quoting from was Jean-Jacques Rousseau, *Eloisa; or, A Series of Original Letters Collected and Published by J. J. Rousseau: Translated from the French*... (London, 1761), 4:157. In the original, the line reads: "[J]'aimerais mieux croire la Bible falsifiée ou inintelligible, que Dieu injuste ou malfaisant."

20. DRO, MS 3237M/F1, October 20, 1761.

21. Robert Boulton, *Letters and Tracts on the Choice of Company* (London, 1761).

22. DRO, MS 3237M/F1, October 20, 1761.

23. DRO, MS 3237M/F1, October 20, 1761.

24. Eliot and Haffensen, eds., *The Letters of T. S. Eliot*, 6:290–91.

INDEX